God in the Labyrinth

God in the Labyrinth

A Semiotic Approach to Christian Theology

ANDREW HOLLINGSWORTH

WIPF & STOCK · Eugene, Oregon

GOD IN THE LABYRINTH
A Semiotic Approach to Christian Theology

Copyright © 2019 Andrew Hollingsworth. All rights reserved. Except for brief quotations in critical publications or reviews, no part of this book may be reproduced in any manner without prior written permission from the publisher. Write: Permissions, Wipf and Stock Publishers, 199 W. 8th Ave., Suite 3, Eugene, OR 97401.

Wipf & Stock
An Imprint of Wipf and Stock Publishers
199 W. 8th Ave., Suite 3
Eugene, OR 97401

www.wipfandstock.com

PAPERBACK ISBN: 978-1-5326-7984-1
HARDCOVER ISBN: 978-1-5326-7985-8
EBOOK ISBN: 978-1-5326-7986-5

Manufactured in the U.S.A.   04/18/19

For Katie, Mom, Grandfaye, and Grandaddy,
for supporting me in all that God has called me.

Contents

Acknowledgments	ix
Introduction	1
1 // A History of Semiotics	14
2 // The Semiotics of Umberto Eco	29
3 // Umberto Eco's Model Encyclopedia	66
4 // The Model Encyclopedia and Theological Epistemology	88
5 // The Model Encyclopedia and the Hermeneutic Nature of Theology	110
6 // The Model Encyclopedia and the Development of Doctrine	139
Conclusion	156
Bibliography	161
Index	175

Acknowledgments

A project like this does not happen without the help and support of family and friends. My Mom, Grandfaye, and Grandaddy, as well as my wonderful aunts, uncles, and cousins, have supported me in countless ways concerning this book. Not only have they provided the prayers and encouragement that have gotten me through some very frustrating moments while researching and writing, but they have provided the bulk of literary resources featured in said research and writing. For your spiritual, emotional, and monetary support, thank you!

A large number of friends have encouraged me throughout this process as well. Meagan Medley, Lou Werkheiser, Cory Barnes, Obbie Todd, Matthew Halsted, Mark Cooper, Jacob Milstead, Ben Hutchison, Tim Walker, Sam Marshall, Jay Mullins, and Kyle Boyd are just a few of the many friends who have helped me think through many of my ideas, navigate the plethora of theological resources that are available, and provide me with the laughter needed to help preserve my sanity when Peirce's and Eco's dense writing nearly drove me insane! And a special thank you goes to my friend, Chelsea Armstrong, for proofreading these chapters, formatting the manuscript, and making me a better writer.

The Theological and Historical Studies faculty at New Orleans Baptist Theological Seminary also were crucial to making this project possible. Thanks belong to Dr. Bob Stewart, Dr. Jeff Riley, and Dr. Adam Harwood for encouraging me and pointing me to useful resources for my work. Thanks also belong to Dr. Page Brooks, my professor and pastor, for the academic and spiritual guidance he has provided. A special thanks belongs to Dr. Rhyne Putman, my Doktorvater and friend. Were it not for him I would have not discovered the wonderful worlds of philosophical hermeneutics, semiotics, and theological method. He has guided and mentored me in more ways than the academic: thank you!

A very special thank you belongs to my best friend and bride-to-be, Katie "The Hobbit" Hodas. She has provided me with more encouragement, affirmation, and laughter than one can imagine. She has supplied the means necessary to procuring books for my research, a number of prepared meals in order to save me time, and countless prayers lifting me and my research up to the Lord. Thank you, Katie, for all of your love, support, and friendship. I eagerly anticipate the day when I call you wife.

The final acknowledgment belongs to my Lord, Jesus of Nazareth. Thank you for the mind you have blessed me with; the family, friends and faculty you have provided me with; the support that I have needed; and your most glorious cross and empty tomb that have given me new life. May this book glorify you and help give you the place in the Academy that you deserve.

Solus Christus. Soli Deo Gloria.

Introduction

This book is an interdisciplinary effort to bring together two disciplines of study: semiotics and systematic theology. It is a slight re-working of my doctoral dissertation, which I wrote under the supervision of Rhyne Putman at New Orleans Baptist Theological Seminary.[1] In short, semiotics is the science, or study, of signs.[2] A sign is something that can stand for something to someone usually for the sake of communication.[3] According to Umberto Eco, a sign is "anything that can be used to lie. If something cannot be used to tell a lie, conversely it cannot be used to tell the truth: it cannot in fact be used 'to tell' at all."[4] Theology is the science, or study, of God.[5] Theology comes in different types: biblical, historical, philosophical, practical, and systematic.[6] In this book, the term *theology* primarily refers to systematic theology. Systematic theology is by nature an interdisciplinary enterprise that includes the insights of other theological disciplines as well as developments in philosophy, the natural sciences, and the social sciences.[7]

Insufficient scholarly attention has been given to the relationship between theology and semiotics. What might the study of signs have to

---

1. Hollingsworth, "'Ecos' in the Labyrinth."
2. Danesi, *Encyclopedic Dictionary of Semiotics, Media, and Communications*, 205.
3. Danesi, *Encyclopedic Dictionary of Semiotics, Media, and Communications*, 209. See also Eco, "Sign," 959–64.
4. Eco, *A Theory of Semiotics*, 7.
5. Pannenberg, *Theology and the Philosophy of Science*, 297.
6. Clark, *To Know and Love God*, 165–74.
7. Pannenberg, *Systematic Theology: Vol. 1*, 8–26.

offer theology? Hermeneutical philosopher Hans–Georg Gadamer pointed out that all thinking and understanding take place through the medium of language.[8] What he does not note, however, is that language itself is a sign system. All words are signs along with the grammar that provides them their structure. As a result, all thinking takes place through the medium of a sign system, including thinking about God. The study of signs and sign systems, therefore, has the potential to make one a better thinker by forcing her to reflect on the medium through which her thinking occurs. Semiotics, therefore, has the potential to aid theologians in their task of thinking about God. This book will show how contemporary developments in semiotics can aid systematic theologians in their task by drawing attention to a single concept in the work of a semiotician, Umberto Eco. Eco is a prime interlocutor for this project due to the prolific contributions he has made in the field of semiotics and their wide acceptance by other semioticians. More specifically, this book will show how the concept of *encyclopedia* in Eco's semiotic project can provide a model for systematic theology, one that will prove especially helpful in matters pertaining to prolegomena.

The research problem of this book is the lack of dialogue between semiotics and theology. I will contribute to the solution of this problem by bringing the work of a prolific semiotician into dialogue with theology. The guiding question of this research is as follows: how might Umberto Eco's semiotic project aid systematic theologians in matters pertaining to theological prolegomena? The research thesis is that Eco's concept of encyclopedia can provide a model for systematic theology, one that is especially useful concerning matters of theological prolegomena. The way this model will be useful is that it will have the capacity to bring together the endeavors of other prominent theologians in the field of prolegomena that have been widely accepted. More specifically, the model of the encyclopedia has the capacity to bring together seminal endeavors by theologians in epistemology, hermeneutics, and doctrinal development. Thinkers who will be discussed include Wolfhart Pannenberg, Alister McGrath, and Anthony Thiselton.

DEFINITIONS OF TERMS

Some preliminary definitions are necessary. First, Eco defined *semiotics* as a discipline that "studies all cultural processes as processes of

---

8. Gadamer, *Truth and Method*, 390.

communication."[9] He further stated that culture "can be studied completely under a semiotic profile."[10] Second, another word that might be used interchangeably with *semiotics* is *semiology*. Third, Eco's definition of the *sign* is important for this project. As he defined it, "A sign is everything which can be *taken* as significantly substituting for something else. This something else does not necessarily have to exist or actually be somewhere at the moment in which a sign stands for it."[11] Fourth, a term that will be used throughout this project is *sememe*. A *sememe* is a "minimal unit of meaning that goes into the composition of the overall meaning of a word. . . . This term is used equivalently for semantic feature."[12] Fifth, Eco's definition of *meaning* is important. His definition of *sememe* as "meaning" or "a cultural unit" will be used here.[13] A *cultural unit* is "simply anything which is culturally defined and distinguished as an entity. It may be a person, place, thing, feeling, state of affairs, sense of foreboding, fantasy, hallucination, hope or idea."[14]

A sixth term that needs to be defined here is *abduction*. *Abduction* is a form of reasoning explicated by the philosopher Charles Sanders Peirce and is to be distinguished from deduction and induction. Deduction begins with a rule, is followed by a case, and leads to a necessary consequent. Induction begins with a case, followed by a result, and concludes with a rule. Abduction, on the other hand, begins with a rule, follows with a result, and concludes with a case. The following are examples of each form of reasoning. Deduction: all of the marbles in this bag are blue. These marbles are from this bag. Therefore, the marbles are blue. Induction: These marbles are from this bag. These marbles are blue. Therefore, all of the marbles from this bag are blue. Abduction: All of the marbles in this bag are blue. These marbles are blue. Therefore, these marbles are from this bag.[15]

A definition for systematic theology is needed as well. Wolfhart Pannenberg noted that the role of systematic theology or dogmatics "must not only unfold the content of church teaching but also attend to the question of

---

9. Eco, *A Theory of Semiotics*, 8.
10. Eco, *A Theory of Semiotics*, 26–27.
11. Eco, *A Theory of Semiotics*, 7 (emphasis mine). See also Eco, "Sign," 959–64.
12. Danesi, *Encyclopedic Dictionary*, 204.
13. Eco, *A Theory of Semiotics*, 67.
14. Magli, "Cultural Unit," 170.
15. Ayim, "Abduction," 1–2.

the truth of dogma."[16] He further wrote, "Claiming that the content of Christian doctrine is true in detail, proclamation implicitly presupposes its inner coherence and its coherence with all that is true. In systematic theology, however, this coherence itself is the object of investigation and presentation of the doctrinal content."[17] This led Pannenberg to understand dogmatic theology as systematic theology. Systematic theology, according to him, is dogmatic theology in which the theme of dogmatic theology is its own truth-value.

Theological prolegomena also needs to be defined. "Theological prolegomena" is essentially the prologue material to systematic theology. The term often is used synonymously with the term *theological method*. Issues discussed in theological prolegomena include, but are not limited to, the nature and task of theology, the sources of theology, and the need for theology.[18]

PREVIOUS DIALOGUES BETWEEN SEMIOTICS AND THEOLOGY

Robert Corrington provides one of the few conversations between semiotics and theology in his monograph *A Semiotic Theory of Theology and Philosophy*. As the title suggests, Corrington aims to use insights from semiotics to frame a new theory for understanding both theology and philosophy. He begins by stating, "The immodest proposal in this book is that the interdisciplinary science and art of semiotics can transform philosophy and theology and pave the way for a new metaphysics."[19] More specifically, Corrington aims to understand the concept of nature through the lens of semiotics and use the implications of that understanding to frame a new theory of theology and philosophy. He writes, "The failure to develop an adequate and compelling conception of nature has haunted thought down through the centuries, but we are now at a historical nexus in which our categorical framework can be broadened through a semiotic cosmology that probes into the ultimate texture of meaning in an evolutionary world."[20] By "semiotic cosmology" he does not mean cosmology as discussed in the fields of physics and astrophysics. Rather, "the 'object' of

---

16. Pannenberg, *Systematic Theology: Vol. 1*, 17.
17. Pannenberg, *Systematic Theology: Vol. 1*, 19.
18. Pannenberg, *Systematic Theology: Vol. 1*, 26–48.
19. Corrington, *A Semiotic Theory of Theology and Philosophy*, ix.
20. Corrington, *A Semiotic Theory of Theology and Philosophy*, ix.

semiotic cosmology is broader in scope than the worlds of energy and matter, and includes anything that is an order in any respect whatsoever, whether discriminated by human sign users or not."[21] Corrington frequently dialogues with psychoanalysis psychology, especially when discussing what he calls "psychosemiotics." Psychosemiotics "starts from the familiar territory of self-consciousness and moves past and through surface structures into the depths that link the unconscious of the self to the underconscious of nature. It also shows how signs and symbols function through structures that are readily available."[22] Corrington adheres more to C. S. Peirce's semiotics rather than the semiotics of Ferdinand de Saussure.[23]

Though Corrington makes a significant contribution to the needed dialogue between semiotics and theology, his contribution is not altogether satisfactory. Wesley Wildman comments, "In fact, the book can be thought of as an essay in the philosophy of nature."[24] He also notes that Corrington's project is ultimately a "posttheistic theology."[25] Corrington's notion of God is grounded on naturalism, specifically his semiotic theory of nature, which is unacceptable for many in the Christian tradition. This reconceiving of both God and theology has sacrificed too much in order to be recognizable to Christian traditions such as Evangelicalism. Wildman claims that the book, most likely, will be ignored, not simply because of its radical claims but because of its level of reading difficulty.[26] Nonetheless, this monograph is one of the few works of theology engaging the field of semiotics.

Andrew Robinson has put forth one of the most useful monographs contributing to the dialogue of theology and semiotics: *God and the World of Signs: Trinity, Evolution, and the Metaphysical Semiotics of C. S. Peirce*.[27] In this monograph, Robinson seeks to approach systematic theological topics from the standpoint of Peircean semiotics. He claims that many others have described Christianity as a religion seeking a metaphysic, and he seeks to use Peirce's philosophy to provide just this metaphysic. He engages Peirce's metaphysical concepts of firstness, secondness, and thirdness to

---

21. Corrington, *A Semiotic Theory of Theology and Philosophy*, ix.

22. Corrington, *A Semiotic Theory of Theology and Philosophy*, 87.

23. The differences between the semiotics of Peirce and Saussure will be discussed in chapter 1 below.

24. Wildman, "A Semiotic Theory of Theology and Philosophy," 657.

25. Wildman, "A Semiotic Theory of Theology and Philosophy," 658.

26. Wildman, "A Semiotic Theory of Theology and Philosophy," 658.

27. Robinson, *God and the World of Signs*.

approach the doctrine of the Trinity, and he shows how these concepts are useful in understanding issues concerning not only the imminent Trinity but the economic Trinity as well. Robinson also utilizes Peirce's semiotics to engage issues surrounding Christology, namely the incarnation, as well as issues concerning theological anthropology. Specifically, he shows where Karl Rahner's notion of Jesus as the real–symbol is lacking and puts forth a much more satisfying semiotic discussion of Jesus. The final section of the work shows how Peirce's metaphysical semiotics can help bridge the gap between science and religion. This section couples Peirce's semiotics along contributions in the field known as biosemiotics in order to discuss issues surrounding evolutionary science and Christian theology.

Robinson puts forth a type of theology of nature using semiotics as his primary conversation partner, according to Yong.[28] Not only does he show the usefulness of Peirce's semiotics for topics of systematic theology, but he also shows its usefulness for understanding evolutionary biology and conversations surrounding the origins of life.

In *Changing Signs of Truth: A Christian Introduction to the Semiotics of Communication*, Crystal Downing sets out to show how understanding the impact of semiotics on theories of communication can be useful for Christians in communicating the gospel and theology to contemporary culture.[29] She interacts with the works of multiple major semioticians throughout the history of modern semiotics such as Ferdinand de Saussure, Charles Sanders Peirce, Mikhail Bhaktin, and Julia Kristeva, though she utilizes the insights of Peirce more than the others. She shows the usefulness of Perice's semiotics in dealing with issues such as understanding the Trinity. Whereas Robinson used the Peircean concepts of firstness, secondness, and thirdness to explicate the doctrine of the Trinity, Downing uses Peirce's triadic model of the sign for this explication, highlighting that even Peirce himself made this connection.

Downing's monograph, similar to Robinson's, is a significant contribution to the dialogue between semiotics and theology. The work at hand, however, is not a dialogue between semiotics and systematic theology per se; however, it does engage some topics of systematic theology. The primary aim of Downing's book is to show how semiotics can inform Christians on how to engage culture with the gospel and Christian doctrine better. Though this topic can fall within the realm of systematic theology, it can

---

28. Yong, "God and the World of Signs," 269–70.
29. Downing, *Changing Signs of Truth*.

fall also within the realm of evangelism studies. Nonetheless, Downing's monograph is still one of few that provides a dialogue between semiotics and theology.

In "Religion and Semiosphere: From Religious to the Secular and Beyond," Rajka Rush sets out to provide a semiotic theory of religion.[30] She engages the works of Charles Sanders Peirce, Umberto Eco, Yuri Lotman, and Jürgen Habermas for her project. One should note that Rush seeks to provide a semiotic theory of *religion*, whereas I seek to provide a new model for understanding and doing *systematic theology*.

Robinson and Christopher Southgate also have published and edited several articles on applying Peirce's metaphysical semiotics to Christian theology. Two issues of the journal *Zygon* were dedicated to this specific topic. Contributors included, but were not limited to, Robinson and Southgate, Bruce Weber, Jesper Hoffmeyer, and F. LeRon Shults. These articles discussed issues such as the transformation of theological symbols,[31] semiotics as a metaphysical paradigm for Christian theology,[32] and the usefulness of biosemiotics and the question of meaning.[33] These essays are all in the same vein of work that Robinson has done in his aforementioned monograph though some new topics are explored also. As with *God and the World of Signs*, the focus of these articles is on dialoging with the semiotic works of Peirce. Neither Umberto Eco nor the model encyclopedia are ever mentioned in any of the articles in these two editions of *Zygon*.

These works are in the minority, as the majority of Christian scholarship that has engaged the field of semiotics falls within the realm of biblical interpretation. The majority of these works focus on issues concerning biblical intertextuality. Though a full review of the literature that dialogues between biblical interpretation and semiotics is not needed here, a brief discussion of some examples of these works can provide a frame of reference to show how semiotics might prove useful for systematic theology.

Stefan Alkier is a New Testament scholar who has appropriated insights from the semiotic works of Peirce and Eco for biblical and theological interpretation of the New Testament. Though his work never deals with systematic theology or theological method, his use of Peirce and Eco can

---

30. Rush, "Religion and Semiosphere."

31. Shults, "Transforming Theological Symbols," 713–32.

32. Robinson and Southgate, "Semiotics as a Metaphysical Framework for Christian Theology," 689–712.

33. Hoffmeyer, "A Biosemiotic Approach to the Question of Meaning," 367–90.

prove helpful in how theologians might go about appropriating their works for theological method purposes. He has shown the usefulness of semiotics in the areas of intertextuality, Pauline studies, and the interpretation of the resurrection discourses of the New Testament. Alkier is a proponent of what he refers to as "categorical semiotics." In categorical semiotics, Alkier couples Peirce's concept of "the universe of discourse" with Eco's "encyclopedia" to explain how authors generate texts and think intertextually.[34] He notes how semiotics, being the study of signs, is also a study of culture since cultures are made up of signs.[35]

In *The Reality of the Resurrection*, Alkier uses his categorical semiotics to explore the New Testament resurrection discourses.[36] Drawing from the concepts of the "universe of discourse" and "encyclopedia," he shows how the New Testament authors indeed discuss the resurrection as a real historical event. Though Alkier is interested primarily in appropriating the semiotics of Peirce and Eco for biblical interpretation, the way he uses their insights can aid in understanding how one can bring semiotics to bear on theological method. His contribution to the interpretation of the resurrection discourses can prove especially helpful to a biblical theology of the resurrection, as well as prove useful for apologetics as well.

Leroy Huizenga is a Catholic biblical scholar who has appropriated semiotics, namely the semiotics of Eco, to biblical interpretation. Following in the line of Alkier, Huizenga's primary interest is in using semiotics to illuminate intertextual phenomena in biblical canon. He has produced both a monograph and an article on the usefulness of semiotics for interpreting and explaining instances of intertextuality in the Gospel of Matthew, namely those pertaining to an Isaac typology.[37] In these works, Huizenga deals primarily with two of Eco's semiotic concepts: "encyclopedia" and "the model reader." He couples these two concepts of Eco's to explain how the author of Matthew uses the Genesis narratives about Isaac as a way of interpreting and explaining Jesus to his audience. Specifically, he notes how the cultural encyclopedia of Matthew's audience would hold many similarities between the promised son of Abraham and Jesus of Nazareth. Like Alkier, though Huizenga does not provide a dialogue between semiotics and

---

34. Alkier, "New Testament Studies on the Basis of Categorical Semiotics," 223–48.

35. Alkier, "New Testament Studies on the Basis of Categorical Semiotics," 230–37.

36. Alkier, *The Reality of the Resurrection*.

37. Huizenga, "The Matthean Jesus and the Isaac of the Early Jewish Encyclopedia," 63–81.

theology, his appropriation of semiotics for biblical interpretation proves useful for showing how semiotics can dialogue with biblical and theological studies.

Like the two aforementioned scholars, Justin Langford has used semiotics to bear on instances of intertextuality in the New Testament. In his dissertation, he uses Alkier's categorical semiotics to explore 1 Peter's intertextual uses of Isaiah.[38] This project is in the same vein as those by Alkier and Huizenga mentioned above. He couples Peirce's concept of "universe of discourse" with Eco's "encyclopedia" to interpret and explain 1 Peter's use of Isaiah texts to encourage his audience to remain in their hope concerning Christ.

Heath Thomas is a biblical scholar who has used insights from Eco's semiotics for Old Testament exegesis. He uses Eco's concepts of "encyclopedia" and "the open text" as a foundational method for exploring the poetry and theology of the book of Lamentations.[39] He shows how the author of Lamentations frequently exploits his cultural encyclopedia in his crafting the poetry of the text. He shows how this exploitation results in an open text that lends itself to an intentional multivalence of meaning resulting in a plurality of possible interpretations.

As this review has shown, there is little dialogue between semiotics and systematic theology. Aside from the three monographs mentioned above and the two issues of *Zygon* edited by Robinson and Southgate, few scholarly works evidence dialogue between the two disciplines. The works by Alkier, Huizenga, Langford, and Thomas deserve mention for a few reasons. First, they show how semiotics has major implications for biblical interpretation, especially in intertextuality. Second, though they do not give direct implications for systematic theology, they do have some indirect implications. Since much of Christian theology is concerned with the meaning of biblical texts and their interpretations, these works do have indirect implications for both dogmatic theology and systematic theology.

IMPORTANCE OF THIS STUDY

Since theologians seek to study the God who is creator of everything, then theology must be a discipline that studies everything. Since the birth of Christian theology, theologians often have dialogued with contemporary

38. Langford, "'Signs' of Hope in the Midst of Suffering."
39. Thomas, *Poetry and Theology in the Book of Lamentations*.

philosophies in order to articulate better the truth of Christian theology to their audiences. Many Christian theologians, however, have neglected the philosophical discipline of semiotics. Though some, such as Mark C. Taylor, have engaged the works of the French semiotic thinker Jacques Derrida in their works on theological method, none have sought to utilize the semiotic works of Umberto Eco for such. To date, the most substantial appropriation of semiotics for systematic theology is Andrew Robinson. Though Robinson contributes to the needed dialogue between semiotics and theology, he does not interact any with Eco's semiotics. I will show that Eco's semiotic project has much to offer theological prolegomena, specifically his theory of encyclopedia.

Eco provides his first thorough treatment of his concept of encyclopedia in his work *Semiotics and the Philosophy of Language*. In the chapter "Dictionary vs. Encyclopedia," he discussed whether a theory of dictionary or encyclopedia is more suited to provide a theory of sememes. Sememes are basic content units, specifically in semantics. Sememes might be understood best as the content of an expression. Every sign has both an expression plane and a content plane. Take for example the verbal sign *dog*. The morpheme, or word, itself serves as the expression of the sign. The content might be something along the lines of "domesticated canine." This content is an example of a sememe. How does one understand sememes? Eco introduced his concept of "dictionary vs. encyclopedia" to answer this question.

Dictionary theories, he demonstrated, are grounded on a type of Porphyrian tree that attempt to generate sememes based on the Aristotelian categories of *genera* and *species*. He then provided multiple counterexamples showing how the Porphyrian tree is an unacceptable model for this task. Unlike the model of the dictionary, the model of the encyclopedia does not seek to generate sememes based on *genera* and *species*. Rather, in the encyclopedia, a sememe presupposes a totality of sememes. An encyclopedia draws on the relatedness and interrelatedness of the sememe to all other sememes. In other words, an entry in an encyclopedia presupposes all of the other entries. Rather than being grounded in a philosophy of substance, like the dictionary, an encyclopedia understands a sememe in its relationships and interrelationships with all other sememes. These relationships and interrelationships constitute sememes.

Whereas the model of the Porphyrian tree best represents the model dictionary, the labyrinth best represents the encyclopedia. The model of the labyrinth that Eco utilizes is that of a rhizomatic net. This net has no set layout; there is no set way that two nodes must be connected. Each node in a net is an intersection of connectors. All of the nodes in a net are connected and interconnected to each other. Also, according to Eco, the potential connections and interconnections between these nodes are *potentially* infinite, though *realistically* finite (as the net is not actually infinite). Translated to the concept of sememes, each sememe would represent a node in a net. As each node in a net has a relationship, direct or indirect, to all of the other nodes in it, a sememe is related to all other sememes, directly or indirectly.

This understanding of encyclopedic semantics can offer a useful model for understanding the nature and task of systematic theology. I will show that this model is beneficial for systematic theology in that it lends itself to doctrinal development, critical realism, the necessary coherence of all knowledge as well as the interconnectedness of all knowledge, and abductive reasoning, all of which feature prominently in issues surrounding theological prolegomena. Also, following theologians such as Pannenberg and Thiselton, this model for systematic theology will lend itself to understanding systematic theology as a hermeneutic endeavor. This semiotic model will provide a better understanding of the nature and task of systematic theology and will demonstrate the practical significance of this research endeavor.

As one can see, this book will be an original contribution to the dialogue between theology and semiotics. This monograph is original in that, though some recent theologians have dialogued with the semiotic projects of Peirce and others, none have engaged the works of Eco. As shown above, the primary engagement with Eco's semiotics has been in the discipline of biblical interpretation, and only a few of these contributing scholars have engaged his concept of encyclopedia. Though Thomas, Alkier, Huizenga, and Langford note the usefulness of Eco's concept of encyclopedia for biblical interpretation and biblical intertextuality, no one has noted its usefulness for systematic theology. This work will be an original contribution to the needed dialogue between theology and semiotics in that it will utilize Eco's semiotic concept of encyclopedia to develop a new model for systematic theology, one that is especially useful for addressing issues in theological prolegomena.

METHODOLOGY

The work at hand is an exercise in constructive theology. I aim to appropriate insights in contemporary semiotics for the use of systematic theology. The primary method that I will utilize is an abductive and dialogical approach that will work along with content analysis to analyze Eco's works in philosophy and semiotics. The research is abductive because it is a creative hypothesis that Eco's concept of the model encyclopedia can offer a new model and method for systematic theology that is especially useful in matters pertaining to theological prolegomena. This conjectured hypothesis will provide better explanations and answers to the phenomena of problems that surround issues in theological prolegomena. The research is dialogical in that these problems that surround theological prolegomena will serve as guiding questions and case studies to test the competency of this new model. Each problem will utilize the space of one chapter to dialogue with this model based on Eco's encyclopedia to show the benefits of said model. This research will take place via content analysis in that the work of Eco will be analyzed and evaluated for its usefulness for systematic theology. I will use this dialogical approach of the guiding questions previously mentioned to evaluate the content being analyzed.

This project begins with an exploration of the corpus of Umberto Eco, especially those texts dealing with semiotics and philosophy, in order to discern and explicate his concept of the model encyclopedia. The primary works in which this concept appears are his *A Theory of Semiotics, The Role of the Reader: Explorations in the Semiotics of Texts, Semiotics and the Philosophy of Language, The Limits of Interpretation,* and *Kant and the Platypus: Essays on Language and Cognition.* This explicated overview will serve as one chapter.

A chapter is devoted to each of three problems in theological prolegomena that will serve as a case study to test the competency of the new model. Each problem will be posed as a question. The first question concerns the usefulness of the encyclopedic model for issues surrounding epistemology, namely those of critical realism and abduction. What role does abductive reasoning play in this new model? How does this model relate to the models of critical realism proposed by other significant theologians? Are there implications of the model encyclopedia for issues surrounding foundationalism and coherentism? These questions are some of the epistemological issues that this chapter will address. Some of the primary interlocuters for Eco in this chapter are Peirce, Quine, and McGrath. These have been chosen due to the prolific works they have dedicated to these issues.

The second question concerns how this new model will work with the hermeneutical nature of theology. *Hermeneutics*, in this monograph, refers to the branch of philosophy that enquires into human understanding, what some refer to as philosophical hermeneutics or hermeneutic philosophy. This branch of philosophy is concerned with all human understanding. More specifically, according to Pannenberg, hermeneutics is concerned with understanding meaning, and meaning is the relationship between particulars and wholes. Gadamer contended that all understanding occurs through the medium of language. How does Eco's model encyclopedia work with these phenomena? Some of the primary interlocuters for Eco in this chapter will include Gadamer, Ricoeur, Pannenberg, and Thiselton.

The final question concerns the implications of this model for doctrinal development. Does Eco's model help explain the phenomenon of doctrinal development? Does Eco's model allow for the continuation of doctrinal development? The primary interlocutors for Eco in this chapter include George Lindbeck, Alister McGrath, Kevin Vanhoozer, Anthony Thiselton, and Rhyne Putman.

I will determine the ability of this new model and method, grounded on Eco's semiotic concept of the model encyclopedia, to serve as a satisfactory model for theology by its ability to answer each of the three problems posed above. Upon answering these problems in a satisfactory manner, one can infer the conclusion that Eco's model encyclopedia is indeed capable of offering systematic theology a new model and method, which implicates the usefulness of semiotics for theology.

1

A History of Semiotics

ANCIENT AND MEDIEVAL SEMIOTICS

Before discussing the semiotics of Umberto Eco, one should understand first the context in which he appears. Though he has been one of the most monumental contemporary figures in the field, his project cannot be grasped without understanding its place in the history of semiotics. This chapter will provide a brief history of semiotics in order to put Eco in his appropriate context.

The word *semiotics* comes from the Greek *semeion*, which means "sign." Its cognate *semeiotikos* means "observant of signs."[1] The ancient philosopher Hippocrates (c. 460–c. 370 BC) was the first to coin the term in his studies in medicine. Specifically, he coined the term for diagnosing bodily symptoms. When a body took on a fever, the fever itself was a manifestation of something else. The fever became a sign as it stood to someone for something else. Langford notes that, for this period in history, the medical symptom was the "paradigm sign."[2]

Plato (*ca.* 427–347 BC) was the first to differentiate between natural signs and conventional signs. Examples of natural signs include smoke, which points to fire, or a fever, as noted above. Conventional signs, on the

---

1. Langford, "'Signs' of Hope in the Midst of Suffering," 8.
2. Langford, "'Signs' of Hope in the Midst of Suffering," 9.

other hand, are man-made constructs. Examples of conventional signs are symbols, words, and traffic lights. Plato was especially interested in how conventional signs, namely words, could refer to specific objects as well as objects of similarity. The word *circle*, for example, does not merely refer to a specific circle, but it can refer to all things possessing the quality of circularity.[3] As Marcel Danesi notes, Plato believed that persons encode ideas with words, and these words do not belong to the everyday world because it is constantly changing. He suggested that words possess inherent properties that mirror the mind's innate forms.[4]

Aristotle (384-322 BC) took on a different understanding of signs than his teacher. Whereas Plato held that words themselves possessed inherent properties of the ideas they encoded, Aristotle claimed that words served as "practical strategies for naming singular things."[5] Only after the discovery that certain things possess similar qualities, or properties, are they classified into categories. Once this classification takes place, persons develop words to unite these different things that possess qualities of similarity. Examples of these categories are animals, plants, objects, etc. Whereas Plato's theory can be understood as *mentalist*, Aristotle's is *empirical*.[6]

Not long after the contributions of Plato and Aristotle, a question arose regarding signs: "Is there any connection between natural and conventional signs?"[7] Thus sparked the famous dispute over signs between the Stoics and the Epicureans. According to the Stoics, there are intrinsic qualities between conventional signs and human emotional and psychological states. In the same way that a fever reveals something intrinsic about the body's biological state, words can reveal something intrinsic to human states. The Epicureans, on the other hand, were not convinced. They discounted the Stoics' inferential theory of signs. Whereas, for the Stoics, signs were essentially propositions, the Epicureans held that signs were something that was observed.[8] For example, one observes that smoke is a sign of a fire, "not the proposition expressed by the sentence 'There is smoke over there.'"[9]

3. Danesi, *The Quest for Meaning*, 6.
4. Danesi, *The Quest for Meaning*, 6.
5. Danesi, *The Quest for Meaning*, 7.
6. Danesi, *The Quest for Meaning*, 7.
7. Danesi, *The Quest for Meaning*, 7.
8. Nöth, *Handbook of Semiotics*, 16.
9. Clarke, *Principles of Semiotic*, 14.

In some ways, Augustine (354–430) represented a sort of middle ground in the Stoic-Epicurean debate. Following the Epicureans, he accepted "the sign as a sense datum representing something that is not presently perceivable."[10] In keeping with the Stoics, he maintained a place for intentionality as well. In *On Christian Teaching*, Augustine held to a fundamental difference between natural signs and conventional signs. This difference lies in that natural signs, being products of nature, do not possess intentionality whereas conventional signs do. For Augustine, conventional signs include not only words but any sign invented by humans to serve communicative, psychological, or social needs, such as gestures. Augustine considered miracles to be conventional signs in that they were "messages from God and thus sacred signs."[11]

Danesi notes that the interest in "linking human understanding with sign production waned after St. Augustine's death."[12] The discussion remained in hibernation until around the eleventh century when many took interest in translating and preserving the works of Plato and Aristotle. Though the majority of scholars in Medieval Scholasticism followed Aristotle in their theory of the sign, some did make important developments during this time, such as nominalists. Whereas many scholastics, such as Thomas (1225–1274), held to a form of Aristotelian realism concerning metaphysics, others, namely William of Ockham (c. 1285–c. 1349), held a different view of reality. Aristotelian realism, following Plato, affirmed the existence of both forms (universals) and particulars. Whereas Plato held that the forms belonged to a separate immaterial reality, which was more real than the material reality, Aristotle argued that the forms were present in the particulars themselves. Nominalists, such as William, rejected the existence of forms altogether. They argued that only particulars exist in reality. Conventional signs, such as words, have an arbitrary relationship to particulars. As Martin Nöth summarizes, "Ockham considered universals to be signs without an existence of their own, but standing for individual objects. In his view, real existence had to be individual and could not be universal."[13] Thomas countered proto-nominalist ideas with the claim that "signs do indeed refer to real things and categories of things, even if

---

10. Nöth, *Handbook of Semiotics*, 17.
11. Danesi, *The Quest for Meaning*, 7.
12. Danesi, *The Quest for Meaning*, 7.
13. Nöth, *Handbook of Semiotics*, 18.

they constitute variable human models of them."[14] Also around this time, Francis Bacon (c. 1214–c.1292) provided one of the earliest typologies of signs. This comprehensive typology of signs contended that "without a firm understanding of the role of signs in human understanding, discussing what truth is or is not can only end up being a trivial matter of subjective opinion."[15]

PRECURSORS TO CONTEMPORARY SEMIOTICS

John Poinsot (1589–1644) is perhaps the most influential Renaissance figure in the history of semiotics. In the *Treatise on Signs* (1632), he defined a sign as a type of intermediary that stands between a thing and a thought. For him, a sign functions psychologically as a type of intermediary form in the mind to make a direct connection, or link, to reality. As a result, reality can be studied via the forms the mind makes.[16]

John Locke (1632–1704) seems to be the most influential contributor to sign theory during the Enlightenment. In his *Essay Concerning Human Understanding* (1690), he developed a plan for incorporating the study of these mental forms, or signs, into the study of philosophy. One should note that Locke was a nominalist rather than a realist. For Locke, signs serve as investigative instruments for philosophers.[17] Signs are instruments of knowledge. They do not, however, serve as a distinct method or discipline. Both ideas and words are signs, according to Locke. As a result, words are simply signs of other signs. Locke's views developed in his *Essay* were not challenged until the contributions of Ferdinand de Saussure.[18]

Though not as influential as John Locke, George Berkeley (1685–1753) is a noteworthy figure in the history of semiotics. A form of extreme nominalism, as well as an ontological idealism, can characterize his semiotics. He also held an extreme dyadic model of the sign.[19] For Berkeley, the word "*matter* is an ontologically meaningless term, whereas sensations or ideas are the only proper subject of philosophical investigation."[20]

14. Danesi, *The Quest for Meaning*, 8.
15. Danesi, *The Quest for Meaning*, 8.
16. Danesi, *The Quest for Meaning*, 9.
17. Danesi, *The Quest for Meaning*, 9.
18. Nöth, *Handbook of Semiotics*, 24.
19. Nöth, *Handbook of Semiotics*, 24–25.
20. Nöth, *Handbook of Semiotics*, 25.

The notion of an object of reference is semiotically meaningless. Unlike Locke, Berkeley rejected the distinction between cognitive objects and objects of the external world.[21]

FATHERS OF CONTEMPORARY SEMIOTICS

Ferdinand de Saussure and Charles Sanders Peirce are, undoubtedly, the fathers of contemporary semiotics. These two took semiotics in a whole new direction. Whereas before the paradigm sign for semiotics was the medical symptom, the paradigm sign became both the written and spoken word.[22]

Ferdinand de Saussure (1857–1913) often is credited with being the first to suggest that the study of signs and sign systems be its own formal discipline of study.[23] He proposed this idea in his work *Cours de linguistique générale* (1916).[24] He referred to this study as *semiology*. According to Saussure, the primary goal of semiology was to provide an understanding of the social functions of signs.[25] He contended that the most complex and universal of all sign systems is language. He stated that his reason for making this claim was that "There are no pre-existing ideas, and nothing is distinct before the appearance of language."[26]

Many of Saussure's insights are in response to the traditional approach to linguistics in the nineteenth century. Whereas the traditional approach to linguistics was diachronic in nature, looking at the changes in languages as they occur through history, Saussure preferred a synchronic approach, in which he "presented an analysis of the state of language in general, an understanding of the conditions for existence of *any* language."[27] He understood the linguistic sign to take on the form of a dyad. In this model, a sign is composed of two sides, like a coin. On one side is what he referred to as the *signifier*. The morpheme *dog*, is an example of a signifier. On the other side is what Saussure referred to as the *signified*. The signified is *not* equivalent to an object, or referent. Rather, the signified, according to Saussure,

21. Nöth, *Handbook of Semiotics*, 25.
22. Langford, "'Signs' of Hope," 13.
23. Danesi, *The Quest for Meaning*, 9.
24. Translated: *Course in General Linguistics*.
25. Danesi, *The Quest for Meaning*, 9.
26. Saussure, *Course in General Linguistics*, 15–16.
27. Cobley and Jansz, *Semiotics*, 9.

should be likened to a mental content.[28] More specifically, the signified of the spoken morpheme *dog* is the mental content, idea, image, or definition of *dog* that appears in the mind of the hearer or interpreter.

In Saussure's dyad, the relationship between a signifier and a signified is arbitrary. Nothing intrinsically relates or grounds the word *dog* to an actual dog. The meaning of signs is determined by their difference(s) from other signs. One of the ways one knows the meaning of *dog* is due to its difference from the word *cat*. The relationship, in languages, between the signifier and the signified is conventional in nature. This concept leads Saussure to make one of his most popular distinctions: the distinction between *langue* and *parole*. According to Paul Cobley, *parole* can be defined as "individual acts of speech," and *langue* can be defined as "a system of differences between signs."[29] The majority of European semiotics has fallen, more or less, in the footsteps of Saussure.

The second father of modern semiotics is Charles Sanders Peirce (1839–1914). Unlike Saussure, who referred to the study of signs as *semiology*, Perice, in keeping with Locke's terminology, referred to it as *semiotics*. Though much of Peirce's work was ignored during his lifetime, many now herald him as the greatest American philosopher. He is known primarily for his contributions to semiotics and logic, and he is known also as the father of *pragmatism*, which he later referred to as *pragmaticism*.

For Peirce, semiotics is essentially the science or study of *semiosis*.[30] He defined a sign, or *representamen*, as "something which stands to somebody for something in some respect or capacity."[31] Unlike Saussure, who understood the sign to be a dyad, Peirce understood the sign as a triad. In this triadic model, the sign is made up of the *representamen*, the *object*, and the

28. Cobley and Jansz, *Semiotics*, 11.

29. Cobley and Jansz, *Semiotics*, 15.

30. Peirce defines *semiosis* as "an action, or influence, which is, or involves, a cooperation of *three* subjects, such as a sign, its object, and its interpretant, this tri-relative influence not being in any way resolvable into actions between pairs." See Peirce, "A Survey of Pragmaticism," 5.484–488. Danesi provides a more basic summary of Peirce's definition: the "innate capacity that underlies the comprehension and production of signs. Semiosis is an activity of the brain that controls the production and comprehension of signs, from simple physiological signals to highly complex symbols." See Danesi, *Encyclopedic Dictionary of Semiotics, Media, and Communications*, 204. Elsewhere, he simplifies this definition to "the comprehension and production of signs" (Danesi, *The Quest for Meaning*, 180). For a more detailed discussion of Peirce's use of the term as well as Charles Morris's, see Ayim, "Semiosis," 910–15.

31. Peirce, "Divisions of Signs," 2.228.

interpretant. The representamen is equivalent to Saussure's *signifier*. Peirce often used the terms *representamen*, *sign-vehicle*, and *sign* interchangeably. This representamen stood for something else, what Peirce referred to as its *object*.[32] The sign, or representamen, also generated another sign, or idea, in the mind of the interpreter, which he called the *interpretant*.[33] The *interpretant* is synonymous with Saussure's *signified*. These three elements together form the "triadic sign relation."[34] Peirce suspected that the entire universe was made up entirely of signs.[35] Nöth notes, "Peirce even went so far as to conclude that 'the fact that every thought is a sign, taken in conjunction with the fact that life is a train of thought, proves that man is a sign.'"[36] Peirce's view of semiosis can be referred to as a pansemiotic understanding of the universe.

Following Kant, Peirce affirmed the existence of universal categories. Whereas Kant held to twelve categories, Peirce claimed only three: firstness, secondness, and thirdness.[37] He defined *firstness* as "the mode of being of that which is such as it is, positively and without reference to anything."[38] *Secondness* is best understood as a comparative category, the "relation of

---

32. Peirce distinguished between two types of object: immediate and dynamical. The dynamical object is understood also as the mediate object. He defined the immediate object as the "Object within the Sign" and "as the Sign itself represents it, and whose Being is thus dependent upon the Representation of it in the Sign." See Peirce, "Apology for Pragmaticism," 4.536. He defined the dynamical, or mediate, object as the "Object outside of the Sign," the "Reality which by some means contrives to determine the Sign to its Representation," (Peirce, "Apology for Pragmaticism," 4.536) or that "which, from the nature of things, the Sign cannot express, which it can only indicate and leave the interpreter to find out by collateral experience." See Peirce, "To William James," 8.314.

33. Peirce held that there were three interpretants. The first is the *immediate interpretant*, which is "the Quality of the Impression that a sign is fit to produce, not any actual reaction" (Peirce, "To William James," 8.314) . He often referred to the immediate interpretant as *semantic potentiality*. The second interpretant is the *dynamical interpretant*, which is the "direct effect actually produced by a Sign upon an Interpreter of it . . . that which is experienced in each act of Interpreation and is different in each from that of any other" (Peirce, "To William James," 8.315). Peirce referred to the third interpretant as the *final interpretant*. The *final interpretant* "is that which would finally be decided to be the true interpretation if consideration of the matter were carried so far that an ultimate opinion were reached." See Peirce, "Lady Welby, *What Is Meaning?*," 8.184.

34. Langford, "'Signs' of Hope," 17.

35. Peirce, "Issues of Pragmaticism," 5.448, ff.

36. Nöth, *Handbook of Semiotics*, 41. See also Peirce, "Some Consequences of Four Incapacities," 5.314.

37. Peirce, "To Lady Welby," 8:328.

38. Peirce, "To Lady Welby," 8.328.

a first to a second."³⁹ Peirce wrote, "It meets us in such facts as another, relation, compulsion, effect, dependence, independence, negation, occurrence, reality, result."⁴⁰ *Thirdness* is what relates a second to a third. Nöth comments, "It is the category of mediation, habit, memory, continuity, synthesis, communication (semiosis), representation, and signs."⁴¹

Peirce wrote substantially more on the topic of semiotics than did his contemporary Saussure. His numerous contributions to semiotics, as well as those of Saussure, are indispensable for the history of semiotics. These two fathers of contemporary semiotics are very different in their approaches to the topic. While the majority of semioticians in Europe have followed in the footsteps of Saussure, the majority of American semioticians have followed in the footsteps of Peirce.

CONTEMPORARY SEMIOTICS

Louis Hjelmslev (1899–1965) was one of the founders of a radically structuralist school of linguistics known as *glossematics*. Glossematics often is referred to as the Copenhagen School of Linguistics. Like the majority of European semioticians, Hjelmslev followed in the footsteps of Saussure, whose semiology project lent itself to structuralism. Hjelmslev's structural glossematics is not the same as the formalism that characterized the Prague School of Linguistics. One of the major contributions of Hjelmslev's glossematics was its "theory of structural homology between the expression and the content lanes of language."⁴² Language is Hjelmslev's departure point for his semiotics. Nöth notes that Hjelmslev often used *semiotic* in a broad sense to denote *language*.⁴³ Hjelmslev wrote, "In practice, a language is a semiotic into which all other semiotics may be translated—both all other languages, and all other conceivable semiotic structures."⁴⁴ Hjelmslev adopted Saussure's dyadic model of the sign.

Perhaps the other contribution for which Hjelmslev is most recognized is his *connotative semiotics*. Danesi defines *connotation* as "The extended or secondary meaning of a sign; the symbolic or mythic meaning of a certain

39. Nöth, *Handbook of Semiotics*, 41.
40. Peirce, "A Guess at the Riddle," 1.356.
41. Nöth, *Handbook of Semiotics*, 41.
42. Nöth, *Handbook of Semiotics*, 64.
43. Nöth, *Handbook of Semiotics*, 65–66.
44. Hjelmslev, *Prolegomena to a Theory of Language*, 109.

signifier (word, image, etc.)."[45] According to Hjelmslev, what characterizes a connotative semiotic is the semantic addition of a stylistic value to the "primary semiotic form."[46] Connotations are essentially stylistic semiotic units. For Hjelmslev, a language semiotic is made up of two planes: an expression plane and a content plane. The immediate content plane, or the content plane of intentionality, is the denotation. But this denotative plane itself becomes a semiotic and has its own expression and content planes. The planes of this denotative plane are the connotative planes. Nöth notes, three forms of a connotation: a denotative form, substance, or both form and substance.[47]

Roman Jakobson (1896–1982) was perhaps the most productive semiotician of the twentieth century. His personal bibliography contains over one thousand titles, and his *Selected Works* comprises eight volumes. Nöth categorizes Jakobson's career into four epochs: the formalist period, the structuralist period, the semiotic period, and the interdisciplinary period.[48] His primary fields of semiotic research concentrated on linguistics and poetics. He was one of the first scholars, if not the first, to discover the usefulness of Peirce's semiotics for linguistics.[49] Though he recognized the usefulness of Peirce's work, he still aligned closer to the school of Saussure, which is seen in his affinity for structuralism. Daniel Chandler notes that Jakobson was the first to coin the term "structuralism."[50]

Concerning semiotics and language, Jakobson wrote,

> The subject matter of semiotic is the communication of any messages whatever, whereas the field of linguistics is confined to the communication of verbal messages. Hence, of these two sciences of man, the latter has a narrower scope, yet on the other hand, any human communication of nonverbal messages presupposes a circuit of verbal messages, without a reverse implication.[51]

He described three types of sign systems: language substitutes, language transforms, and idiomorphic systems.[52] These three sign systems are re-

---

45. Danesi, *The Quest for Meaning*, 173.
46. Nöth, *Handbook of Semiotics*, 72. See also Hjelmslev, *Prolegomena*, 119.
47. Nöth, *Handbook of Semiotics*, 72.
48. Nöth, *Handbook of Semiotics*, 75.
49. Nöth, *Handbook of Semiotics*, 75.
50. Chandler, *Semiotics*, 5.
51. Jakobson, *Main Trends in the Science of Language*, 32.
52. Nöth, *Handbook of Semiotics*, 75.

lated to verbal, or spoken, language. Even though Jakobson is one of the most interdisciplinarian semioticians in modern semiotics, he did not hold a pansemiotic view of the universe or of the sciences as Peirce did. He did hold, however, that three branches of science constantly overlapped one another, thus showing their generality: linguistics, semiotic, and social anthropology.[53]

Charles Morris (1901–1979) was an American semiotician and one of the foremost advocates of the Peircean school of semiotics. Cobley notes that Morris began his semiotic work in a time when behaviorism was the intellectual trend, and that this trend can be seen in his work.[54] Following Peirce, Morris saw the semiotic problem as broader than the problems surrounding communication and language. Whereas Saussure and his intellectual offspring focused on discovering "'deep structures' underlying the 'surface features' of sign systems,"[55] Peirce and his intellectual children broadened the problem from culture and language to include all types of signs, both natural and conventional.[56] Morris is clearly in the latter of these two camps.

According to Morris, semiotics had two relationships to science: "It is both a science among the sciences and an instrument of the sciences."[57] Morris also slightly deviated from Peirce in his model of the sign. Whereas Peirce held that the three elements of a sign were the representamen, the object, and the interpretant, Morris referred to these as the *sign vehicle*, the *designatum*, and the *interpretant*.[58] Perhaps what he is best known for is his division of the three components of semiotics: syntax, semantics, and pragmatics. These are the three components not only of semiotics but of semiosis as well.[59] Nöth summarizes, "Accordingly, *syntactics* studies the relation between a given sign vehicle and other sign vehicles, *semantics* studies the relations between sign vehicles and their designata, and *pragmatics*

---

53. Nöth, *Handbook of Semiotics*, 76.
54. Cobley and Jansz, *Semiotics*, 106.
55. Chandler, *Semiotics*, 5.
56. Cobley and Jansz, *Semiotics*, 36.
57. Morris, *Foundations of the Theory of Signs*, 2.

58. Morris, *Foundations of the Theory of Signs*, 3. Morris also noted that some consider the *interpreter* to be one of the semiosic relationships as well.

59. Morris, *Foundations of the Theory of Signs*, 6–7. See also Nöth, *Handbook of Semiotics*, 50.

studies the relation between sign vehicles and their interpreters."[60] Morris also developed an elaborate typology of signs, one much more elaborate than that developed by Peirce. He is recognized also for making some early pioneering efforts in the field of zoosemiotics.[61]

Claude Lévi-Strauss (1908–2009) was one of the pinnacles of structuralism in the twentieth century. He took many insights from the semiotics of Saussure and Jakobson and applied them to anthropology. He referred to his project as *structural anthropology*.[62] He is well known for applying these insights from structuralism to the study of myth, which, according to Nöth, "has become a significant contribution to text semiotics."[63] Concerning anthropology, Lévi-Strauss wrote, "Structural linguistics will certainly play the same renovating role with respect to the social sciences that nuclear physics, for example, has played for the physical sciences."[64] He was convinced that the linguistic structures that form and shape a culture's mind provided the most general way to understand said culture. More important than the signs used, according to Lévi-Strauss, were the relations between them, the general laws that exist within the sign system. He goes on to apply this structuralism to institutions such as marriage, religious rites, and even cuisine preferences.[65]

Jacques Lacan (1901–1981) is known for his contributions in the structuralism of psychoanalysis. Following Saussure, he maintained a dyadic model of the sign, as well as Saussure's interest in binary oppositions. Nöth comments that Lacan applied several of Saussure's binary oppositions such as *langue–parole*, *signifier–signified*, and *metaphor–metonymy*, to his reading of Freud's psychology.[66] Following Freud, he affirmed that humans use language on two different levels: the message of the conscious subject and the message of the unconscious subject.[67] Nöth summarizes, "For Lacan, the language of the unconscious is a system of dyadic signs in which the psychoanalytic symptom functions as a signifier that points to the unconscious

---

60. Nöth, *Handbook of Semiotics*, 50. See also Morris, *Foundations*, 6–7.
61. Cobley and Jansz, *Semiotics*, 106–09.
62. Lévi-Strauss, *Structural Anthropology*.
63. Nöth, *Handbook of Semiotics*, 301.
64. Lévi-Strauss, *Structural Anthropology*, 58.
65. For a more comprehensive survey of Lévi-Strauss, see Rossi, *The Unconscious in Culture*.
66. Nöth, *Handbook of Semiotics*, 303.
67. Lacan, *The Language of the Self*, 27ff.

thought process."⁶⁸ Lacan argued that in the dyad of the sign, the signifier dominated the signified.⁶⁹ Since, within speech, many intrasystematic references develop, meaning "insists" in a chain of signifiers. None of the elements of meaning consist in the signification.⁷⁰ One can see affinities here between Lacan and Jacques Derrida, who will be discussed below.

Though he is not a semiotician per se, Michel Foucault (1926–1984) has made some insights into the structuralism of the history of ideas that has had an impact in the field of semiotics. Nöth notes that his contributions are not centered on the structuralism of linguistics like many are, but that they focus on differential structures, such as emic units, oppositions, and other types of structures that occur throughout the history of ideas.⁷¹ Foucault did, however, make the sign his primary emphasis and the center of his research. More specifically, he focused on the sign and "the disappearance of the subject in an anonymous system."⁷²

Concerning signs, for Foucault, signs are representative systems that make up three primary areas: economics, language, and natural history. He concludes that the sign has no actual connection to external reality. As a result, the sign is no more than a connection "between the idea of one thing and the idea of another."⁷³ A gap exists between a sign and its object. Language is not able to relate directly to reality. Foucault writes, "Language was a form of knowing and knowing was automatically discourse. Thus, language occupied a fundamental situation in relation to all knowledge: it was only by the medium of language that the things of the world could be known."⁷⁴ Foucault appears as one of the early figures of poststructuralism.

Jacques Derrida (1930–2004) is one who has gained semiotics a lot of popular attention. He is known primarily as the father of deconstruction. Deconstruction is programmatically poststructuralist, according to Nöth.⁷⁵ Similar to Foucault's project, deconstruction rejects a direct relation of signs to reality, especially linguistic signs. For Derrida, no actual something lies behind a sign; only other signs lie behind signs. There is an "absence of

---

68. Nöth, *Handbook of Semiotics*, 303.
69. Lacan, *Ecrits: A Selection*, 149.
70. Lacan, *Ecrits: A Selection*, 153.
71. Nöth, *Handbook of Semiotics*, 304.
72. Nöth, *Handbook of Semiotics*, 304.
73. Foucault, *The Order of Things*, 63.
74. Foucault, *The Order of Things*, 295–96.
75. Nöth, *Handbook of Semiotics*, 306.

26 \\ God in the Labyrinth

the transcendental signified."[76] More specifically, the meaning of a sign is found in a combination of what Saussure called *différence* and what Derrida referred to as *différance*. For Saussure, *différence* was the structural principle through which a sign takes on meaning. On the other hand, for Derrida, a sign contains *traces* of all other signs in it because the meaning of a sign is no more than the deferment a sign has to the other signs it is related to within a syntagm.[77] This trace slips into an infinite regress of sign deferment. While this notion might sound similar to Peirce's concept of *unlimited semiosis*, the two are not the same; rather, they are quite different.[78]

Roland Barthes (1915–1980) is best known for his work in text semiotics and visual communication. His early work was thoroughly structuralist, but after encountering the work in intertextuality by his pupil, Julia Kristeva, he too shifted into the poststructuralist camp. Again, he was known primarily for his structuralist work in visual advertisements and his dictum of the death of the Author.[79]

Key to Barthes's text semiotics was Hjelmslev's theory of connotation. He differed from Hjelmslev, however, by disregarding the notions of form and substance.[80] More specifically, Hjelmslev's theory of connotation was key to his semiotic analysis of culture. Barthes defined a sign as "a system consisting of E, an expression (or signifier), in relation (R) to C, a content (or signified)."[81] He also popularized the idea that objects systems were secondary systems.[82] As noted above, he would shift eventually from structuralism into poststructuralism. This shift took place after his *The Fashion System*.[83]

Algirdas Julien Greimas (1917–1992) is best known for his *Structural Semantics* and founding of the semiotic School of Paris.[84] His rigorous structuralism has become very influential for text semiotics following him. Influenced by the work by Lévi-Strauss and others, Greimas became

---

76. Derrida, *Writing and Difference*, 280.

77. Nöth, *Handbook of Semiotics*, 306.

78. See Eco, "Unlimited Semiosis and Drift: Pragmaticism vs. Pragmatism," 23–43.

79. Barthes's most systematic work was Barthes, *Fashion System*. This contains one of the most comprehensive sources of Barthes semiotic thought. See also Barthes, *Elements of Semiology*.

80. Nöth, *Handbook of Semiotics*, 310.

81. Barthes, *Semiology*, 90.

82. Nöth, *Handbook of Semiotics*, 312.

83. Nöth, *Handbook of Semiotics*, 313.

84. Nöth, *Handbook of Semiotics*, 314.

interested in the place of structuralism in concrete existence. More specifically, he became fascinated with the placement of structuralism in semantics. He sought to apply some of the methods utilized in structural linguistics to analyze texts.[85] Nöth summarizes, "His linguistic framework is determined by Saussure's concept of structure as difference, the principle of binary oppositions and distinctiveness of functional phonology, and Hjelmslev's glossamatic sign model."[86] Greimas rejected the definition of semiotics as "the theory of signs" and, instead, defined it as "a theory of signification."[87] Greimas also made key insights into generative discourse analysis and isotopy. Danesi notes that Greimas's model of generative discourse analysis has been used widely in narrative theory and hermeneutics.[88] In many senses, he represents a type of pinnacle of structuralism in the twentieth century.

Thomas Sebeok (1920–2001) was a pupil of Charles Morris and subsequently followed in the footsteps of Peirce's semiotics. He held a faculty position at Indiana University Press for many years, and he was an editor of the major journal in semiotics, *Semiotica*. Cobley credits Sebeok as the reason that the term *semiotics* has superseded *semiology*.[89] He is best known for his work in the field of *zoosemiotics*. This would later come to be known as *biosemiotics*, which studies the role of semiotics in all life forms.[90] Zoosemiotics is distinct from anthroposemiotics, according Sebeok, because the former does not utilize language.[91] Important for Sebeok's project is the concept of *Umwelt*, or environment. Specifically, this concept is important for understanding how semiosis occurs in specific environments. According to Sebeok, there are two universal sign systems in which semiosis occurs: genetic and verbal.[92]

Julia Kristeva (b. 1941) originally sought to study the work of the Russian postformalist Mikhail Bakhtin under the guidance of Roland Barthes.

---

85. Nöth, *Handbook of Semiotics*, 315.
86. Nöth, *Handbook of Semiotics*, 315.
87. Greimas and Courtés, *Semiotics and Language*, 287.
88. Danesi, *The Quest for Meaning*, 107–8.
89. Cobley and Jansz, *Semiotics*, 120.
90. Danesi defines *zoosemiotics* as "the branch of semiotics studying semiosis in animals," and he defines *biosemiotics* as "the branch of semiotics that studies semiosis in all life forms." See Danesi, *Quest for Meaning*, 172; 182.
91. Cobley and Jansz, *Semiotics*, 122.
92. Cobley and Jansz, *Semiotics*, 126.

Early in her work, however, Kristeva became prominent in poststructuralism. For her, semiotics was primarily concerned with making models.[93] Semiotics, therefore, became a type of autocritical metatheory for Kristeva. She defined *models* as "formal systems whose structure is isomorphic or analogous to the structure of another system."[94] This definition provided her with the foundation for her developments in what is now known as *intertextuality*, a term that she coined. She is best known for her developments in intertextuality and for her approach to studying texts in light of these developments, which is referred to as *semanalysis*.[95]

Since a text is an important concept in semiotic research, it becomes a central concept for Kristeva's semanalysis. Nöth notes that, for Kristeva, language system and text are opposed to one another in a dialectical relationship.[96] Concerning intertextuality, a text is "the absorption and transformation of another text."[97] Kristeva also applied her work in intertextuality and semanalaysis to psychoanalysis, and she is also popular for her "logic of negativity."[98]

This chapter has put forth a brief history of semiotics in order to establish the appropriate context for understanding Eco's contributions. Eco himself has engaged in a broad semiotic project. Foundationally, Eco adopts Peirce's pragmaticist concerns; however, he adopts Hjelmslev's dyadic model of the sign. Also, like Peirce, Eco is a realist, affirming that signs indeed relate to reality. Methodologically, however, he is a structuralist, though he does not adopt a structuralist ontology. He primarily adopts insights from the structuralism projects of Hjelmslev and Jakobson, citing the former more than the latter. Eco has contributed to text semiotics and the relationship between semiotics and the philosophy of language. He has written also on the relationship of semiotics to cognition. This next chapter will overview Eco's semiotic project in order to provide a holistic context for his concept of the model encyclopedia.

---

93. Nöth, *Handbook of Semiotics*, 321.
94. Kristeva, *The Kristeva Reader*, 76.
95. Nöth, *Handbook of Semiotics*, 322.
96. Nöth, *Handbook of Semiotics*, 322.
97. Kristeva, *Desire in Language*, 37.
98. Nöth, *Handbook of Semiotics*, 323.

2

The Semiotics of Umberto Eco

This chapter will provide a detailed overview of the semiotics of Umberto Eco. Though my thesis focuses on Eco's model encyclopedia, one needs a general understanding of his semiotic project to provide the appropriate context. This chapter will proceed by working through each of Eco's major works in semiotics. I will deal with these works in Eco's written chronological order: *A Theory of Semiotics, The Role of the Reader, Semiotics and the Philosophy of Language, The Limits of Interpretation,* and *Kant and the Platypus*.[1] Eco published the first

---

1. These books are not the only works that comprise Eco's contributions to the field of semiotics; however, space does not allow for a thorough interaction with all of Eco's works. The works discussed in this chapter are more than adequate for providing a comprehensive overview of Eco's semiotics. One might notice that I have not included Eco's first monograph in semiotics, *La struttura assente* (The Absent Structure*)*, which never was translated into English. I have several reasons for this decision. First, all of Eco's contributions to semiotics in this work can be found in his *A Theory of Semiotics*, which originally was intended to be an English translation of *La struttura assente*. As Michael Caesar notes, every time Eco attempted this translation, he ended up writing a different book. He eventually accepted the new work, *A Theory of Semiotics*, which he wrote first in English and translated later into his native Italian language. Second, as Caesar also notes, *A Theory of Semiotics* includes Eco's more mature semiotic theory. Eco made several corrections to the theory provided in *La struttura assente*, many of which are discussed in Caesar, *Theory*, 76–80. As a result, I have chosen to exclude it from the list of works summarized in this chapter. Also, concerning the works discussed in this chapter, the reader will notice that I am working from the English versions of said works rather than the original Italian versions. The reasons for this decision are as follows: *A Theory of Semiotics, The Role of the Reader, Semiotics and the Philosophy of Language,* and *The Limits*

four of these works through Indiana University Press in the series *Advances in Semiotics*, edited by his friend and fellow semiotician, Thomas Sebeok. The fifth work, however, does not appear in this series.[2] *Kant and the Platypus* also merits mention in this chapter due to Eco's exploration of the implications of his semiotic theory for issues surrounding cognition and language. Though he discusses a large amount of the material in these essays in the four prior works, he develops a lot of new material that he does not discuss in those works. As a result, it has a place in this chapter.

Some of the following works receive more attention than others—specifically *A Theory of Semiotics* and *Kant and the Platypus*. *Theory* receives more attention because the foundational nature it provides for the following works. The four following works serve as applications and endeavors into different areas of semiotics using the insights from *Theory*. Even within the works discussed below, certain chapters and essays from Eco receive more detail than others. I will provide more attention to areas that are more central to Eco's semiotics while only briefly discussing the less pertinent ones. Several essays in *The Role of the Reader* and *The Limits of Interpretation* receive little-to-no mention due to their lack of either theoretical material or centrality to Eco's project.

A THEORY OF SEMIOTICS

A Theory of Semiotics[3] is the first installment in Eco's semiotic project.[4] In this monograph, he provides his general theory of semiotics.[5] He divides

---

of Interpretation were either written in English by Eco prior to his writing them in Italian, such as the case of *Theory*, or they were translated into English by Eco himself. As a result, working and translating from the Italian is not necessary. Though *Kant and the Platypus* is translated by someone else, it is a very reliable translation. In his summary and discussion of the work, Caesar does not note any differences in the English from the Italian.

2. Eco published *Kant and the Platypus* through Harcourt publishers, whom he primarily uses to publish his popular-level essay collections.

3. Eco, *A Theory of Semiotics*.

4. Michael Caesar notes that Eco wrote the English text prior to the Italian *Trattato di semiotica generale*. He writes, "Despite the dates of publication, however, the English version is the prior of the two texts, the outcome of failed attempts to translate *La struttura assente* and the decision to rewrite the book directly in English, with the help of David Osmond Smith; the Italian is 're-translated' from the English. The one place in which the texts differ, as might be expected, is in the prefaces to the respective editions." Caesar, *Umberto Eco*, 78.

5. Unlike many before him, Eco seeks to discuss issues of semiotics not based on

the work into three major chapters: Signification and Communication, Theory of Codes, and Theory of Sign Production. Eco presents his thesis for the book:

> The aim of this book is to explore the theoretical possibility and the social function of a unified approach to every phenomenon of signification and/or communication. Such an approach should take the form of a *general semiotic theory*, able to explain every case of sign–function in terms of underlying systems of elements mutually correlated by one or more codes.[6]

He notes that a general semiotic theory must take into account both a theory of codes and a theory of sign production.[7] He states, "In principle, a semiotics of signification entails a theory of codes, while a semiotics of communication entails a theory of sign production."[8] Concerning the scope of semiotics, Eco states,

> Semiotics is concerned with everything that can be *taken* as a sign. A sign is everything which can be taken as significantly substituting for something else. This something else does not necessarily have to exist or to actually be somewhere at the moment in which a sign stands in for it. Thus *semiotics is in principle the discipline studying everything which can be used in order to lie.*[9]

If something *cannot* be used to lie then it *cannot* be used to tell the truth either. Eco also notes that semiotics is concerned both with signification and communication because every form of communication presupposes a system of signification.[10] He defines a communicative process as "the passage of a signal (not necessarily a sign) from a source (through a

---

linguistics but on information theory. Caesar comments, "Eco's first important move, following up the research already embarked upon in *Opera aperta*, is to establish the key notions of semiology (sign, meaning, code, message, etc.) on the basis not of linguistics but of information theory. . . . If every cultural fact is communication, it is necessary to identify the elementary structure of communication where communication takes place, so to speak, at its most basic level: the transmission of information between two machines. This is not because more complex forms of communication can be reduced to the most simple, but because the latter serves to help us construct an exemplary *model*." Caesar, *Umberto Eco*, 55.

6. Eco, *A Theory of Semiotics*, 3.
7. Eco, *A Theory of Semiotics*, 3.
8. Eco, *A Theory of Semiotics*, 4.
9. Eco, *A Theory of Semiotics*, 7.
10. Eco, *A Theory of Semiotics*, 8.

transmitter, along a channel) to a destination."[11] He defines a code as "a system of signification, insofar as it couples present entities with an absent unit. When—on the basis of an underlying rule—something actually presented to the perception of the addressee *stands for* something else, there is *signification*."[12] Eco defines a signification system as "an autonomous semiotic construct that has an abstract mode of existence independent of any possible communicative act it makes possible."[13] He also notes the two major understandings of the sign that exists within semiotics: those of Saussure and Peirce. The former proposed a dyadic model of the sign where the sign was composed of the signifier and the signified "or sign-vehicle and meaning."[14] Peirce, on the other hand, proposed a triadic model of the sign where the sign is composed of the representamen (signifier), the interpretant (signified or meaning), and, in the case of icons and indices, the object. Eco adopts Peirce's understanding of the semiotic task, claiming that "the definition given by Peirce seems to me more comprehensive and semiotically more fruitful."[15] He does not, however, adopt Peirce's triad; rather, he adopts a dyadic model, but not that of Saussurre. Eco adopts the dyad of Louis Hjelmslev, who claimed that a sign is composed of two functive planes: an expression plane and a content plane, but more will be said on this below. He also discusses issues concerning epistemological boundaries, information theory, and signals before concluding his introduction.

Eco discusses the topic of signification and communication in chapter one. He states the following: "If every communication process must be explained as relating to a system of signification, it is necessary to single out *the elementary structure of communication* at the point where communication may be seen in its most elementary terms."[16] Eco's communication model is composed of the following components: source, transmitter, signal, channel, signal, receiver, message, and destination. He provides the following example of a watergate as an example for this elementary model of communication:

> Whether there is water or not; whether it is above or below the danger level; how much above or below; at what rate it is rising:

11. Eco, *A Theory of Semiotics*, 8.
12. Eco, *A Theory of Semiotics*, 8.
13. Eco, *A Theory of Semiotics*, 9.
14. Eco, *A Theory of Semiotics*, 14.
15. Eco, *A Theory of Semiotics*, 15.
16. Eco, *A Theory of Semiotics*, 32.

all this constitutes pieces of information which can be transmitted from the watershed, which will therefore be considered as a *source* of information.

> So the engineer puts in the watershed a sort of buoy which, when it reaches danger level, activates a *transmitter* capable of emitting an electric *signal* which travels through a *channel* and is picked up downstream by a *receiver*; this device converts the signal into a given string of elements that constitute a *message* for a *destination* apparatus. The destination, at this point, can release a mechanical response in order to correct the situation at the source.... In this model the code is the device which assures that a given electric signal produces a given mechanical message, and that this elicits a given response.[17]

Next, Eco discusses systems and codes. In the watergate model above, under the name *code* the engineer considers four things:

> (a) A set of signals ruled by internal combinatory laws.... They could be called a *syntactic system*. (b) A set of states of the water which are taken into account as a set of *notions* about the state of the water and which can become a set of possible communicative contents.... Let me call this set of 'contents' a *semantic system*. (c) A set of possible *behavioral responses* on the part of the destination.... (d) A *rule* coupling some items from the (a) system with some from the (b) or the (c) system."[18]

Eco highlights that one must be able to distinguish between two types of codes: codes and s–codes. He defines s–codes as follows:

> S–codes are systems or 'structures' that can also subsist independently of any sort of significant or communicative purpose, and as such may be studied by information theory or by various types of generative grammar. They are made up of finite sets of elements oppositionally structured and governed by combinational rules that can generate both finite and infinite strings or chains of these elements.[19]

S–codes function as structures. Eco discusses issues of information theory and how they pertain to codes and s–codes. As noted above, information

---

17. Eco, *A Theory of Semiotics*, 33.
18. Eco, *A Theory of Semiotics*, 37.
19. Eco, *A Theory of Semiotics*, 38.

theory provides a basic foundation for the way Eco understands communication, although he is aware that communication is often more than the transmission of information. Though communication is more than the transmission of information, it is never less.

Eco provides his theory of codes in chapter two. He begins by discussing sign–function. More specifically, he distinguishes between a sign and a signal:

> A signal is a pertinent unit of a system that may be an expression system ordered to a content, but could also be a physical system without any semiotic purpose; as such it is studied by information theory in the stricter sense of the term. A signal can be a stimulus that does not mean anything but causes or elicits something; however, when used as the recognized *antecedent* of a foreseen *consequent* it may be viewed as a sign, inasmuch as it stands for its consequent (as far as the sender is concerned). On the other hand a sign is always an element of an *expression plane* conventionally correlated to one (or several) elements of a *content plane*.[20]

Eco also provides the following explanation of sign–functions as they pertain to a theory of codes:

> Properly speaking there are not signs, but only *sign–functions*. . . . A sign–function is realized when two *functives* (expression and content) enter into a mutual correlation; the same functive can also enter into another correlation, thus becoming a different functive and therefore giving rise to a new sign–function. Thus signs are the provisional result of coding rules which establish *transitory* correlations of elements, each of these elements being entitled to enter –under given coded circumstances—into another correlation and thus form a new sign."[21]

Codes do not organize signs as much as they "provide the rules which *generate* signs as concrete occurrences in communicative intercourse."[22] Eco then discusses *expression* and *content*. All expressions have contents, and all contents have an expression. He states,

> Thus (a) a code establishes the correlation of an expression plane with a content plane; (b) a sign-function establishes the correlation of an abstract element of the expression system with an

---

20. Eco, *A Theory of Semiotics*, 48.
21. Eco, *A Theory of Semiotics*, 49.
22. Eco, *A Theory of Semiotics*, 49.. See also Caesar, *Umberto Eco*, 85.

abstract element of the content system; (c) in this way a code establishes general *types*, therefore producing the rule which generates concrete *tokens*, i.e., signs such as usually occur in communicative processes; (d) both the continua represent elements which precede the semiotic correlation and with which semiotics is not concerned.[23]

Subsequently, Eco explains the concepts of denotation and connotation. Every sign has a denotation that has multiple connotations. This discussion pertains to the notions of expression and content because every expression plane, separate from the content plane to which it is connected, has a further expression plane that has its own content plane, and that expression plane has a further expression plane that has its own content plane ad infinitum.[24] Eco clarifies, "A connotative code, insofar as it relies on a more basic one, can be called a *subcode*."[25]

He then explicates the notions of message and text: "A single sign–vehicle conveys many intertwined contents and therefore what is commonly called a 'message' is in fact a *text* whose content is a multileveled *discourse*. . . . A text represents the result of the coexistence of many codes (or, at least, many subcodes)."[26] Eco's discussion of the referent is important as it relates to what he calls *the referential fallacy*.

Concerning the referent and the referential fallacy, Eco explains,

> The problem in question is that of the *referent*, in other words the problem of the possible states of the world supposedly corresponding to the content of a sign–function. Although of considerable importance within its proper domain, the notion of 'referent' has most unfortunate results within the framework of a theory of codes, and to underestimate this malignant influence leads to the *referential fallacy*.[27]

Specifically, Eco is discussing the idea that signs must have a referent, an object that exists in reality to which it corresponds. He reverts back to his watergate model, noting that the state of the water level appeared to be present as the object of the sign AB. He admits that this state of the world

23. Eco, *A Theory of Semiotics*, 50–51.
24. Eco, *A Theory of Semiotics*, 55.
25. Eco, *A Theory of Semiotics*, 56.
26. Eco, *A Theory of Semiotics*, 57.
27. Eco, *A Theory of Semiotics*, 58.

is "a necessary condition for the entire model."[28] He counters, "But even though it certainly was a necessary condition for the *design* of the model, it is not a necessary condition for its semiotic *functioning*.[29]

Again, a theory of codes is concerned primarily with *sign-functions* rather than *sign-production*. One must remember Eco's definition of the sign as anything that can be used to lie. The signal AB could have been sent as a form of deception, not corresponding to any state of the world. Signification still occurs though the referent is absent:

> Every time there is a lie there is signification. Every time there is signification there is the possibility of using it in order to lie. If this is true (and it is methodologically necessary to maintain that it is true) then semiotics has found a new threshold: between *conditions of signification* and *conditions of truth*, in other words the threshold between an *intensional* and *extensional* semantics.[30]

An intensional semantics is the concern of a theory of codes, while an extensional semantics is the concern of a theory of mentions or a theory of truth-values.[31] A theory of sign-production, which Eco discusses in the next chapter, will be concerned with an extensional semantics. Since Eco is dealing with a theory of codes in the present chapter, he is concerned only with how codes relate to intensional semantics.[32] As a result, the referent does not have a place here. Rather, the focus is on the relationship

---

28. Eco, *A Theory of Semiotics*, 58.
29. Eco, *A Theory of Semiotics*, 58.
30. Eco, *A Theory of Semiotics*, 59.
31. Eco, *A Theory of Semiotics*, 59.
32. Eco clarifies that a theory of codes is not concerned with a theory of truth-values. This is not to say that he is not concerned with a theory of truth-values as he will focus more on this when discussing a theory of sign-production. He states, "It must be absolutely clear that the following argument has nothing to do with a theory of the t-values of an expression, that is, with an extensional semantics; within this framework, even if the meaning of an expression is independent of the actual presence of the objects it refers to, the verification of the actual presence of these objects (or states of the world) is necessary in order to satisfy the t-value of the given expression and thus to consider it within the framework of propositional calculus. But from the point of view of the functioning of a code (or many codes), the referent must be excluded as an intrusive and jeopardizing presence which compromises the theory's theoretical purity. Thus, even when the referent could be the object named or designated by the expression when language is used in order to mention something, one must nonetheless maintain that an expression does not, in principle, designate any object, but on the contrary *conveys a cultural content*" (Eco, *A Theory of Semiotics*, 60–61).

between a signifier and its *content*. This discussion of content leads Eco to his discussion of *meaning*.

Eco defines meaning as a *cultural unit*:

> *Every attempt to establish what the referent of a sign is forces us to define the referent in terms of an abstract entity which moreover is only a cultural convention*. . . . What, then, is the meaning of a term? From a semiotic point of view it can only be a *cultural unit*. In every culture 'a unit . . . is simply anything that is culturally defined and distinguished as an entity.'[33]

Eco then discusses the notion of interpretant as it appears in the semiotics of Peirce. The interpretant is that which appears in the quasimind of the interpreter; it is what grounds the meaning of the sign. Michael Caesar observes the connection between Eco's understanding of meaning as *cultural unit* and Peirce's concept of the *interpretant*: "The idea of cultural unit . . . is intimately linked in Eco's reasoning with the (for him) fruitful notion of *interpretant*, as posited by Peirce, and with it that of *unlimited semiosis*."[34] The *interpretant* grounds the meaning of a sign, or guarantees its validity.[35]

Next, Eco remarks on different models of codes as they pertain to signs. He explains different concepts as they pertain to code models, such as dictionary and encyclopedia. He notes the KF model, which ultimately fails because it stands on a model dictionary that is grounded on a Porphyrian Tree of substance that attempts to determine the meaning in the essential attributes of a sign.[36] Eco opts for the model known as the Model Q due to its reliance on the model encyclopedia, which seeks to ground the content of signs in their connections and interconnections to all other signs.[37] This is a

33. Eco, *A Theory of Semiotics*, 66–67 Caesar notes that *cultural unit* is used interchangeably with the term *semantic unit*. Caesar, *Umberto Eco*, 87.

34. Caesar, *Umberto Eco*, 87.

35. Caesar, *Umberto Eco*, 87.

36. This model receives its name from its creators: Katz and Fodor, "The Structure of a Semantic Theory." Eco characterizes this model with following six criteria: "i. a dictionary–like rigidity; ii. the Platonism of the markers; iii. the disregard of connotations; iv. the refusal to consider settings; v. the extensional impurity of the distinguishers; vi. limitations to the verbal and the categorematic." See Eco, *A Theory of Semiotics*, 98.

37. This model receives its name from its creator: Ross Quillian (cf. Quillian, "Semantic Memory"). Eco comments, "The Revised Model [the Model Q] does not escape a criticism to which the model KF has also been subjected. Componential analysis isolates within the sememe paths or readings composed of different nodes representing semantic markers. In the KF model these markers could still at times be complex definitions (the distinguishers); in the Revised Model they have been reduced to elementary cultural

self-contained system that grounds and checks itself.[38] He then comments on issues concerning semantic space[39], overcoding and undercoding,[40] and the interplay of codes and the message as an open form.[41]

In the third chapter, Eco provides his theory of sign production. As he claimed earlier in the book, a theory of codes concerns a semiotics of signification while a theory of sign production concerns a semiotics of communication, though these cannot be separated so easily. Eco provides a general survey of a theory of sign production, observing issues concerning productive labor and types of labor. By *labor*, Eco denotes "first of all the labor of *producing* the signal; then the labor of *choosing*, among the set of signals that I have at my disposal, those that must be articulated in order to compose an expression, as well as the labor of isolating an expression-unit in order to compose an expression-string, a message, a text."[42]

Next, Eco provides comment on "semiotic and factual statements,"[43] adding, "To communicate means to concern oneself with extra-semiotic circumstances.... The fact that *semiosis lives as a fact in a world of facts* limits the absolute purity of the universe of codes. Semiosis takes place among events, and many events happen that no code could have anticipated."[44] He acknowledges the age-old discussion concerning analytic and synthetic judgments before commenting on semiotic and factual judgments. He asserts, "Let us call *semiotic* a judgment which predicates of a given content (one or more cultural units) the semantic markers already attributed to it by a previous code; let us call *factual* a judgment which predicates of a given content certain semantic markers that have never been attributed to it by a previous code."[45] Eco provides the following example: "Therefore /every unmarried man is a bachelor/ is a semiotic judgment solely because there exists a conventional code which refers to a compositional tree which possesses among its markers <never married>. Instead /Louis is a bachelor/ is undoubtedly a factual

---

units such as <fish> or <close>." See Eco, *A Theory of Semiotics*, 121.

38. Eco, *A Theory of Semiotics*, 124.
39. Eco, *A Theory of Semiotics*, 125.
40. Eco, *A Theory of Semiotics*, 129.
41. Eco, *A Theory of Semiotics*, 139.
42. Eco, *A Theory of Semiotics*, 151. Caesar also provides a helpful, though lengthy, commentary on this concept of Eco. See Caesar, *Umberto Eco*, 91.
43. Eco, *A Theory of Semiotics*, 158.
44. Eco, *A Theory of Semiotics*, 158.
45. Eco, *A Theory of Semiotics*, 159.

judgment."[46] He also discusses issues concerning statements and nonverbal statements before moving on to his discussion of *mentioning*.

Mentioning is a type of factual judgment, according to Eco. He comments, "Let us now consider another type of factual judgment, the *index-sensitive* one, i.e. the act of mentioning something actually present, as in /this pencil is blue/ or /this is a pencil/."[47] Eco connects mentioning to *referring*: "The act of *referring* places a sentence (or the corresponding proposition) in contact with an *actual circumstance* by means of an *indexical device*. We shall call these indexical devices *pointers*."[48] Pointing-fingers, analogue hands on a clock, and indices in a book are all examples of pointers, or indexical devices. Eco also discusses the notion of ideas as signs in this chapter. He states, "In order to assert that objects (insofar as they are perceived) can also be approached as signs, one must also assert that even the concepts of the objects (as the result or as the determining schema of every perception) must be considered in a semiotic way. Which leads to the straightforward assertion that *even ideas are signs*."[49]

Eco then explicates "the problem of a typology of signs."[50] He begins by discussing issues surrounding verbal and nonverbal signs: "Without a doubt verbal language is the most powerful semiotic device that man has invented; but that nevertheless other devices exist, covering portions of a general semantic space that verbal language does not."[51] Eco then discusses "the origins and purposes of signs.[52]" He notes that signs are distinguished from one another based on their origin, namely whether they "originate from a *sender* or a natural *source*."[53] He also writes, "Signs are also distinguished according to their *semiotic specificity*. Some signs are objects explicitly produced in order to signify, others are objects produced in order to perform a given function."[54] He progresses to Peirce's trichotomy of semiotic modality: symbols, icons, and indices, holding that

---

46. Eco, *A Theory of Semiotics*, 159.
47. Eco, *A Theory of Semiotics*, 162.
48. Eco, *A Theory of Semiotics*, 163.
49. Eco, *A Theory of Semiotics*, 166.
50. Eco, *A Theory of Semiotics*, 172.
51. Eco, *A Theory of Semiotics*, 174.
52. Eco, *A Theory of Semiotics*, 177.
53. Eco, *A Theory of Semiotics*, 177.
54. Eco, *A Theory of Semiotics*, 177.

this trichotomy is ultimately untenable.⁵⁵ Concerning Peirce's trichotomy, he writes, "The reason is simple: such a trichotomy postulates the presence of the referent as a discriminant parameter, a situation which is not permitted by the theory of codes proposed in this book."⁵⁶ He concludes with a discussion on the replicability of signs, doubles of signs, expression-clusters, and content-nebulas.

Next, Eco provides a "critique of iconism."⁵⁷ He notes that if one is going to discuss the "mode of production of the signal itself,"⁵⁸ then she must also discuss its, the signal's, "mode of correlation to its content."⁵⁹ Eco explains "a typology of modes of production."⁶⁰

In this section, Eco provides a "four-dimensional classification."⁶¹

i. the *physical labor* needed to produce expressions (ranging from the simple recognition of a pre-existent object or event as a sign to the invention of previously non-existent object or event as a sign to the invention of previously non-existent and un-coded expressions);

ii. the *type/token-ratio*, whether *facilis* or *difficilis*;

iii. the type of *continuum* to be shaped; this continuum can be either *homomaterial* or *heteromaterial*. . . .

iv. the mode and complexity of *articulation*, ranging from systems in which there are precise combinational units that are duly coded or

---

55. Eco, *A Theory of Semiotics*, 178.
56. Eco, *A Theory of Semiotics*, 178.
57. Eco, *A Theory of Semiotics*, 191.
58. Eco, *A Theory of Semiotics*, 191.
59. Eco, *A Theory of Semiotics*, 191. Caesar comments, "But the question of iconism is in the first place an important test-case for the idea of sign-function itself: given that iconic signs exhibit a natural resemblance or kinship, a relationship that is in some sense motivated, with the referent, the proposed definition of sign-function will only remain valid if it can be shown that in the iconic sign also the correlation of expression and content is conventional and culturally determined. Having analysed the concept of similarity (Morris) and the more precise one, used by Peirce, of 'similitude', Eco goes on to show that they are not based on properties common to the icon and the object but to 'a network of cultural stipulations that determine and direct ingenuous experience.' Thus what motivates the organization of the expression is not the object but the corresponding cultural content." Caesar, *Umberto Eco*, 92. The quotations from Eco in the above comment from Caesar can be found in Eco, *A Theory of Semiotics*, 195.
60. Eco, *A Theory of Semiotics*, 217.
61. Eco, *A Theory of Semiotics*, 217.

overcoded to those in which there are texts whose possible compositional units have not yet been further analyzed.[62]

He advances to a discussion of the role of *recognition* in his typology: "Recognition occurs when a given object or event, produced by nature or human action (intentionally or unintentionally), and existing in a world of facts as a fact among facts, comes to be viewed by an addressee as the expression of a given content, either through a pre-existing and coded correlation or through the positing of a possible correlation by its addressee."[63] Eco also discusses issues concerning *ostension*, "which occurs when a given object or event produced by nature or human action (intentionally or unintentionally and existing in a world of facts as a fact among facts) is 'picked up' by someone and *shown* as the expression of the class of which it is a member."[64]

Eco also remarks on *inventions* in this chapter:

a. *Moderate inventions* occur when one projects directly from a perceptual representation into an expression-continuum, thereby realizing an expression-form which dictates the rules producing the equivalent content-unit. . . .

b. The case of *radical inventions* is rather different, in that the sender more or less bypasses the perceptual model, and delves directly into the as yet unshaped perceptual continuum, mapping his perception as he organizes it.[65]

Eco asserts that no one ever really witnesses a total radical invention, or moderate invention for that matter. The reason is that "texts are maze-like structures combining inventions, replicas, stylizations, ostentions and so on. Semiosis never rises *ex novo* and *ex nihilo*. No new culture can ever come into being except against the background of an old one."[66] Eco concludes,

---

62. Eco, *A Theory of Semiotics*, 217. Caesar summarizes *ratio facilis* and *ratio difficilis* as follows: "In *ratio facilis*, the occurrence (token) possesses all or some of the pertinent features or of the properties of the type, as in the case of doubles and replicas. . . . This second kind of relation, the *ratio difficilis*, is one that is less immediate: the expression is not modeled on an already existing type but has to be established on the basis of a type (both expression-type and content-type) which does not yet exist in codified form in the culture." Caesar, *Umberto Eco*, 92–93. For more details, see Eco, *A Theory of Semiotics*, 180–89.
63. Eco, *A Theory of Semiotics*, 221.
64. Eco, *A Theory of Semiotics*, 224–25.
65. Eco, *A Theory of Semiotics*, 252–54.
66. Eco, *A Theory of Semiotics*, 256.

"Man is continuously making and re-making codes, but only insofar as other codes already exist. In the semiotic universe there are neither single protagonists nor charismatic prophets. Even prophets have to be socially *accepted* in order to be right; if not, they are wrong."[67] Eco further concludes this chapter with discussions on "the aesthetic text as invention,"[68] "the rhetorical labor,"[69] and "ideological code switching."[70]

Eco provides the conclusion to *A Theory of Semiotics* as a fourth chapter, "The Subject of Semiotics."[71] He concludes,

> In this book semiotics has been provided with a paramount subject matter, *semiosis*. Semiosis is the process by which empirical subjects communicate, communication processes being made possible by the organization of signification systems. Empirical subjects, from a semiotic point of view, can only be defined and isolated as manifestations of this double (systematic and processual) aspect of semiosis.... Semiotics treats subjects of semiosic acts in the same way: either they can be defined in terms of semiotics structures or—from this point of view—they do not exist at all.[72]

Semiotics attempts to analyze culture and communication through its own categories. Eco has shown that a general semiotics can be divided into two subcategories: a theory of codes and a theory of sign-production. Each of these presupposes and relies upon the other. Through his developments in these two subcategories, Eco has attempted to provide a theory of semiotics, one that is able to explain adequately how persons and cultures communicate, i. e. semiosis.

THE ROLE OF THE READER

The *Role of the Reader* is a collection of essays in which Eco explores the implications of his *A Theory of Semiotics* for textual semiotics.[73] He organizes these essays into three categories: I. Open; II. Closed; III. Open/Closed.

---

67. Eco, *A Theory of Semiotics*, 256.
68. Eco, *A Theory of Semiotics*, 261–76.
69. Eco, *A Theory of Semiotics*, 276–89.
70. Eco, *A Theory of Semiotics*, 289–98.
71. Eco, *A Theory of Semiotics*, 314–17.
72. Eco, *A Theory of Semoitics*, 316.
73. Eco, *Role of the Reader*.

These categories pertain to the type of texts that readers encounter. Eco provides a lengthy introduction that outlines the rest of the work at hand.

In the introduction, Eco highlights issues concerning texts and their interpreters. He commences, "The very existence of texts that can not only be freely interpreted but also cooperatively generated by the addressee (the 'original' text constituting a flexible *type* of which many *tokens* can be legitimately realized) posits the problem of a rather peculiar strategy of communication based upon a flexible system of signification."[74]

Eco examines several important concepts in this introduction: the Model Reader, the Open Text, and the Closed Text:

> To organize a text, its author has to rely upon a series of codes that assign given contents to the expressions he uses. To make his text communicative, the author has to assume that the ensemble of codes he relies upon is the same as that shared by his possible reader. The author has thus to foresee a model of the possible reader (hereafter Model Reader) supposedly able to deal interpretatively with the expressions in the same way as the author deals generatively with them.[75]

The Model Reader is integral in the generation of texts since different model readers are envisioned for different types of texts. Eco asserts that both open and closed texts presuppose different model readers: "Those texts that obsessively aim at arousing a precise response on the part of more or less precise empirical readers . . . are in fact open to any possible 'aberrant' decoding. A text so immoderately 'open' to every interpretation will be called a *closed* one."[76] Examples of closed texts include, but are not limited to, Superman comics and James Bond novels. On the other hand, concerning open texts, Eco remarks,

> An author can foresee an 'ideal reader affected by an ideal insomnia' . . . able to master different codes and eager to deal with the text as with a maze of many issues. But in the last analysis what matters is not the various issues in themselves but the maze-like structure of the text. You cannot use the text as you want, but only as the text wants you to use it. An open text, however 'open' it be, cannot afford whatever interpretation.[77]

---

74. Eco, *Role of the Reader*, 3.
75. Eco, *Role of the Reader*, 7.
76. Eco, *Role of the Reader*, 8.
77. Eco, *Role of the Reader*, 9.

Eco next provides comment on the concepts of *author* and *reader* as textual strategies.[78] He also discusses *textual levels* such as narrative and nonnarrative texts.[79] He also remarks on discursive structures.[80] Here, he discusses codes, overcoding, and frames. Subtopics that Eco explains here include "basic dictionary,"[81] "rules of co-reference,"[82] "contextual and circumstantial selections,"[83] "rhetorical and stylistic overcoding,"[84] "inferences by common frames,"[85] "inferences by intertextual frames,"[86] and "ideological overcoding."[87]

The concept of *encyclopedia*, though not thoroughly explicated here, is an important topic in the introduction as well. In his discussion on *semantic disclosures*, Eco writes,

> When faced with a lexeme, the reader does not know which of its virtual properties has to be actualized so as to allow further amalgamations.... They are *virtually* present in the encyclopedia, that is they are socially *stored*, and the reader picks them up from the semantic store only when required by the text. In doing so the reader implements *semantic disclosures* or, in other words, actualizes nonmanifested properties.[88]

He also comments on the concepts of "topics and isotopies."[89]

---

78. Eco, *Role of the Reader*, 10. One should note that Eco distinguishes between the *empirical author* and the *model author*. The *empirical author* is the actual author, or generator, of the text, to which Eco claims that readers do not have access, especially if said author is deceased. The *model author* is a textual strategy that the reader employs in her process of interpreting a text. This author does not exist in reality but *only as a textual strategy in the mind of the reader*. For more on the distinction between empirical and model authors, and their roles in textual interpretation, see Eco, "Between Author and Text," 67–88. See also Thomas, *Poetry and Theology in Lamentations*, 61–66.

79. Eco, *Role of the Reader*, 11.
80. Eco, *Role of the Reader*, 17.
81. Eco, *Role of the Reader*, 18.
82. Eco, *Role of the Reader*, 18.
83. Eco, *Role of the Reader*, 19.
84. Eco, *Role of the Reader*, 19.
85. Eco, *Role of the Reader*, 20.
86. Eco, *Role of the Reader*, 21.
87. Eco, *Role of the Reader*, 22.
88. Eco, *Role of the Reader*, 23.
89. Eco, *Role of the Reader*, 24.

Eco also notes the role of *narrative structures* in textual interpretation. He highlights the journey from "plot to *fabula*."[90] *Fabula* is Eco's word for the notion of *story*: "The *fabula* is the basic story stuff, the logic of actions or the syntax of characters, the time–oriented course of events. It need not necessarily be a sequence of human actions (physical or not), but can also concern a temporal transformation of ideas or a series of events concerning inanimate objects."[91] He then discusses "forecasts and inferential walks"[92] and "open and closed *fabulae*."[93] He remarks on "the sememe and the *fabula*"[94] and "deeper levels" of reading.[95] In his concluding remarks to the introduction, Eco highlights the inherent limitations to theories about texts:

> As far as the problem of the textual levels is concerned, one could say that there are more things in a text than are dreamt of in our text theories. But there are also *fewer* things than are dreamt of. The structure of the compositional spectrum of a given *sememe* is the same as the structure of a *frame* and the *actantial structure*. The world structures are dominated by the opposition of presence and absence, necessity or accidentality of properties. Ideological structure oppositions can be translated into truth assignments (True vs. False)—and vice versa, as logicians hardly suspect. There are ideological structures also in logical *fabulae*.[96]

Though there might be more in a text than one realizes, there are often fewer things as well. All approaches to texts, whether composition or interpretation, are governed by ideological structures, and these structures permeate the entire *fabulae*.

The rest of *The Role of the Reader* is a compilation of essays that discuss more specific instances of the contents provided in the introduction. Perhaps the most important portion of the work at hand is the introduction itself. Concerning open texts, Eco provides essays, such as his famous "The Poetics of the Open Work," in which he remarks on poetry and the function of language as it pertains to poetics. He notes that, in poetics, authors produce signs with typical as well as atypical sign functions, which

---

90. Eco, *Role of the Reader*, 27.
91. Eco, *Role of the Reader*, 27.
92. Eco, *Role of the Reader*, 31.
93. Eco, *Role of the Reader*, 33.
94. Eco, *Role of the Reader*, 34.
95. Eco, *Role of the Reader*, 37.
96. Eco, *Role of the Reader*, 39.

create a multivalence of meaning. In so doing, authors exploit the semantic encyclopedia in order to lead their readers through the labyrinth of potential meanings.[97] Also, in these essays concerning open texts, Eco discusses "the semantics of metaphor" in which he looks at theories of metaphor, noting that a theory of metaphor is necessarily connected to a theory of metonymy.[98] Concerning closed texts, Eco provides essays analyzing the closed nature of Superman comics, Sue's *Les Mystères de Paris*, and "narrative structures in Fleming."[99] He asserts, in "The Myth of Superman,"[100] that the author generates the text in order to meet specific expectations on the reader's part, though some instances exist when the author intentionally subverts the expectations of the reader, providing a dimension of openness to the text.[101]

In the third section, Eco comments on "Open/Closed" texts. His essay "Peirce and the Semiotic Foundations of Openness: Signs as Texts and Texts as Signs" is especially important. He writes, "*A sememe is in itself an inchoative text, whereas a text is an expanded sememe.*"[102] In this essay, Eco focuses on Peirce's concept of *interpretants* and *unlimited semiosis* as they pertain to textual meaning. According to Peirce, a sign is composed of a representamen, an interpretant, and an object. The intepretant itself becomes a sign whose meaning is grounded in more interpretants, which become signs on their own and whose meaning is grounded in other interpretants, ad infinitum. This provides the foundations for *openness*.[103] Eco concludes this essay with the following explanation:

97. Eco, *Role of the Reader*, 47–65.

98. Eco, *Role of the Reader*, 67–88.

99. Eco, *Role of the Reader*, 144.

100. Lubomir Dolež provides a brief summary of the importance of this essay: "Eco reveals the absurdity of the myth by pointing out the inexplicable discrepancy between the hero's virtual omnipotency and the small-scale field of his operations. If we consider the gigantic, historical deeds that Superman could accomplish, his activities are 'paradoxical waste of means.' But this paradox is inevitable, if the myth is to carry its basic ideological message. . . . Eco thus reveals that narrative submitted to ideology is stereotyped by necessity: ideology creates a well-serving narrative structure and this structure is perpetuated *ad infinitum* by the never-ending demand for ideological reinforcement." Dolež, "The Themata of Eco's Semiotics of Literature," 112.

101. Eco, *Role of the Reader*, 109.

102. Eco, *Role of the Reader*, 175.

103. See also Caesar's brief discussion on Peirce's notion of *unlimited semiosis* as it pertains to *The Role of the Reader*. Caesar, *Umberto Eco*, 111–12.

Interpretants are the testable and describable correspondents associated by public agreement to another sign. In this way the analysis of content becomes a cultural operation which works only on physically testable cultural products, that is other signs and their reciprocal correlations. Therefore the process of unlimited semiosis shows us how signification, by means of continual shiftings which refer a sign back to another sign or string of signs, circumscribes *cultural units* in an asymptotic fashion, without even allowing one to touch them directly, though making them accessible through other units. Thus one is never obliged to replace a cultural unit by means of something which is not a semiotic entity, and no cultural unit has to be explained by some platonic, psychic, or objectal entity. Semiosis explains itself by itself: this continual circularity is the normal condition of signification and even allows communicational processes to use signs in order to mention things and states of the world.[104]

The final essay is Eco's "*Lector in Fabula*: Pragmatic Strategy in a Metanarrative Text."[105]

SEMIOTICS AND THE PHILOSOPHY OF LANGUAGE

In this work, Umberto Eco applies the theory of semiotics developed in *A Theory of Semiotics* to the philosophy of language.[106] This volume is the third installment in his semiotics project. Eco divides the book into eight chapters, each discussing an important dimension of how semiotics pertains to the philosophy of language.[107]

In the Introduction, Eco writes, "This is a book on philosophy of language for the very simple reason that a general semiotics is nothing else but *a* philosophy of language and that the 'good' philosophies of language, from *Cratylus* to *Philosophical Investigations*, are concerned with all the semiotic questions."[108] He differentiates between general and special semiotics: "A

---

104. Eco, *Role of the Reader*, 198.

105. One should also reference Eco's essay "Two Problems in Textual Interpretation." In this essay, Eco further elaborates some of the topics of *The Role of the Reader*, namely those of *isotopy* and *use and interpretation*. Eco, "Two Problems in Textual Interpretation," 34–52.

106. Eco, *Semiotics and the Philosophy of Language*.

107. For a briefer treatment on semiotics and the philosophy of language by Eco, see Eco, "Semiotics and the Philosophy of Language," 1–13.

108. Eco, *Semiotics and the Philosophy of Language*, 4.

specific semiotics is, or aims at being, the 'grammar' of a particular sign system, sand proves to be successful insofar as it describes a given field of communicative phenomena as ruled by a system of signification. . . . These systems can be studied from a syntactic, a semantic, or a pragmatic point of view."[109] Concerning the aims of a general semiotics, Eco states,

> Thus the basic problem of a general semiotics splits into three different questions: (a) Can one approach many, and apparently different, phenomena as if they were all phenomena of signification and/or of communication? (b) Is there a unified approach able to account for all these semiotic phenomena as if they were based on the same system of rules (the notion of system not being a mere analogical one)? (c) Is this approach a 'scientific' one? If there is something which deserves the name of general semiotics, this something is a discourse dealing with the questions above, and this discourse is a philosophical one.[110]

Eco concludes by commenting on a general semiotics and how it pertains to philosophy of language:

> A general semiotics studies the whole of the human signifying activity—languages—and languages are what constitutes human beings as such, that is, as semiotic animals. It studies and describes languages through languages. By studying the human signifying activity it influences its course. A general semiotics transforms, for the very fact of its theoretical claim, its own object.[111]

In chapter one, Eco revisits his position on the sign.[112] He maintains the Peircean definition that "a sign is 'something which stands to somebody for something in some respect or capacity.'"[113] All events, whether intentional or unintentional, can be a sign. He notes "the deconstruction of the linguistic sign," highlighting specific dialogues such as the sign vs. *figura*, sentences, text, the sign as difference, and the predominance of the signifier.[114] Eco also highlights the conversation of signs vs. words.[115] He references Aristotle's

---

109. Eco, *Semiotics and the Philosophy of Language*, 5.
110. Eco, *Semiotics and the Philosophy of Language*, 7.
111. Eco, *Semiotics and the Philosophy of Language*, 12.
112. Michael Caesar notes that this chapter is Eco's most comprehensive treatment of his position on the sign. Caesar, *Umberto Eco*, 112.
113. Eco, *Semiotics and the Philosophy of Language*, 14.
114. Eco, *Semiotics and the Philosophy of Language*, 20–26.
115. Eco, *Semiotics and the Philosophy of Language*, 26.

understanding of words, both spoken and written, as *symbols*.[116] Eco also comments on "strong codes and weak codes"[117] and "abduction and inferential nature of signs."[118] He remarks that abduction is the primary form of reasoning that one uses in interpretation and how the nature of the sign is necessarily inferential.[119] Eco also asserts that a hypothesis is an overcoded abduction.[120] He stresses the "criterion of interpretability":

> Thus substitution ... is not the only necessary condition for a sign: the possibility of *interpretation* is necessary as well. By interpretation (or criterion of interpretability) we mean the concept elaborated by Peirce, according to which every *interpretant* (either a sign or an expression or a sequence of expressions which translate a previous expression), besides translating the Immediate Object or the content of the sign, also increases our understanding of it. The criterion of interpretability allows us to start from a sign in order to cover, step by step, the entire circle of semiosis.[121]

Eco titles chapter two "Dictionary vs. Encyclopedia." How is a sememe determined? The model dictionary seeks to determine sememes via a Porphyrian Tree of substance that determines a sememe based on its essential attributes, namely *genera* and *species*.[122] The problem with this method is that it does not allow one to differentiate between a horse and a man; in order to do so, she would need to include accidental attributes, or *differentiae*, in the definition. The problem is that there are no criteria one can consult when deciding which *differentiae* to include and which to exclude. Instead, the model encyclopedia provides a better foundation for understanding how sememes are constructed. Eco writes,

> The tree of genera and species, the tree of substances, blows up in a dust of differentiae, in a turmoil of infinite accidents, in a nonhierarchical network of *qualia*. The dictionary is dissolved into a potentially unordered and unrestricted galaxy of pieces of

---

116. Eco, *Semiotics and the Philosophy of Language*, 27.
117. Eco, *Semiotics and the Philosophy of Language*, 36–39.
118. Eco, *Semiotics and the Philosophy of Language*, 39.
119. Eco, *Semiotics and the Philosophy of Language*, 39.
120. Eco, *Semiotics and the Philosophy of Language*, 41.
121. Eco, *Semiotics and the Philosophy of Language*, 43.
122. Eco, *Semiotics and the Philosophy of Language*, 58–61.

world knowledge. The dictionary thus becomes an encyclopedia, because it was in fact *a disguised encyclopedia*.[123]

The best representation of the model encyclopedia[124] is the labyrinth, more specifically a rhizome or net. Each node represents an expression, and its content, or sememe, is determined by the connections and interconnections it has with all of the other nodes. This net has no outer boundary and is ever growing. No one has access to the global encyclopedia, for it contains all that has ever been thought or said. One has access only to a local encyclopedia. Whether the situation is an author generating a text, or a reader interpreting a text, one must navigate the labyrinth of the semantic encyclopedia via abduction. The remaining chapters in the book reveal the implications of this encyclopedia for other issues surrounding semiotics and the philosophy of language.[125]

In chapter three, Eco discusses the phenomenon of metaphor. If one uses the model dictionary to ground a sememe, then it is unable to account for metaphor. If, however, one understands that the semantic network is grounded in its connections and interconnections, then she can account for this phenomenon. Eco acknowledges historical treatments on the topic of metaphor, namely that of Aristotle.[126] He likewise remarks on issues of metaphor and metonymy, and the implications of metaphor for symbolic interpretation.[127]

Eco explicates *symbols* in chapter four. He comments that symbols are conventional expressions and that symbols are expressions that indirectly convey meaning.[128] He discusses symbols as diagrams and as tropes. He uses the Romantic symbol to discuss a theory and example of an aesthetic text.[129] He concludes the chapter on symbols by discussing a

---

123. Eco, *Semiotics and the Philosophy of Language*, 68.

124. Heath Thomas provides the following summary definition of Eco's model encyclopedia: "The encyclopedia is a descriptor of the cumulative amount of cultural knowledge present to a creator of a message at the time of its genesis" (Thomas, *Poetry and Theology in Lamentations*, 54).

125. See also Eco, "Dictionary vs. Encyclopedia," 209–14; and Caesar, *Umberto Eco*, 113–17.

126. Eco, *Semiotics and the Philosophy of Language*, 91–96.

127. Eco, *Semiotics and the Philosophy of Language*, 124–27.

128. Eco, *Semiotics and the Philosophy of Language*, 136.

129. Eco, *Semiotics and the Philosophy of Language*, 141–43.

semiotics of the symbolic mode.[130] Contra the deconstructionists, everything cannot be a symbol.[131]

In chapter five, Eco writes on the role of code in a philosophy of language. He specifically stresses the relationship codes and communication[132] along with the relationship between codes and s–codes:[133]

> Thus, at its very birth, the idea of code appears wrapped in ambiguity: bound to a pancommunicative hypothesis, it is not a guarantee of communicability but, rather, of structural coherence and of access between different systems. An ambiguity rooted in the twofold meaning of communication: communication as a *transfer* of information between two poles, and as *accessibility* or *passage* between spaces. The two concepts imply one another.[134]

Concerning s–codes, Eco argues that they are the types of codes that information theorists discuss. These codes are *monoplanar systems* as well are they non–correlational devices.[135] S–codes are not capable of lying,[136] and s–codes are institutional codes.[137] The genetic code is an example of an s–code.[138]

Eco discusses the notion of isotopy as it pertains to semiotics and the philosophy of language. In chapter seven, he talks about whether or not mirror images are signs. He highlights multiple examples of how a mirror image might be a sign, but he concludes that mirror images, though they are images, are not signs. They do not stand for something to something else, and they are not indexical devices.

THE LIMITS OF INTERPRETATION

In this monograph, Eco appropriates insights from his work in semiotics to defend the limits of interpretation.[139] By *the limits of interpretation*, Eco

130. Eco, *Semiotics and the Philosophy of Language*, 156–62.
131. Eco, *Semiotics and the Philosophy of Language*, 157.
132. Eco, *Semiotics and the Philosophy of Language*, 167.
133. Eco, *Semiotics and the Philosophy of Language*, 169.
134. Eco, *Semiotics and the Philosophy of Language*, 168.
135. Eco, *Semiotics and the Philosophy of Language*, 169.
136. Eco, *Semiotics and the Philosophy of Language*, 177.
137. Eco, *Semiotics and the Philosophy of Language*, 179.
138. See also Heath Thomas's summary of Eco on s–codes in Thomas, *Poetry and Theology in Lamentations*, 54.
139. Eco, *Limits of Interpretation*.

does not mean that there is a limit on how far interpretation can get a reader in grasping the meaning of a text. *The limits of interpretation*, rather, refers to the idea that a limit exists on the valid interpretations a text can have. Eco begins his Introduction by making reference to John Wilkins's work *An Essay towards a Real Character, and a Philosophical Language*.[140] In this monograph, Wilkins discusses the multivalence of meaning that texts have while maintaining that texts cannot mean, potentially, everything. Regarding Wilkins's model of the location of certain prepositions and other particles, Eco writes, "It shows that in interpreting syncategorematic terms we must follow certain 'directions.' Even if the world were a labyrinth, we could pass through it by disregarding certain directional constraints."[141] Though texts have a plurality of possible meanings, one is not justified in taking them to mean anything they, the readers, desire them to mean. Eco further remarks, "But the interpreter would not be entitled to say that the message can mean *everything*. It can mean many things, but there are senses that would be preposterous to suggest."[142] He concludes the introduction with the following point:

> Even the most radical deconstructionists accept the idea that there are interpretations which are blatantly unacceptable. This means that the interpreted text imposes some constraints upon its interpreters. The limits of interpretation coincide with the rights of the text (which does not mean the rights of its author).... If there is something to be interpreted, the interpretation must speak of something which must be found somewhere, and in some way respected.[143]

The rest of *The Limits of Interpretation* is a compilation of essays defending the argument that Eco has proposed in the introduction. The first essay discusses two models of interpretation. The first model of interpretation reflects the approach used by patristic and medieval interpreters of Scripture. "Pansemiotic metaphysics" grounds this model.[144] He writes, "There is, in the patristic and medieval tradition, an idea of symbolism as a way of speaking of something unknowable."[145] He considers the nature of

140. Wilkins, *An Essay Towards a Real Character, and a Philosophical Language*.
141. Eco, *Limits of Interpretation*, 2.
142. Eco, *Limits of Interpretation*, 5.
143. Eco, *Limits of Interpretation*, 7.
144. Eco, *Limits of Interpretation*, 9.
145. Eco, *Limits of Interpretation*, 9.

religious language following the Neoplatonic tradition. More specifically, he elaborates on one's ability to speak *symbolically*:

> The semiosic process involved in the reading of Scripture was rather complicated: there was a first book speaking allegorically of the second one, and a second one speaking through parables of something else. Moreover, in this beautiful case of unlimited semiosis, there was a puzzling identification among the sender (the divine Logos), the signifying message (words, Logoi), the content (the divine message, Logos), the referent (Christ, the Logos)—a web of identities and differences, complicated by the fact that Christ, as Logos, insofar as he was the ensemble of all the divine archetypes, was fundamentally polysemous.[146]

This method of interpretation is best represented by the fourfold approach to interpretation: literal, allegorical, moral, and anagogical. This approach to interpretation allows not only for literal readings of Scripture but also for symbolic, or spiritual, ones. The Hermetic model, as used by the Romanticists, has challenged this traditional model of interpretation.

The main features of the Hermetic model are as follows: (1) "the refusal of the metric measure, the opposition of the qualitative to the quantitative, the belief that nothing is stable and that every element of the universe acts over any other through reciprocal action";[147] (2) "the refusal of causalism, so that the reciprocal action of the various elements of the universe does not follow the linear sequence of cause to effect but rather a sort of spiral-like logic of mutually sympathetic elements. If the universe is a network of similitudes and cosmic sympathies, then there are no privileged causal chains";[148] (3) "the refusal of dualism, so that the very identity principle collapses, as well as the one of the excluded middle; as a consequence, *tertium datur*";[149] (4) "the refusal of agnosticism";[150] and (5) "the hermetic tradition is based on the principle of similitude."[151] Eco then concludes,

> Medieval interpreters were wrong in taking the world as a univocal text; modern interpreters are wrong in taking every text as an unshaped world. Texts are the human way to reduce the world to

146. Eco, *Limits of Interpretation*, 11.
147. Eco, *Limits of Interpretation*, 19.
148. Eco, *Limits of Interpretation*, 19.
149. Eco, *Limits of Interpretation*, 19.
150. Eco, *Limits of Interpretation*, 19.
151. Eco, *Limits of Interpretation*, 20.

a manageable format, open to an intersubjective interpretive discourse. Which means that, when symbols are inserted into a text, there is, perhaps, no way to decide which interpretation is the "good" one, but it is still possible to decide, on the basis of the context, which one is due, not to an effort of understanding "that" text, but rather to a hallucinatory response on the part of the addressee.[152]

In chapter two, Eco differentiates the concept of unlimited semiosis from the concept of the hermetic drift. The former derives from the pragmaticism of Peirce while the latter derives from the neo–pragmatism utilized in the Hermetic tradition. Major proponents of the Hermetic tradition include theorists such as Jacques Derrida and Richard Rorty.[153] According to the deconstructionists and neo–pragmatists, one understands a sign only by way of other signs. As a result, the interpreter only drifts further away from a meaning of the starting sign, and she knows practically nothing of it. Eco, on the other hand, advocates for Peirce's unlimited semiosis. In unlimited semiosis, using more signs in order to interpret a sign does not lead one further away from the original sign; rather, it allows the reader to know a lot about said sign, for the labyrinth of the semantic encyclopedia is a self–checking system. The concept of unlimited semiosis may not always reveal which reading is a "good" one, but it can help to show which readings are "bad" ones.[154] In judging which interpretations are good and which are bad, the reader engages in the process of reasoning known as abduction. Not only does the reader engage in abduction when making interpretative judgments, but the act of interpreting itself is an exercise in abduction, since, as Eco notes, abduction is the means by which one navigates her way through the labyrinth of the encyclopedia.[155]

In the third essay, "*Intentio Lectoris*: The State of the Art," Eco focuses "on the change of paradigm *in literary theories*."[156] He comments, "I shall claim that a theory of interpretation—even when it assumes that texts are open to multiple readings—must also assume that it is possible to reach

152. Eco, *Limits of Interpretation*, 21.

153. See also Eco et al., *Interpretation and Overinterpretation*. This work contains the Tanner Lectures that Eco gave at Cambridge University. Others were able to provide responses to Eco's work throughout the lectures, including Richard Rorty. See Rorty's response to Eco: Rorty, "The Pragmatist's Progress," 89–108.

154. Eco, *Limits of Interpretation*, 42. For more on Eco's use of Peirce in textual interpretation, see Tejera, "Eco, Peirce and the Necessity of Interpretation," 147–62.

155. See Caesar, *Umberto Eco*, 117–19.

156. Eco, *Limits of Interpretation*, 45.

an agreement, if not about the meanings that a text encourages, at least about those that a text discourages."[157] Eco privileges the Reader over the Author. He recognizes, "To privilege the initiative of the reader does not necessarily mean to guarantee the infinity of readings. If one privileges the initiative of the reader, one must also consider the possibility of an active reader who decides to read a text univocally."[158] He then provides an apology for reading a text for its literal sense: "Every discourse on the freedom of interpretation must start from a defense of a literal sense. . . . If texts have intentions, *p* had the intention to say so."[159]

Eco differentiates between two types of interpretation: semantic and critical, or semiosic and semiotic:

> Semantic interpretation is the result of the process by which an addressee, facing a Linear Text Manifestation, fills it up with a given meaning. . . . Critical interpretation is, on the contrary, a metalinguistic activity—a semiotic approach—which aims at describing and explaining for which formal reasons a given text produces a given response.[160]

He acknowledges that every text has two model readers: the semantic and the critical. Eco also converses on the role abduction plays in interpretation as well as "the falsifiability of misinterpretations."[161]

These first three essays provide the foundational concepts and arguments that Eco makes in the work at hand. The remaining essays, save essays thirteen and fourteen, apply the material of the first three essays to different case studies. These latter essays concern the interpretation of drama, serials, and animals. He also examines the role of abduction in reading Uqbar. He discusses the importance of "small worlds" within the maximal world. He also acknowledges semiotic issues concerning fakes and forgeries.

He provides some new content, however, in the thirteenth essay: "Semantics, Pragmatics, and Text Semiotics." His primary argument is that all studies in semantics are ultimately studies in pragmatics. He remarks, "If the relation to the interpreter is crucial for the very definition of a sign, and if the

---

157. Eco, *Limits of Interpretation*, 45.
158. Eco, *Limits of Interpretation*, 51.
159. Eco, *Limits of Interpretation*, 53.
160. Eco, *Limits of Interpretation*, 53.
161. Eco, *Limits of Interpretation*, 58.

object of pragmatics is this relation to an interpreter that characterizes a sign as such, in which sense would pragmatics then differ from semiotics?"[162]

Eco discusses presuppositions in essay fourteen. He begins this essay by explicating "the problem of presuppositions," which he claims begins with the problem of "the delimitation of the objects under investigation."[163] He asserts that not all presuppositions are valid and that some, if not many, can be denied.[164] He summarizes the "delimitation of the objects under investigation" as follows: "Thus presuppositions are characterized by two different features: first, they are tied to particular aspects of surface structure; second, they are context-sensitive, since they can be challenged under given textual conditions."[165] He then discusses how presuppositions pertain to the encyclopedic framework,[166] the "encyclopedic differences between presuppositions and other inclusions,"[167] and "encyclopedic representation of p-terms."[168] P-terms are "presuppositions conveyed by lexical items . . . whose presuppositional power depends on their intensional structure, that is, it is a part of their coded content, irrespective of the context in which they are used, and also when they are considered out of any context."[169] Eco also comments on the problem of existential presuppositions and concludes the essay by summarizing contextual presuppositions.[170] Eco concludes *The Limits of Interpretation* at hand with the essay "On Truth: A Fiction."

KANT AND THE PLATYPUS

This work is a compilation of essays written by Eco on cognition and language.[171] Though it does not belong to the series of works he has published in the Advances in Semiotics series, this work does approach issues of cognition, mental representation, and language from a semiotic horizon, thereby deserving consideration in this chapter. The majority of

---

162. Eco, *Limits of Interpretation*, 205.
163. Eco, *Limits of Interpretation*, 222.
164. Eco, *Limits of Interpretation*, 233–37.
165. Eco, *Limits of Interpretation*, 236.
166. Eco, *Limits of Interpretation*, 237.
167. Eco, *Limits of Interpretation*, 238.
168. Eco, *Limits of Interpretation*, 242.
169. Eco, *Limits of Interpretation*, 229.
170. Eco, *Limits of Interpretation*, 253–61.
171. Eco, *Kant and the Platypus.*

the content of these essays does not appear in the four works overviewed above and is original to the work at hand.[172]

The first essay in *Kant and the Platypus* is an essay on ontology: "On Being." Eco begins by restating the ontological question that Martin Heidegger posed in *Being and Time*: "What is the meaning of 'Being?'"[173] For the purposes of this essay, Eco defines *being* thus: "Here is what we mean by the word *Being*: Something."[174] Eco quickly refocuses his attention to the relationship of semiotics and being, writing, "Why should semiotics deal with this something? Because one of the problems of semiotics is to say whether and how we use signs to refer to something, and a great deal has been written on this. But I do not think that semiotics can avoid another problem: What is that something that induces us to produce signs?"[175] He then examines the word *being*. If persons use language to refer to things, then to what are they referring when they use this sign? Not only does this question arise but so does another—"What makes us talk?"[176] In other words, what causes the need to communicate, to refer to things?

According to Eco, the external world gives rise to the need to communicate and reference. Moreover, one presupposes that language relates to reality. He highlights the contributions of Peirce on his concept of the *object* as it pertains to signs. For Peirce, the *object* belongs to the triad of the sign. Eco asserts Peirce's distinction between the immediate object and the dynamical object.[177] He summarizes Peirce:

> A Dynamical Object drives us to produce a *representamen*, in a quasi-mind this produces an Immediate Object, which in turn is translatable into a potentially infinite series of interpretants and sometimes, through the habit formed in the course of the interpretative process, we come back to the Dynamical Object, and we make something of it.[178]

---

172. Michael Caesar provides a helpful summary guide through the work at hand. See Caesar, *Umberto Eco*, 162–70.
173. Eco, *Kant and the Platypus*, 9. See also Heidegger, *Being and Time*, 1–35.
174. Eco, *Kant and the Platypus*, 12.
175. Eco, *Kant and the Platypus*, 12.
176. Eco, *Kant and the Platypus*, 13.
177. Eco, *Kant and the Platypus*, 13.
178. Eco, *Kant and the Platypus*, 13.

He notes that the dynamical object is what drives persons "to produce semiosis."[179] The external world arouses the attention of persons, resulting in their need to speak of it. All experience of the external world, however, takes place through the medium of signs via semiosis. *Being* itself is one of these things that arouses one's attention and is sought after through the long chain of semiosis.[180]

Next, Eco remarks that the problem of *being* is the most unnatural semiosic problem one faces.[181] When one claims, "*Being* is . . ." already she has assumed a sort of definition by using the verb *is*. Subsequently, Eco reverts back to the classical question posed by metaphysics: "Why is there something (whether it is being as such, or the plurality of entities that may be experienced or thought of, and the totality of the immense flaw that has deprived us of the divine tranquility of nonbeing) rather than nothing?"[182] He answers, "*Because there is*."[183] Eco then writes,

> The very fact that we can pose the question (which we could not pose if there were nothing, not even the posers of the question) means that the condition of every question is that being exists. Being is not a problem for common sense (or, rather, common sense does not see it as a problem), because it is the condition for common sense itself. . . . That is, we could not think if not by starting from the (implicit) principle that we are thinking something.[184]

As Eco recaps, "There is being because we can pose the question of being, and this being comes before every question, and therefore before every answer and every definition."[185]

Eco remarks on further problems of defining *being*. He makes recourse to his discussion of the model dictionary and model encyclopedia, showing that *being* cannot be broken down into categories of *genera* and *species*: "Being is not a genus, not even the most general of them all, and it therefore eludes all definition, if it is necessary to use the genus and the *differentia* in order to make a definition. Being is that which enables

---

179. Eco, *Kant and the Platypus*, 14.
180. Eco, *Kant and the Platypus*, 15.
181. Eco, *Kant and the Platypus*, 15.
182. Eco, *Kant and the Platypus*, 17.
183. Eco, *Kant and the Platypus*, 17.
184. Eco, *Kant and the Platypus*, 17–18.
185. Eco, *Kant and the Platypus*, 19.

all subsequent definitions to be made."[186] *Being* is the precondition for language, defining, and cognition.[187]

In the second essay, "Kant, Peirce, and the Platypus," Eco redirects his attention to matters of cognition. He begins by making recourse to "Marco Polo and the unicorn."[188] When Polo laid eyes on a rhinoceros for the first time, he recognized it as something different; he recognized it as a unicorn. The reason for this is that he did not have the cognitive category appropriate to make sense of his sensory data of the rhinoceros. As a result, Polo made sense of this phenomenon with the category that he possessed that made the best sense of it; he understood this phenomenon as a unicorn.[189] Eco then poses the question as to what Polo would have done had he landed in Australia and laid eyes on the platypus. How would he have begun to understand this animal?

Eco then directs his attention to Kant's schematism. He notes that Kant sought a transcendental ground for judgments based on sensory perception.[190] Eco shows that, in *The Critique of Pure Reason*, Kant is concerned more with scientific knowledge as opposed to everyday knowledge, what Aristotle refers to as *phronesis*.[191] He writes, "The first *Critique* fails to deal with the problem of how we understand that a dog is a dog, and it does not even explain how we are able to say that a dog is a mammal."[192] The problem is that Kant has reduced knowledge to propositional knowledge. Eco comments, "Therefore, even if he realized that he was reducing knowledge to the knowledge of propositions (and therefore to linguistic knowledge), Kant could not have posed himself the problem, which Peirce was to set himself, that the nature of knowledge was not linguistic but *semiosic*."[193] Therefore, Kant's table of categories and schemata is still not able to provide an adequate theory of everyday knowledge; it does not allow one to recognize that "a stone is a stone."[194]

---

186. Eco, *Kant and the Platypus*, 24.
187. See also Caesar's helpful summary of this essay; Caesar, *Umberto Eco*, 166–70.
188. Eco, *Kant and the Platypus*, 57.
189. Eco, *Kant and the Platypus*, 57–59.
190. Eco, *Kant and the Platypus*, 68.
191. Eco, *Kant and the Platypus*, 69.
192. Eco, *Kant and the Platypus*, 70.
193. Eco, *Kant and the Platypus*, 71.
194. Eco, *Kant and the Platypus*, 73.

Eco turns his attention to Kant on perceptual judgments. He claims that, for Kant, "perceptual judgments are a lower-order logical activity that creates the subjective world of personal consciousness."[195] Judgments are a form of knowledge that always undergoes mediation; they are not directly perceivable or accessible. Eco comments, "In short, Kant postulates a notion of empirical concept and of perceptual judgment, but he does not manage to pull either of them out of the mire, from that muddy ground between sensible intuition and the legislator activity of the intellect."[196] He concludes that Kant's concepts of the schemata fail to provide an adequate theory of everyday knowledge. They do not allow one to know that a rock is a rock or that a dog is a dog. The reason is that the schemata are not transcendental things known innately. Whenever someone comes across something she has never perceived before, she does not have an innate category or schema to make sense of it. Rather, she understands this new phenomenon based on the other things she knows. This phenomenon is why Marco Polo reverted to understanding the rhinoceros as a unicorn. Eco concludes, "*What happens when we must construct the schema of an object that is as yet unknown?*"[197] What would Kant have done had he stumbled across a platypus?

Eco concludes this essay by noting that Kant was indeed on to something with his notion of schemata, though his theory ultimately proved unsatisfactory. Though these schemata are in some sense unnatural, they are motivated.[198] Some sort of category or form seems to be in the mind by which persons are able to understand objects that they have never perceived before.

Eco titles his third essay "Cognitive Types and Nuclear Content." In this essay, he develops his own theory of the mind's categories by which it understands new phenomena. He begins by discussing "perception and semiosis," asking the question, "Can we detach the phenomenon of semiosis from the idea of a sign?"[199] He references the example of smoke signifying a fire, remarking that there seems to be a gap between the perception of smoke and the judgment that there is a fire. The first is a perception and the second an inference: "Therefore any phenomenon, for it to be understood as a sign of something else and from a certain point of view, must first of all be

---

195. Eco, *Kant and the Platypus*, 76.
196. Eco, *Kant and the Platypus*, 77.
197. Eco, *Kant and the Platypus*, 89.
198. Eco, *Kant and the Platypus*, 122.
199. Eco, *Kant and the Platypus*, 125.

perceived. The fact that the perception may be successful precisely because we are guided by the notion that the phenomenon is hypothetically understood as a sign does not eliminate the problem of how we perceive it."[200] The process by which one makes a perceptual judgment happens via abduction.

Eco references the story of the Aztecs' first encounter with the Spanish conquistadors, specifically their first encounter with horses. Up until this point, Montezuma and the Aztecs never had encountered horses before. When the first warriors return to Montezuma to tell of these strangers, they describe them as riding atop deer as tall as their homes. The Aztecs did not have any experience with horses and were not sure how to identify them. They attempted to understand these new creatures with what they already know about deer: "Oriented therefore by a system of previous knowledge but trying to coordinate it with what they were seeing, they must have soon worked out a perceptual judgment. *An animal has appeared before us that seems like a deer but isn't.*"[201]

The *concept* of deer that the Aztecs used as a way of understanding this new phenomenon leads Eco to discuss *cognitive types*: "At the close of their first perceptual process, the Aztecs elaborated what we shall call a Cognitive Type (CT) of the horse. If they had lived in a Kantian universe, we should say that this CT was the schema that allowed them to mediate between the concept and the manifold of the intuition."[202] Unlike Kantian schemata, however, CTs are not innate. One comes to possess CTs via sensory perception and what Hans–Georg Gadamer referred to as the *sensus communis*, thus leading Eco to begin his semiotic discussion of CTs. [203]

Eco uses the semiotic terminology of *tokens* and *types* to discuss CTs. A *token* is a specific occurrence of a *type*. For example, *this* golden retriever is a token of the type golden retriever. He states, "It is precisely the phenomenon of recognition that induces us to talk of *type*, in fact, as a parameter of the comparison of tokens. This type has nothing to do with an Aristotelian Scholastic "essence.""[204] In the language of Kantian schematism, a CT would be "a rule, a procedure for constructing the image of the horse rather than a sort of multimedial image."[205]

200. Eco, *Kant and the Platypus*, 125.
201. Eco, *Kant and the Platypus*, 128.
202. Eco, *Kant and the Platypus*, 130.
203. Gadamer, *Truth and Method*, 17–27.
204. Eco, *Kant and the Platypus*, 131.
205. Eco, *Kant and the Platypus*, 131. See also Caesar, *Umberto Eco*, 165.

Eco progresses to his discussion of *nuclear content*. *Nuclear Content* (NC) is the basic content attached to CTs.[206] Nuclear contents are not determined by an independent subjectivity but a communal intersubjectivity:

> At first the area of consensus could be postulated only to explain the fact that they understood one another by using the same word. But bit by bit they must have proceeded to *collective interpretations* of what they understood by that word. They associated a 'content' with the expression *maçtal*. . . . In other words, the Aztecs gradually interpreted the features of their CT, in order to homologate it as much as possible.[207]

NCs are always public, or intersubjective, whilst CTs can be private, or subjective.[208] NCs as well as CTs are *interpretants*.[209] Eco states, "But if these interpretants were available integrally, as is the case with the scientists who saw a platypus for the first time, the Aztecs would not only make clear what their CT was but also circumscribe the meaning they assigned to the expression *maçtal*."[210]

Eco carefully distinguishes NC from *meaning*: "I prefer to speak of Nuclear Content rather than Meaning, because by time–honored tradition one tends to associate meaning with a mental experience."[211] He makes this distinction due to the ambiguity of the word *meaning*, contending that often it is used to reference mental experiences, denotations, intentions, as well as significance.[212] The term *content* is not as ambiguous, and one can use it "in a public sense and not a mental one."[213] Eco emphasizes that CTs are private while their NCs are public, or shared. All CTs have NCs.

A final concept to note from this essay is Eco's term *molar content* (MC). Eco provides the following lengthy definition of MC:

> When, having seen horses in the flesh and having talked with Spaniards, Montezuma acquired other information about horses, he could have reached the point where he knew what a Spaniard knew about them. In this case he would have had what is called

206. Eco, *Kant and the Platypus*, 136–37.
207. Eco, *Kant and the Platypus*, 136.
208. See also Caesar, *Umberto Eco*, 165.
209. Eco, *Kant and the Platypus*, 137.
210. Eco, *Kant and the Platypus*, 137.
211. Eco, *Kant and the Platypus*, 137.
212. Eco, *Kant and the Platypus*, 137.
213. Eco, *Kant and the Platypus*, 137.

a *complex* knowledge of them. Note that I am talking not about an "encyclopedic" knowledge, in the sense of a difference between Dictionary and Encyclopedia, but about "broadened knowledge," which includes notions that are not indispensable for perceptual recognition (e. g., that horses are reared in such and such a way or that they are mammals). With regard to this broadened competence I shall talk of Molar Content (MC).[214]

MCs, like CTs and NCs, are also interpretants; and like NCs, they are intersubjective, though the community possessing them might be substantially smaller. An example of a MC is the knowledge that a zoologist has of a horse. These "experts" have a special, broadened, knowledge of horses, albeit their differences. MCs are not universal, as are not NCs. The difference between NCs and MCs is the communities that possess them. Broader communities possess NCs whilst localized communities within these broader communities possess MCs. Unlike MCs, NCs represent *encyclopedic* contents rather than specialized ones: "Let us say that the sum of the MCs coincides with the Encyclopedia as a regulative idea and a semiotic postulate."[215] Eco also discusses semiosic primitives, empirical cases and cultural cases, and other issues surrounding these concepts of CTs, NCs, and MCs.

The next essay is "The Platypus between Dictionary and Encyclopedia." Eco utilizes his concepts of *dictionary* and *encyclopedia* to discuss the determination of NCs and MCs. MCs tend de facto to follow the model dictionary while the encyclopedia best represents NCs, though not *per se*. Again, MCs are a type of localized, or specialized, content within the larger content of NCs. This description is a gross overgeneralization to be further explored.

Eco begins this essay by discussing "mountains and mountains."[216] He comments that if he were to give Sandra directions on recognizing "the mountain" Ayers Rock, she would have no problem doing so due to the CT that she has of mountains even though it, Ayers Rock, is not technically a mountain. Ayers Rock bears many of the characteristics one has of mountains; however, from a scientific perspective, it is a stone: "Ayers Rock is a mountain from the point of view of the CT, but it is not from the point of view of the MC, i.e., of a competence definable as petrological or lithological or what have you."[217]

214. Eco, *Kant and the Platypus*, 141.
215. Eco, *Kant and the Platypus*, 142.
216. Eco, *Kant and the Platypus*, 224.
217. Eco, *Kant and the Platypus*, 225.

Sandra is able to recognize Ayers Rock as a mountain according to her CT because she has extralinguistic knowledge about mountains, which Ayers Rock resembles. Eco elaborates,

> The supporters of a dictionary representation maintain that such representations take account of relations within the language, leaving aside elements of knowledge of the world, while knowledge in an encyclopedic format presupposes extralinguistic knowledge. In order to provide a rigorous explanation of the functioning of language, the supporters of a dictionary representation maintain that we must turn to a package of semantic categories that are organized hierarchically and that are of such a kind that—even when we have no knowledge of the world—various inferences can be made of the type.[218]

Unlike dictionary knowledge, which is organized hierarchically, encyclopedic knowledge is, by nature, uncoordinated. Eco notes, "The dictionary schema is an instrument of classification, not an instrument of definition."[219] He also reminds his reader that NCs are public knowledge, implying that encyclopedic knowledge is also public, or intersubjective, knowledge.[220] Eco summarizes,

> Perhaps it would be sufficient to state that the NC is mostly composed of features of an encyclopedic nature, often disorganized, while forms of dictionary competence appear only in representations of MC. But it's not that simple. The authors of the medieval bestiaries would perhaps fail a zoology exam, but it cannot be denied that in their own way they were trying to constitute categories when they defined the crocodile (in terms of NC) as a water snake, evidently by taking for granted that this category was opposed to that of land snakes.[221]

Eco then discusses the notions of "files and directories." He shows that when someone perceives something, she recognizes it by a set of properties; but these recognizing properties do not function hierarchically. In order to recognize something, a perceiving subject creates a *file* of that something. When the subject needs to locate this file, she might consult a sort of cognitive directory. As she creates more files and the directories

218. Eco, *Kant and the Platypus*, 226.
219. Eco, *Kant and the Platypus*, 228.
220. Eco, *Kant and the Platypus*, 226.
221. Eco, *Kant and the Platypus*, 228–29.

become more complex: "it becomes necessary to split certain directories up into subdirectories, and at a certain point we may decide to restructure the entire tree of directories."[222] Eco also comments on issues of "wild categorization,"[223] "indelible properties,"[224] and understanding meaning as a contract or negotiation.[225]

Eco provides "notes on referring as contract."[226] As one can infer from the title of the essay, he primarily focuses on how one uses language to reference things. He reverts back to the story of the Aztecs beholding horses for the first time. Since the Aztecs did not have a CT of a horse, they navigated their way through their encyclopedia to locate a CT that best represented this new phenomenon as well as the NC that came with it: the deer. They were not, however, looking at deer but horses. In this case, the Aztecs did not have a CT or NC of a horse in order to grasp what they were seeing, so they utilized the CT and NC of a deer to attempt to understand these creatures. In this instance, their referencing was a case of *negotiation*.[227] This negotiation is the same sort of process that scientists went through when trying to identify the platypus.

In the final essay of this work, Eco revisits the debate on iconism and hypoiconism. He discusses his differences with Peirce on what constitutes an icon and how icons are to be understood. This material is discussed more thoroughly in his *A Theory of Semiotics*.

CONCLUSION

This chapter provided a detailed overview of Eco's semiotic project and has been necessary in providing the appropriate context in which one should understand Eco's model encyclopedia. As the reader should have noticed, this concept has been mentioned multiple times throughout Eco's works. I will turn now to providing a detailed explication of the model encyclopedia. This next chapter will follow a similar format as this chapter has, tracing the development of this concept throughout Eco's overall semiotic project.

    222. Eco, *Kant and the Platypus*, 229.
    223. Eco, *Kant and the Platypus*, 232–35.
    224. Eco, *Kant and the Platypus*, 235–41.
    225. Eco, *Kant and the Platypus*, 248–79. Eco elsewhere applies this concept of *negotiation* to translation. See Umberto Eco, *Mouse or Rat?*.
    226. Eco, *Kant and the Platypus*, 280.
    227. Eco, *Kant and the Platypus*, 287.

3

Umberto Eco's Model Encyclopedia

This chapter will provide a detailed explication of Eco's model encyclopedia and its role in his semiotic project. Eco does not discuss the encyclopedia in all of his semiotic works, though he does in most of them. The primary monographs consulted in this chapter are *A Theory of Semiotics*, *The Role of the Reader*, and *Semiotics and the Philosophy of Language*. Two essays, in addition to these monographs, will be consulted as well: "From the Tree to the Labyrinth" and "The Platypus between Dictionary and Encyclopedia." The former is a historical discussion on the model dictionary and the model encyclopedia, and the latter is an essay showing the role of the encyclopedia in cognition, specifically in recognition. Eco's most thorough discussions and explications of the model encyclopedia appear in *Semiotics and the Philosophy of Language* and "From the Tree to the Labyrinth." Though these works are his two major treatments of the topic, I will not begin by discussing them. Instead, I will trace the development of this concept as it appears in his writings chronologically. This order will be as follows: *A Theory of Semiotics*, *The Role of the Reader*, *Semiotics and the Philosophy of Language*, "From the Tree to the Labyrinth," and "The Platypus between Dictionary and Encyclopedia." I will conclude by summarizing Eco's model encyclopedia and discussing his best summary representation of it: the labyrinth of the library in *The Name of the Rose*.

A THEORY OF SEMIOTICS

Eco briefly treats the topic of encyclopedia in *A Theory of Semiotics*. He first mentions the concept when discussing the KF Model for semiotic theory in his chapter where he develops his theory of codes. Again, he only briefly treats the topic here. He begins by discussing "the sememe as encyclopedia."[1] He notes the possibility of incomplete codes concerning "hierarchical scientific componential spectrums, of disconnected lists of semantic properties attributed to a sememe by the layman, and so on."[2] He uses the example of the sememe <whale>. Specifically, Eco discusses possible denotations and connotations for <whale>: "For a modern layman <whale> is probably a very disconnected sememe in which such properties as <fish> and <mammal> coexist and its semantic spectrum should probably be a network of superimpositions of possible readings in which the contextual selections are not very well established."[3] He shows how this phenomenon can lead to "a certain cultural level at which /whale/ gives rise to a contradictory sememe considering both medieval, the scientific and the popular system of units."[4]

Eco discusses the competence of the encyclopedia as opposed to the dictionary:

> The sign-vehicle /whale/ corresponds to a content unit (a sememe) <whale> which can be decomposed in different ways. It depends on the context whether a whale will be considered a fish or a mammal, and this decision precedes the isolation of the first immediate denotation. In fact, in order to conceive of a whale as being something like a fish, a culture must set it in a given semantic field in which <whale> is opposed and interconnected with <shark> and <dolphin> for example, those cultural units having certain elements in common and others in mutual opposition, exactly as in a structured field of phonemes, mutually correlated and opposed by means of distinctive features (Jakobson–Halle, 1956). If on the other hand a whale is viewed as a mammal (or at least as an aquatic animal although not a fish) it will have to be posited as the pertinent unit of another semantic field.[5]

1. Eco, *A Theory of Semiotics*, 112.
2. Eco, *A Theory of Semiotics*, 112.
3. Eco, *A Theory of Semiotics*, 113.
4. Eco, *A Theory of Semiotics*, 113.
5. Eco, *A Theory of Semiotics*, 113–14.

Fundamental differences exist in the nature of the model dictionary and the model encyclopedia. One should note, however, that Eco does not develop or provide the content for these concepts of model dictionary or model encyclopedia in *A Theory of Semiotics*. He, rather, only shows the role of the model encyclopedia as it pertains to developing a theory of codes. One of the failures of the KF Model is that it does not escape the pitfalls of presupposing the model dictionary as the grounds for the development of sememes.

The Model Q, for which Eco advocates, utilizes more insights from the model encyclopedia and thus offers a stronger model for grounding sememes as they pertain to a theory of codes: "The real problem is that *every semantic unit used in order to analyze a sememe is in its turn a sememe to be analyzed*."[6] Commenting on the relationship of Eco's theory of codes and this notion of encyclopedia, Heath Thomas writes,

> If a theory of codes frames how one might understand the structure of potential communicative acts, then the encyclopedia proffers a way to describe the global material from which s–codes and codes are constructed that give insight to specific communicative acts. The encyclopedia is a descriptor of the cumulative amount of cultural knowledge present to a creator of a message at the time of its genesis.[7]

The encyclopedia is the total sum of cultural knowledge that sign producers possess, which provides the grounding content for the theory of codes that makes the production of signs possible.

THE ROLE OF THE READER

Eco briefly discusses the model encyclopedia in *The Role of the Reader*. In the introduction, Eco has been showing how semiotic categories can aid readers in understanding the nature of texts and the phenomenon of reading. He discusses the model encyclopedia in the context of *discursive structures* as it pertains to his model of the "hierarchy of operations performed to interpret a text."[8] Leading up to his brief discussion of the encyclopedia, he converses on matters pertaining to a theory of codes and overcoding. He writes, "At box 4 the reader confronts the text linear manifestation with the system of

---

6. Eco, *A Theory of Semiotics*, 121.
7. Thomas, *Poetry and Theology in the Book of Lamentations*, 54.
8. Eco, *Role of the Reader*, 13.

codes and subcodes provided by the language in which the text is written (box 1). Such a system is presupposed by the present research in the format of an encyclopedia, structured as the Model Q proposed in *Theory* (2.12)."[9] Box 4 concerns the matters of the "individuation of topics," "reduction of frames," and "blowing up and narcotizing properties," all of which fall under the bracket of semantic disclosures.[10] Isotopies also find a home in box 4.

In the process of interpretation, when the reader reaches the stage depicted in box 4, "this begins the transformation of the expression into content, word by word, phrase by phrase."[11] One should remember from chapter two that, according to Eco, the sign is made up of an expression plane and a content plane, according to his theory of codes. Written words, just as spoken words, represent *expression planes*. In Speech Act Theory, expression planes find a sort of parallel with locutionary acts. Each expression plane has a coinciding content plane. These content planes are sememes. When writing a text, authors have a certain content plane in mind for which they choose a certain expression plane. In doing so, the author supposes that the reader will attach a similar, if not the same, content plane to the expression plane when reading. In the process of decoding, the reader reads, or actualizes, a text, and she attaches content planes to the expression planes that she reads.. These content planes are derived from her, the reader's encyclopedia. This content is what Eco means by the phrase "transformation of the expression into content."[12]

Eco quickly discusses a *basic dictionary* and its role in reading: "The reader resorts to a lexicon with the format of a basic dictionary and immediately detects the most basic semantic properties of the sememes involved, so as to make a first tentative amalgamation."[13] As will be discussed more below, the dictionary serves only as a tool to be utilized in determining the content of an expression; it does not provide an adequate theory for determining sememes themselves. Eco refers to the example of the expression <princess>:

> If the text says that /once upon a time there was a young princess called Snow White. She was very pretty/, the reader detects by a first semantic analysis of <princess> that Snow White is surely

9. Eco, *Role of the Reader*, 17.
10. Eco, *Role of the Reader*, 14.
11. Eco, *Role of the Reader*, 17.
12. Eco, *Role of the Reader*, 17.
13. Eco, *Role of the Reader*, 18.

> a <woman>. The sememe <princess> is virtually much more complex (for instance, <woman> entails <human female>, and a human female should be represented by many properties such as having certain body organs, and so on). At this point the reader does not know as yet which of these *virtual* properties must be *actualized*.[14]

What will determine which properties to actualize while reading are matters of "rules of co-reference,"[15] "contextual and circumstantial selections,"[16] "rhetorical and stylistic overcoding,"[17] "inferences by common frames,"[18] "inferences by intertextual frames,"[19] and "ideological overcoding."[20]

Eco begins his discussion of semantic disclosures as follows: "Should every virtual property be taken into account in the further course of the text, the reader would be obliged to outline, as in a sort of vivid mental picture, the whole network of interrelated properties that the encyclopedia assigns to the corresponding sememe. Nevertheless (and fortunately), we do not proceed like that."[21] The reader does not exhaust her encyclopedia when decoding a lexeme. Again, issues of co-reference, context, isotopies, and intertextual frames determine which semantic properties are actualized. All of the semantic properties, however, are present in one's encyclopedia though she may not utilize them all. Eco states, "They are *virtually* present in the encyclopedia, that is they are socially *stored*, and the reader picks them up from the semantic store only when required by the text. In doing so the reader implements *semantic disclosures*, in other words, actualizes nonmanifested properties (as well as merely suggested sememes)."[22] Semantic disclosures perform two roles: "they *blow up* certain properties (making them textually relevant or pertinent) and *narcotize* some others."[23] Eco clarifies that *narcotized* does not mean *abolished*. The reader could actualize all

---

14. Eco, *Role of the Reader*, 18.
15. Eco, *Role of the Reader*, 18–19.
16. Eco, *Role of the Reader*, 19.
17. Eco, *Role of the Reader*, 19–20.
18. Eco, *Role of the Reader*, 20–21.
19. Eco, *Role of the Reader*, 21–22.
20. Eco, *Role of the Reader*, 22–23.
21. Eco, *Role of the Reader*, 23.
22. Eco, *Role of the Reader*, 23.
23. Eco, *Role of the Reader*, 23.

of these virtual properties, exhausting her encyclopedia; but just because she does not do so does not mean that these properties have been obliterated.[24]

Readers utilize their encyclopedias, their stores of cultural knowledge, when determining the coinciding contents to written expressions. When one reads, she interprets the meaning, or content units, of the words on the page by navigating her way through her encyclopedia. This navigation takes place via what Eco, borrowing from Peirce, calls *abduction*.

SEMIOTICS AND THE PHILOSOPHY OF LANGUAGE

Eco provides his first *thorough* treatment of the model encyclopedia in the chapter "Dictionary vs. Encyclopedia," which appears in *Semiotics and the Philosophy of Language*.[25] As one can see, the encyclopedia plays an important role in Eco's project, though he has yet to provide a thorough explication of it up to this point. In "Dictionary vs. Enyclopedia," Eco shows why the model dictionary fails as an adequate model for the determination of *sememes*. One understanding of a *sememe* is a "minimal unit of meaning that goes into the composition of the overall meaning of a word."[26] In other words, a sememe is a basic content unit. This language of *unit of meaning* echoes back to Eco's own definition of *meaning* that he provides in *A Theory of Semiotics*, where he defines meaning as *a cultural unit*. Eco considers a sememe itself to be a potential encyclopedia. As such, a sememe is not necessarily a basic content unit, as if it possessed the essential attributes of a term. Rather, a sememe becomes simply a content unit, which Eco uses synonymously with his term *cultural unit*. The concepts of *sememe* and *cultural unit* go hand-in-hand with each other, as Eco seems to understand them as identifiable with one another.[27]

---

24. Eco, *Role of the Reader*, 23.

25. Eco, *Semiotics and the Philosophy of Language*, 46–86.

26. Danesi, *Encyclopedic Dictionary of Semiotics, Media, and Communications*, 204.

27. In her entry for the term *cultural unit*, Patrizia Magli notes the interchangeable uses of *cultural unit* and *sememe*: "According to different authors, cultural units can be identified with the whole sememe . . . or with the elementary component of the sememe, semes. . . . Cultural units can be isolated either according to a *dictionary-like representation, or to an encyclopedia-like representation. Eco considers cultural units as components of the content of expressions, in an encyclopedia-like semantics, and identifies them with *interpretants." See Magli, "Cultural Unit," 170. I will use the terms *sememe, content*, and *cultural unit* interchangeably throughout this chapter and the rest of the book.

Eco begins this chapter by reminding the reader that a sign is something that stands for something else, and as such this sign must be interpreted.[28] The fact that signs must be interpreted "allows us to start from a given sign to cover, step by step, the whole universe of semiosis."[29] Eco notes that Hjelmslev was most likely the first semiotician to provide an outline of the model dictionary. He states, "Hjelmslev's proposal for a dictionary leaves unsolved two important questions: how to define the meaning of the components or *figurae* (in other words, if *ram* means male sheep, what does *sheep* mean?) and how to obtain a finite or unrestricted inventory."[30]

Eco goes on to note other major contributors to the model dictionary, namely Katz. Discussing the contribution of Katz, Eco states the following: Naturally, the ideal condition for a dictionary is that this dictionary, being "the reconstruction of an aspect of the speaker's semantic competence," storing "only finitely many bits of information about a particular lexical item," be "a finite list of entries" so that "each entry consists of a finite number of lexical readings, and that each lexical reading contains a finite number of semantic markers."

The dictionary model ultimately depends on a Porphyrian Tree (PT) in order to determine a sememe. This PT ultimately presupposes a philosophy of substance in order to construct sememes. The PT also relies on the hierarchical categories of Aristotle, further developed by Porphyry, to determine sememes, namely those categories of *genus* and *species*.[31]

28. Eco, *Semiotics and the Philosophy of Language*, 46.

29. Eco, *Semiotics and the Philosophy of Language*, 46.. "Semiosis" is a word that refers to "the process of meaning–making—specifically to the interaction between the representamen, the object and the interpretent." See Chandler, *Semiotics the Basics*, 259. Eco also develops the concept of "unlimited semiosis" "to refer to the way in which, for Peirce (via 'the interpretant'), for Barthes (via connotation), for Derrida (via 'freeplay') and for Lacan (via 'the sliding signified'), the signified is endlessly commutable—functioning in its turn as a signifier for a further signified" (Chandler, *Semiotics*, 264).

30. Eco, *Semiotics and the Philosophy of Language*, 49.

31. Eco, *Semiotics and the Philosophy of Language*, 55–57. Eco also states the following: "Porphyry lists five predicables: genus, species, differentia, property, and accident. The five predicables establish the modes of definition for all the ten categories (substance plus nine accidents). It is therefore possible to think of ten Porphyrian trees: one for substances, which allows for instance, the definition of man as a rational mortal animal, and one for each of the other nine categories; for instance, a tree of qualities will allow the definition of purple as a species of the genus 'red'. Aristotle said that even accidents are susceptible to definition, even though an accident can be said to have an essence only in reference to substances. There are, thus, ten possible trees, but there is not a tree of the ten trees, because the Being is not a summum genus."

Eco notes that Porphyry held that a definition should take into account only a limited number of primitives. Primitives are those qualities that are essential to the thing being defined, i.e., essential attributes. Anything not essential to the thing being defined was an accidental attribute, i.e., a property, and one ought not include it in a definition.[32]

Eco next turns his attention to a critique of the PT.[33] He notes, "Porphyry designed a *unique* tree for substances, and it is from this model that every subsequent idea of a dictionary–like representation stems."[34] He shows that if one follows the PT, then one is ultimately never able to define the difference between a man and a horse. In order to do so, one must include an attribute of either *horse* or *man* that is not essential to its substance.[35] At this point, the PT fails its own delimitations of relying solely on *genus* and *species* to establish a sememe. If one seeks to establish a sememe according to the PT then many definitions will be incomplete. Though some might argue that certain accidental attributes could be included in the definition of a sememe, there are no set guidelines or standards as to determine which ones should be used and which ones should not. Eco then shows how each node on the PT is filled ultimately with differentiae rather than primatives.[36] He goes on to conclude, "Genera and species are only the names that we assign to the nodes represented by disjunctions of differentiae."[37] These differentiae, according to Eco, are no more than accidents and signs.[38] Eco concludes his critique of the dictionary model founded on the PT,

> The tree of genera and species, the tree of substances, blows up in a dust of differentiae, in a turmoil of infinite accidents, in a nonhierarchical network of *qualia*. The dictionary is dissolved into a potentially unordered and unrestricted galaxy of pieces of

---

Undoubtedly, the substance–tree proposed by Porphyry aims at being considered a *finite* set of genera and species (we will see in which sense this assumption is tenable); it is not said whether the other nine possible trees are to be finite or not, and Porphyry is rather elusive on this subject" (59).

32. Eco, *Semiotics and the Philosophy of Language*, 57, 59.
33. Eco, *Semiotics and the Philosophy of Language*, 57–68.
34. Eco, *Semiotics and the Philosophy of Language*, 59.
35. Eco, *Semiotics and the Philosophy of Language*, 61.
36. Eco, *Semiotics and the Philosophy of Language*, 64.
37. Eco, *Semiotics and the Philosophy of Language*, 65.
38. Eco, *Semiotics and the Philosophy of Language*, 67.

world knowledge. The dictionary thus becomes an encyclopedia, because it was in fact a *disguised encyclopedia*.[39]

Eco begins his discussion on the model encyclopedia by discussing the registration of contexts and topics:

> If a dictionary is a disguised encyclopedia, then the only possible representation of the content of a given lexical item cannot be provided except in terms of an encyclopedia. If the so-called universals, or metatheoretical constructs, that work as markers within a dictionary-like representation are mere linguistic labels that cover more synthetic properties, an encyclopedia-like representation assumes that the representation of the content takes place only by means of *interpretants*, in a process of unlimited semiosis.[40]

In other words, the represented content is a chain of linked interpretants, each which interprets the others. Perhaps an easier way to summarize this idea is that each sememe finds itself in its interpretant, which finds its meaning in its relationships and interrelationships with all other interpretants. The differentiae of the interpretants ground the content of said interpretants.

Eco writes, "These interpretants being in their turn interpretable, there is no bidimensional tree able to represent the global semantic competence of a given culture. Such a global representation is only a semiotic postulate, a regulative idea, and takes the format of a multidimensional network that has been described as the Model Q."[41] In *The Role of the Reader*, he insists that each sememe is a potential text. Every text is the expansion of at least one sememe.[42] Eco further comments, "The encyclopedic representation of the sememe has been reinforced with the reference to frames, scripts, and other instructions concerning coded circumstantial and contextual occurrences. As a consequence, it is clear that an encyclopedic representation, insofar as it is text-oriented, must take into account this kind of so-called pragmatic factor as well."[43] All sememes are established in their connections and interconnections to all other sememes and their interpretants. In the same way that every entry in the model encyclopedia presupposes the totality of all other encyclopedic entries, so does the sememe because it itself is a potential encyclopedia.

39. Eco, *Semiotics and the Philosophy of Language*, 68.
40. Eco, *Semiotics and the Philosophy of Language*, 68.
41. Eco, *Semiotics and the Philosophy of Language*, 68. See also Eco, *Theory of Semiotics*, 121–25.
42. Eco, *Role of the Reader*, 175.
43. Eco, *Semiotics and the Philosophy of Language*, 69.

Eco notes that an encyclopedic semantics blurs the line that separates analytic from synthetic properties, referencing W. V. Quine's "Two Dogmas of Empiricism" for support.[44] He comments, "Naturally, nothing prevents one from using analytical markers, provided one knows that they are shorthand devices used in order to include other analytic properties they entail and to summarize all the synthetic markers they name.... Semantic markers are pseudoanalytic shorthand labels."[45] In other words, Eco is claiming that the elements utilized by the model dictionary to ground a sememe, i.e. analytic properties, are ultimately only a tool to be used in the encyclopedia. He sums up,

> A semiotic encyclopedia, even though only designed under the form of local examples, is subjected to the same restrictions. However, the choice of the encyclopedia over the dictionary is not a free one: we have shown that dictionaries cannot exist if not as theoretical figments. The universe of natural languages (and not only of verbal ones) is the universe of semiosis. The regulative idea of encyclopedia is the only way to outline a possible format of such a universe and to try tentative devices for describing part of it.[46]

What Eco means by "local examples" is that every example one can give of an encyclopedic entry will be a specific one within a certain context, for in order to give a complete, or global, example would be to provide a model that utilized *all* existing sememes. These local examples can also be referred to as "clusters."[47]

Eco shifts his attention to the role of context in the model encyclopedia. He begins by stating, "According to the last representation we have examined, it is clear that, when the content of an expression is represented in the format of encyclopedia, there is no way to establish—out of any context—a hierarchy among properties."[48] In other words, in the model encyclopedia, there is no one property one must begin with when establishing a sememe. Rather, the context of the sememe plays a more determinative role here. He provides the following example:

---

44. Eco, *Semiotics and the Philosophy of Language*, 73. See also Quine's "Two Dogmas of Empiricism," 31–53.
45. Eco, *Semiotics and the Philosophy of Language*, 73–74.
46. Eco, *Semiotics and the Philosophy of Language*, 77–78.
47. Eco, *Semiotics and the Philosophy of Language*, 78.
48. Eco, *Semiotics and the Philosophy of Language*, 78.

> During the night, looking out of the window of her home in the countryside, a wife tells her husband: *Honey, there is a man on the lawn near the fence!* Now, suppose that her husband controls the situation and answers: *No, honey, it's not a man....* It would be absolutely unclear what the husband means, what he is negating and what survives his negation.[49]

Eco shows that the husband could mean that there is something in the yard, though it is not a man; also, he could mean that there is no one or nothing in the yard:

> Naturally, the husband can have the intention of scaring his wife by producing a feeling of uneasiness and suspense; but, in this case, we are no longer concerned with semantic questions, but with a more complex pragmatic strategy based on *reticence*. The husband, in this case, exploits the nature of the encyclopedia in order to achieve a rhetorical effect.[50]

Suppose, however, that the husband does intend to say something clear concerning what is in the yard. Eco writes,

> He should then say that that thing is not a man but (alternatively) a boy, a dog, a spatial creature, a tree, and so on.... He must simply build up and presuppose the same 'local' portion of dictionary he assumed as implicitly outlined by his wife in uttering her sentence. The husband must make some conjecture or abduction about the *ad hoc* dictionary that both speakers, in that situation, take for granted.[51]

Again, the context, or the locality within the encyclopedia, of the situation grounds the meaning of the husband's speech act. Eco concludes this thought experiment with the following:

> The encyclopedia is the regulative hypothesis that allows both speakers to figure out the 'local' dictionary they need in order to ensure the good standing of their communicative interaction.... A natural language is a flexible system of signification conceived for producing texts, and texts are devices for blowing up or narcotizing pieces of encyclopedic information.[52]

---

49. Eco, *Semiotics and the Philosophy of Language*, 79.
50. Eco, *Semiotics and the Philosophy of Language*, 79.
51. Eco, *Semiotics and the Philosophy of Language*, 79.
52. Eco, *Semiotics and the Philosophy of Language*, 80.

Eco next illustrates the model that best represents the model of the encyclopedia: the labyrinth. Whereas the model that best represents the dictionary is a tree, namely the Porphyrian tree, the model that best represents the encyclopedia is a labyrinth. Eco discusses three models, or versions, of the labyrinth. The first version he discusses is the classical labyrinth where, once one entered, she is only able to make her way to the center where she must face the Minotaur.[53] Eco comments, "Such a labyrinth is ruled by a blind necessity. Structurally speaking, it is simpler than a tree: it is a skein, and, as one unwinds a skein, one obtains a continuous line."[54] This labyrinth is linear, providing only one path that one can travel.

The second model of the labyrinth is the "German *Irrgärten* or *Irrweg*."[55] In English, this model is known as the maze. In the maze multiple paths exist that one can choose to take in order to find her way to the exit on the other side of said maze. Some of these paths lead only to dead ends. Like the classical labyrinth, if one were to unwind this maze, it too would be linear. Eco states, "If one unwinds a maze, one gets a particular kind of tree in which certain choices are privileged in respect to others. Some alternatives end at a point where one is obliged to return backwards, whereas others generate new branches, and only one among them leads to the way out."[56]

The third type of labyrinth that Eco discusses and appropriates for his model encyclopedia is that of a net, more specifically, a rhizome. He writes, "The main feature of a net is that every point can be connected with every other point, and, where the connections are not yet designed, they are, however, conceivable and designable. A net is an unlimited territory. A net is not a tree."[57] In a net, the intersections of the threads are nodes. These nodes represent sememes. In this model, each sememe is established by its connections and interconnections with all of the other nodes. This net has no definable boundary, and it is ever growing, as there are always new sememes coming into existence.[58]

Eco comments on this concept of rhizome, "A rhizome can be broken off at any point and reconnected following one of its own lines."[59] If a con-

---

53. Eco, *Semiotics and the Philosophy of Language*, 80.
54. Eco, *Semiotics and the Philosophy of Language*, 80.
55. Eco, *Semiotics and the Philosophy of Language*, 80.
56. Eco, *Semiotics and the Philosophy of Language*, 81.
57. Eco, *Semiotics and the Philosophy of Language*, 81.
58. Eco, *Semiotics and the Philosophy of Language*, 81.
59. Eco, *Semiotics and the Philosophy of Language*, 81.

necting line is weak in the rhizome, then it can be disconnected and reconnected with another in order to form a stronger connection:

> No one can provide a global description of the whole rhizome; not only because the rhizome is multidimensionally complicated, but also because its structure changes through the time; moreover, in a structure in which every node can be connected with every other node, there is also the possibility of contradictory inferences.[60]

Because one is not able to produce a global rhizome, the rhizome can only "be described as a potential sum of *local* descriptions."[61] One is able only to view the rhizome from within the rhizome. Eco further comments, "A labyrinth of this kind is a *myopic algorithm*; at every node of it no one can have the global vision of all its possibilities but only the local vision of the closest ones: every local description of the net is a *hypothesis*, subject to falsification, about its further course; in a rhizome blindness is the only way of seeing (locally), and thinking means to *grope one's way*."[62]

One can conceive also of this type of labyrinth as a road atlas, though one that, theoretically, has no outside or inside borders. All of the different cities on a road atlas are connected and interconnected to each other via interstates, highways, and local roadways. If one were to choose to drive from New Orleans to Dallas, there is a large number of ways that she could go. She could drive north on I-55 to Jackson and then drive west on I-20 until she arrives in Dallas. Another possible route would be to drive west on I-10 to Houston and then drive north on I-45 until she gets to Dallas. A third way would be to drive west on I-10 until one arrived at San Antonio and the take I-35 north until she gets to Dallas. These example routes are only three of *many*! Though some of these routes are more convenient than others, the point to be made is that there exists a plethora of ways one could drive to Dallas from New Orleans; there is no set way. This analogy, however, does breakdown in that one can view the road atlas only from the outside. The net concept that Eco lays out might be better represented as the interstate system in general without reference to an atlas. One can view and navigate the interstate system only from within the system, i.e., driving the interstates. This model of the labyrinth represents the Model Q that Eco discussed in *A Theory of Semiotics*.

---

60. Eco, *Semiotics and the Philosophy of Language*, 81–82.
61. Eco, *Semiotics and the Philosophy of Language*, 82.
62. Eco, *Semiotics and the Philosophy of Language*, 82.

Eco provides the following concluding comments to end this essay in *Semiotics and the Philosophy of Language*:

> The universe of semiosis, that is, the universe of human culture, must be conceived as structured like a labyrinth of the third type: (a) It is structured according to *a network of interpretants*. (b) It is virtually *infinite* because it takes into account multiple interpretations realized by different cultures: a given expression can be interpreted as many times, and in as many ways, as it has been actually interpreted in a given cultural framework; it is infinite because every discourse about the encyclopedia casts in doubts the previous structure of the encyclopedia itself. (c) It does not register only 'truths' but, rather, what has been said about the truth or what has been believed to be true as well as what has been believed to be false or imaginary or legendary, provided that a given culture had elaborated some discourse about some subject matter; . . . . (d) Such a semantic encyclopedia is never accomplished and exists only as a *regulative idea*; it is only on the basis of such a regulative idea that one is able actually to isolate a given portion of the social encyclopedia so far as it appears useful in order to interpret certain portions of actual discourses (and texts). (e) Such a notion of encyclopedia does not deny the existence of structured knowledge; it only suggests that such a knowledge cannot be recognized and organized as a global system; it provides only 'local' and transitory systems of knowledge; which can be contradicted by alternative and equally 'local' cultural organizations; every attempt to recognize these local organizations as unique and 'global'—ignoring their partiality—produces an *ideological* bias.[63]

Once one realizes that the universe of semiosis functions as the labyrinth of the encyclopedia, then she is free to utilize the dictionary as a tool in times of need; but the dictionary is just that: a tool.[64] Eco states, "We presuppose a local dictionary every time we want to recognize and to circumscribe an area of consensus within which a given discourse should stray, because no single discourse is designed to change globally our world view."[65] He concludes with the following:

> Thus, if the encyclopedia is an unordered set of markers (and of frames, scripts, text-oriented instructions), the dictionary-like arrangements we continuously provide are transitory and

63. Eco, *Semiotics and the Philosophy of Language*, 83–84.
64. Eco, *Semiotics and the Philosophy of Language*, 84.
65. Eco, *Semiotics and the Philosophy of Language*, 85.

pragmatically useful hierarchical reassessments of it. In this sense one should turn upside down a current distinction between dictionary (strictly semantic) and encyclopedia (polluted with 'pragmatic' elements); on the contrary, *the encyclopedia is a semantic concept and the dictionary is a pragmatic device.*[66]

Whereas many view the dictionary as pertaining to semantics and the encyclopedia to pragmatics, Eco's understanding of the nature of language reverses this conception.

"FROM THE TREE TO THE LABYRINTH"

Eco provides the lengthiest discussion of the encyclopedia in his essay "From the Tree to the Labyrinth."[67] In this essay, he primarily rehashes what he has previously said in *Semiotics and the Philosophy of Language*. The primary distinction between his treatment in the former work and the essay at hand is that he provides a more historical treatment to the topics of both dictionary and encyclopedia. He provides insights concerning the historical developments of both the dictionary and encyclopedia, providing major examples of each, such as D'Alembert's *Encyclopédie* and the *Encyclopedia Britannica*. However, Eco does provide some new insights to his theory of encyclopedia in the essay at hand.

Eco provides the useful distinctions between the maximal encyclopedia, the median encyclopedia, and the special encyclopedia. The maximal encyclopedia represents the model encyclopedia that he discusses in *Semiotics and the Philosophy of Language*. He points out that not until the work of Quillian does the concept of a semantic network surfaces.[68] This semantic network is structured as a labyrinth made up of interconnected nodes, as the rhizome that he, Eco, promotes above. He states, "Any node can be taken as the point of departure or *type* of a series of other nodes (*tokens*) that define it. . . . Each of the defining terms may in its turn become the *type* of another series of *tokens*."[69] Every concept in the semantic network implies a relationship to every concept in the semantic network. Eco further notes,

66. Eco, *Semiotics and the Philosophy of Language*, 85.
67. Eco, "Labyrinth,," 3–94. This volume functions as a sort of *summa* for Eco's work in semiotics.
68. Eco, "Labyrinth," 57. See also Quillian, "Semantic Memory."
69. Eco, "Labyrinth," 57.

It has been said that, if we assume a maximal notion of competence about the world, the meaning of a term would then consist of all the true propositions in which it has appeared or could appear. In fact, this would presuppose the ideal model of the encyclopedia. But in scientific practice and the way in which, in our daily lives, we try to make sense of sentences, we do not make a global appeal to the encyclopedia for every sentence, and it is the content that selects the local zones of competence that must be activated.[70]

This idea of the "local zone" is what Eco refers to as the *specialized encyclopedia*. Concerning the nature of the specialized encyclopedia, he states, "The format of the network to be activated is prescribed by the contexts and the circumstances of the proposition."[71] Take for example the word /strike/. In the context of baseball, /strike/ means one thing while in bowling it means something else. That is because, in both instances of the sememe, one utilizes a different specialized encyclopedia. Eco further comments, "Often, however, in order to construct and presuppose a local portion of encyclopedia needed for the comprehension of a determined context, we must resort to simplified local representations that set aside many properties that are otherwise (in other contexts) resistant."[72]

Eco points out that each use of the individual, or specialized, encyclopedia presupposes the maximal encyclopedia.[73] He reminds the reader that the maximal encyclopedia cannot be consulted because it is made up of "the sum total of everything that was ever thought or said."[74] Heath Thomas summarizes this concept: "Describing the encyclopedia can only be accomplished from a localized level, and there is no etic perspective by which to empirically perceive and assess the whole. The encyclopedia, then, remains theoretical yet knowable via localized descriptions of it."[75] As noted above, in instances of individual statements, one assumes a local encyclopedia, or specialized encyclopedia.

In conjunction with the concept of local encyclopedia, Eco also discusses "the Median Encyclopedia:"

70. Eco, "Labyrinth," 58.
71. Eco, "Labyrinth," 58.
72. Eco, "Labyrinth," 59.
73. Eco, "Labyrinth," 70.
74. Eco, "Labyrinth," 70.
75. Thomas, *Lamentations*, 55.

> But as a rule ... out of considerations of economy we have recourse to what we consider to be a Median Encyclopedia. Though its extent is difficult to measure, a Median Encyclopedia is identified with the contents of a given culture. ... The fact that it is a Median Encyclopedia does not mean that all of its contents are shared by all members of a given culture, but rather that it is *shareable*.[76]

A full-fledged library, or the maximal encyclopedia for that matter, does not represent the Median Encyclopedia. Rather, the Median Encyclopedia is a sort of abridged version of the encyclopedia. Eco refers to a "mid-sized one-volume encyclopedia" as opposed to the 2010 *Encyclopedia Britannica*, which numbers thirty-two volumes.[77] He then goes on to discuss issues such as "the vertigo of the labyrinth" and memory as they pertain to the encyclopedia, but these topics go beyond the scope of the present essay.

In summary, the model encyclopedia serves as a regulative idea in the philosophy of language. More specifically, the model encyclopedia, working in conjunction with a theory of codes, provides one with the instructions and cultural knowledge necessary to speak and interpret speech. As Paolo Desogus comments, "The encyclopedia is the intersubjective memory that preserves the knowledge that we use in semiosic processes. Without the encyclopedia, from which we draw on the elements that form our competence, we will not be able to interpret or produce signs, since their mechanism is rule-governed by cultural conventions."[78] The rigidness of the model dictionary does not explain adequately how one can use words in such a variety of ways, such as metaphor, without contradicting the definition provided by the word's genus and species. The model encyclopedia better explains how this is possible (descriptive) via the connections and interconnections of all words and their contents to all others, and the model encyclopedia, namely the maximal encyclopedia, functions as a regulative idea (normative) for how one produces signs and interprets them.

"THE PLATYPUS BETWEEN DICTIONARY AND ENCYCLOPEDIA"

In this essay, found in *Kant and the Platypus*, Eco discusses his concept of encyclopedia as it pertains to cognition and recognition. As noted in the

76. Eco, "Labyrinth," 73.
77. Eco, "Labyrinth," 73.
78. Desogus, "The Encyclopedia in Umberto Eco's Semiotics," 520.

previous chapter, Eco begins by discussing how Sandra is able to recognize Ayers Rock as a mountain even though it is not technically a mountain. Sandra, however, is able to recognize it as a mountain due to the nuclear content (NC) attached to her cognitive type (CT). According to the molar content (MC) of a mountain, Ayers Rock is not a mountain but only a stone. This NC is an intersubjective encyclopedic knowledge; it is an encyclopedic representation.

Eco writes, "The supporters of a dictionary representation maintain that such representations take account of relations within the language, leaving aside elements of knowledge of the world, while knowledge in an encyclopedic format presupposes extralinguistic knowledge."[79] Encyclopedic knowledge is not a mere linguistic knowledge; rather, it includes world knowledge. As a result, this knowledge does not function in a hierarchical way but in an uncoordinated manner. Eco states, "Encyclopedic knowledge, on the other hand, would be uncoordinated by nature, with an uncontrollable format, and the encyclopedic content of *dog* would have to include practically all that is and could be known about dogs."[80] He continues, "Naturally it is not quite like this, because we can consider as encyclopedic knowledge only those items that the Community has in some way registered publicly (and moreover it is maintained that encyclopedic competence is shared across sectors, according to a sort of linguistic division of labor, or activated in different ways and formats according to the context)."[81] Though encyclopedic content, theoretically, contains all that one can know about *dog*, this does not mean that all of this extralinguistic knowledge is activated in each use of *dog*.

Eco notes that many seem to view dictionaries as an indispensible tool for language use while encyclopedias contain more complex descriptions of things. This observation, however, is not the case. He provides the following lengthy statement:

> Nonetheless the curious accident has occurred whereby, given that the repertoires that succinctly record the properties of terms are called 'dictionaries' while those that indulge in complex descriptions are called 'encyclopedias,' everybody thinks that dictionary competence is the indispensable one for the use of language. Instead, what the story of Ayers Rock tells us is that, in order to

---

79. Eco, "Dictionary and Encyclopedia," 226.
80. Eco, "Dictionary and Encyclopedia," 226.
81. Eco, "Dictionary and Encyclopedia," 226.

recognize that object and to be able to talk about it every day, the perceptual (not linguistic) characteristic of appearing like a mountain (on the basis of many factual properties) counts for a very great deal, while the fact that it is not a MOUNTAIN but a STONE is a datum reserved only for an elite that shares a vast encyclopedic competence. Therefore Sandra would point out to me that people, when speaking plainly, run on encyclopedia mode, while only the learned turned to the dictionary. Nor would she be wrong.[82]

As noted above, the MC is a more specialized content than NC; however, MCs are not possible without NCs. The dictionary is only a tool one uses to categorize certain contents of the totality of the NC into a brief description.[83] The dictionary is not merely concerned with linguistics while the encyclopedia has a more global focus. In the case of Ayers Rock and Sandra's ability to recognize it as a mountain, though it is not a MOUNTAIN, the content is perceptual content rather than linguistic. Both perceptual and linguistic contents, however, are signs, and one necessarily engages in the task of semiosis when navigating them.

Eco notes that associating NC with encyclopedic knowledge and MC with dictionary knowledge is intriguing but ultimately a gross oversimplification. He writes, "The authors of the medieval bestiaries would perhaps fail a zoology exam, but it cannot be denied that in their own way they were trying to constitute categories when they defined the crocodile (in terms of NC) as a water snake, evidently by taking for granted that this category was opposed to that of land snakes."[84] The knowledge that a zoologist has of an animal is specialized knowledge, or MC, different than that of a non–zoologist. However, this MC derives from within the encyclopedic NC.

Eco then discusses the notions of files and directories as they pertain to encyclopedic knowledge. As one accumulates more knowledge of something, she ends up creating a sort of cognitive file for it. As she continues to accumulate more knowledge of the world in general, she formulates a sort of cognitive directory to help her in navigating her cognitive files and the contents therein. This seems to work well, especially with MCs. However, this does not always happen with NCs. NCs often take on a form of *wild categorization*.[85] Eco states,

---

82. Eco, "Dictionary and Encyclopedia," 226–27. Words in all caps stand for the MC of mountain and stone.

83. Eco, "Dictionary and Encyclopedia," 228.

84. Eco, "Dictionary and Encyclopedia," 228–29.

85. Eco, "Dictionary and Encyclopedia," 232.

At the level of NC there is a continuous organizing and reordering of 'wild' categories, most of which spring from the recognition of constant precategorial features. For example, in the Western world the chicken is considered one of the edible animals while the dog is not, but in some Asiatic regions the dog is a fully fledged member of the edible category and is kept around the house much like a turkey or a pig in the West, in the knowledge that at a certain point it will have to be eaten. But it is in the specialized sector of the MC that negotiations become more punctilious.[86]

One eventually, however, assimilates these wild categories into her cognitive files and directories. Their organization, as is the organization of all NCs, however, is not hierarchical but disorganized.[87]

Eco goes on to discuss the notion of *contracting* as it pertains to cognition and the encyclopedia. Contracting represents "the dialectic both of cognition and understanding, that is, of understanding and knowledge."[88] Important to the concept of contracting is *negotiation*. Concerning the example of the discovery and categorization of the platypus, Eco notes that "the story of the platypus is the story of a long negotiation, and in this sense it is an exemplary tale."[89] For a long time, scientists were not exactly sure how to classify the platypus, as it possessed the properties of multiple types of animals. Here was a mammal with a bill that laid eggs and secreted milk from pores on its skin. How was one to classify this animal? The process of determining its classification was that of negotiation and contracting. This process of negotiation, or navigating the encyclopedia, is what Peirce calls *abduction*.

In summary, the encyclopedia plays an important role in cognition, specifically as it pertains to matters of recognition. When one sees a dog, she recognizes it via a CT. Attached to CTs are NCs, encyclopedic knowledge by which one understands CTs. NCs are sememes. When Montezuma and the Aztecs saw horses for the first time, they navigated their encyclopedia of CTs and NCs to find the appropriate word to describe them. The best they could come across was *deer*. This CT best represented horses, as well did its attached NC. As one accumulates more knowledge, her encyclopedia grows and she eventually begins to form cognitive files for said knowledge

---

86. Eco, "Dictionary and Encyclopedia," 232.
87. Eco, "Dictionary and Encyclopedia," 234.
88. Eco, "Dictionary and Encyclopedia," 249.
89. Eco, "Dictionary and Encyclopedia," 250.

and cognitive directories for navigating said files. This navigation tends to take on the form of negotiation, which is what Peirce refers to as *abduction*.

SUMMARY: *THE NAME OF THE ROSE* AND THE LABYRINTH OF THE LIBRARY

The concept of encyclopedia plays an important role in Eco's semiotic project. The labyrinth of the encyclopedia grounds sememes rather than the Porphyrian tree of the model dictionary. Each sememe, in the encyclopedia, is grounded in the connections and interconnections it has with all other sememes. This labyrinth, which is represented best by the rhizome or net, has no actual boundary and is ever growing. The different connections and interconnections of all of the sememes comprising this semantic network, being interchangeable, are potentially infinite. Though each sememe presupposes its interconnectedness to all other sememes, the maximal encyclopedia is ultimately inaccessible, for it is comprised of everything that has ever been said or thought throughout history. Individuals presuppose a local encyclopedia, as well as the Median Encyclopedia, when performing speech–acts. The Median Encyclopedia is a type of abridged encyclopedia to which the speaker assumes the hearer essentially has access.

Eco provides a practical example of his model encyclopedia in his first novel, *The Name of the Rose*. *The Name of the Rose* is a murder–mystery story set at a monastery in Northern Italy in the year 1327 CE.[90] The protagonist of the story is a Franciscan friar, William of Baskerville, a former inquisitor of the Catholic Church. His companion, Adso of Melk, a Benedictine novice, narrates the story. William and Adso travel to the monastery in order to attend an upcoming disputation concerning Jesus's poverty. Upon arriving they learn of a mysterious death, ruled as a suicide, and begin to investigate. As they investigate, more mysterious deaths occur, ultimately leading them to the monastery's library. No one but the librarian is allowed into the library, which is constructed in the form of a labyrinth, and only the librarian knows the secret to navigating the labyrinth.

Multiple times throughout the novel, William and Adso are able to sneak into the library. Upon entering it for the first time, the two protagonists discover that the library is a labyrinth, namely a rhizomatic labyrinth. The library has multiple rooms, each with multiple hallways connecting them to other rooms. Some rooms have only two hallways connected

---

90. Eco, *The Name of the Rose*.

to them while others have as many as four. As the characters attempt to navigate the labyrinth, they formulate theories to establish the location of certain rooms and the contents they contain. This trial–and–error form of conjecturing a hypothesis and testing it represents abduction.

Each of the rooms of the library has certain books. Each book, obviously, contains contents. Each room, being filled with certain books and their contents, is connected and interconnected to every other room in the library. This represents Eco's model encyclopedia. In the novel, the monastery is known for its vast library. Each room has books pertaining to a certain subject. The subject room represents the morpheme while all the books within the room represent the sememe. What the labyrinth of the library highlights is the connectedness and interconnectedness of all subjects and contents with all other subjects and contents. The subject of physics and all its contents are connected and interconnected to the subjects of biology, sociology, philosophy, theology, and all of their contents. The library itself represents the model encyclopedia.

As the above sections have shown, one can find the concept of the model encyclopedia throughout Eco's semiotic project. The model encyclopedia plays an important role in a general theory of semiotics, especially concerning a theory of codes; it plays an important role in the generation and interpretation of texts; it plays an important role in the philosophy of language; and it plays an important role in cognition and recognition. The rhizomatic labyrinth best represents this encyclopedia by highlighting how all morphemes, lexemes, sememes, cognitive types, nuclear contents, and molar contents are connected and interconnected with one another.

This concept of semantic network has major implications for epistemology as well as hermeneutics and theology. In the following chapters, I will show how Eco's model encyclopedia lends itself to issues of epistemology, hermeneutics, and doctrinal development, all of which are important dialogue partners for systematic theology. Again, my thesis is that Eco's model encyclopedia can provide a new and more useful model for systematic theology, namely because of how it lends itself to areas concerning the aforementioned items.

4

The Model Encyclopedia and Theological Epistemology

As I stated in the Introduction above, my aim is to appropriate Umberto Eco's semiotic model encyclopedia as a new model for theology. Also, as stated in the Introduction, three areas pertaining to matters of theological prolegomena that will be used as dialogue partners with the model encyclopedia in order to determine whether or not it will serve as an appropriate model for theology. This chapter will bring the model encyclopedia into dialogue with the first of these prolegomena matters: theological epistemology. The model encyclopedia adds to the widespread critique that has come against foundationalist epistemology, especially classical foundationalism. The model encyclopedia lends itself to both a postfoundationalist epistemology as well as the philosophy of science known as critical realism. Postfoundationalism, as will be demonstrated below, does not imply antifoundationalism, nor does it imply anti–realism; rather, one can be both a committed postfoundationalist and a committed realist. This position will be further demonstrated by showing how well the model encyclopedia works with critical realism.

THE MODEL ENCYCLOPEDIA AND POSTFOUNDATIONALISM

That epistemological foundationalism has come under heavy attack in the twentieth and twenty-first centuries is no secret. This attack has been, perhaps, one of the most common fads of postmodernity. However, to treat foundationalism as a single monolithic concept or theory would be a gross occurrence of equivocation. In his monograph *The Foundations of Knowledge*, Timothy McGrew rightly highlights that the term *foundationalism* refers not to a single theory of epistemic justification but to a family of theories of epistemic justification. He writes, "'Foundationalism' is the name not of a theory of justification but of a family of such theories, all of which share certain structural features. Since versions of foundationalism may vary widely, reports that foundationalism has been refuted should always be met with a certain amount of healthy doubt."[1] McGrew rightly highlights that foundationalism is not a monolithic concept or theory; rather, multiple types or forms of foundationalism exist. He makes special reference to classical foundationalism.[2]

Classical foundationalism finds its birth in the philosophy of René Descartes, who sought to ground knowledge on one basic belief, a belief that was incorrigible and indubitable.[3] Even here, as McGrew points out, not even classical foundationalism is monolithic. Rather, classical foundationalism is "a variety of foundationalism."[4] Not all forms of classical foundationalism claim one single indubitable and incorrigible belief as the foundation for all other beliefs. Some variations claim a plurality of basic beliefs, and these beliefs together are incorrigible. McGrew writes, "Classical foundationalism . . . involves a very strong claim for its foundations, the claim that *all* of the basic beliefs are incorrigible."[5] This is the primary thesis of classical foundationalism: some beliefs are basic, and basic beliefs are incorrigible.

As noted above, foundationalism has come under severe attack throughout postmodernity, even within evangelical theology. However, as McGrew shows, many of the arguments leveled against foundationalism

---

1. McGrew, *Foundations of Knowledge*, 45.
2. McGrew, *Foundations of Knowledge*, 45–59.
3. See Descartes, *A Discourse on the Method*.
4. McGrew, *Foundations of Knowledge*, 57.
5. McGrew, *Foundations of Knowledge*, 57 (italics mine).

make the straw man fallacy. Many who attack foundationalism, such as Stanley Grenz, attack what is actually the classical foundationalism of Descartes and attribute this attack to foundationalism in general.[6] This attack is an instance of the straw man fallacy in that it attacks one form of a position as though it were representative of all the forms of said position. As demonstrated above, there are multiple forms of foundationalism, and there are even multiple forms of classical foundationalism. Nonetheless, postmodernism's attack against the foundationalism of Descartes has been accepted widely, even in more conservative circles.[7] Popular in many postmodern circles is the adoption of *coherentism* as the epistemology of choice.[8] Several problems arise for coherentism as well.

In *Warrant and Proper Function*, epistemologist Alvin Plantinga notes the problems inherent in coherentism as well as both ordinary and classical foundationalism. He notes that the primary dividing factor between foundationalism and coherentism is the role of *evidence* in warranting beliefs.[9] By *evidence*, Plantinga means *propositional evidence*. For foundationalism,

> There is a *basic* or foundational level of beliefs or propositions that are not accepted on the evidential basis of other beliefs. . . . Other beliefs—beliefs not in the foundations—will be accepted *on the evidential basis* of foundational beliefs; and these beliefs, if things are going properly, will be *evidentially supported* by the foundational beliefs.[10]

This propositional evidence tends to take the form of a chain of evidence.[11] For foundationalism, this propositional evidence stemming from basic,

---

6. Grenz, *Renewing the Center*, 193–98.

7. Again, one need look no further than Stanley Grenz's work in theological method. See especially Grenz, *Renewing the Center*, 193–225; Grenz and Franke, *Beyond Foundationalism*, 28–54. Here, Grenz attacks the classical foundationalism of Descartes and then claims the demise of foundationalism in general. One should note that Grenz refers to Descartes's variation of foundationalism simply with the term *foundationalism*. He is not clear whether he means that classical foundationalism has been usurped or whether he means foundationalism in general.

8. Willard V. O. Quine is, perhaps, one of the most popular coherentists of the twentieth century. See Quine and Ullian, *The Web of Belief*.

9. Traditionally, *knowledge* has been defined as *justified true belief*, but several epistemologists, including Plantinga, have come to question the concept of *justification* and instead prefer to think in terms of *warrant*. For more on this, see Plantinga, *Warrant: The Current Debate*.

10. Plantinga, *Warrant and Proper Function*, 177–78.

11. See also McGrew, *Foundations of Knowledge*, 45–53. McGrew notes the concept

or foundational, beliefs provides warrant for non-basic beliefs. This is not the case for coherentism.[12]

Plantinga distinguishes between pure and impure coherentism: "The *pure* coherentist eschews warrant transfer, holding that no belief will be accepted on the evidential basis of any other belief; instead, each belief will be accepted in the basic way, the warrant accruing to it (if any) arising by way of coherence."[13] He continues, "The *impure* coherentist, on the other hand, will allow that there can be warrant transfer, all right, but the warrant transferred arises originally by way of coherence."[14] Whether pure or impure, coherentism grounds the warrant for beliefs solely in their coherence with the other beliefs in the belief system, or belief web. For coherentism, coherence is both the necessary and sufficient conditions for epistemic warrant. Plantinga shows, however, that this position is untenable, and he notes that coherence is neither necessary nor sufficient for warrant.[15] One of the primary reasons is due to coherence being limited only to the coherence between the propositions within the belief system. Were one to broaden coherence to concern the coherence between propositions and experience, or evidence, then coherentism can function as a sort of modified version of foundationalism.[16] The reason is that, as Plantinga states, "The ordinary foundationalist can hold in perfect consistency that many beliefs get at least some warrant by way of coherence, and even that *some* beliefs get *all* their warrant solely by coherence."[17]

Continental philosophers like Gadamer have shown the lack of tenability inherent in strong forms of foundationalism, and they highlight the role of community and tradition in epistemic matters.[18] According to these philosophers, an individual's community and tradition play a much stronger role in shaping her rationality than she realizes. All knowledge, as well as all cognition, occurs via a language, i.e., a sign system. Languages are

---

of the evidence chain as well as the concept of *evidence trees*.

12. Early on, Plantinga discusses his dissatisfaction with the way many portray coherentism and seeks to portray it in the best possible light. Even so he still rejects it as an adequate theory of epistemic warrant. See Plantinga, *Warrant and Proper Function*, 176; 178–82.

13. Plantinga, *Warrant and Proper Function*, 179.

14. Plantinga, *Warrant and Proper Function*, 179.

15. Plantinga, *Warrant and Proper Function*, 179–80.

16. Plantinga, *Warrant and Proper Function*, 181–82.

17. Plantinga, *Warrant and Proper Function*, 180.

18. Gadamer, *Truth and Method*, 17–27; 273–85.

inherited from traditions and are therefore part of those traditions.[19] One is not capable of knowing or understanding something apart from her inherited sign systems. As a result, all knowledge is, in some part, determined by tradition, including the single incorrigible basic beliefs of Descartes. As a result, postmodernity has claimed the death of foundationalism and sought a different epistemological avenue.

J. Wentzel van Huyssteen notes that, following the rejection of foundationalism, postmodernity has opted typically for *nonfoundationalism*, or *antifoundationalism*, as its epistemology of choice. Huyssteen defines *nonfoundationalism* as a theory that denies "that we have any of those alleged strong foundations for our belief-systems."[20] He continues, "Nonfoundationalists . . . argue instead that all of our beliefs together form part of a groundless web of interrelated beliefs. . . . Nonfoundationalism also highlights the crucial epistemic importance of community, arguing that every community and context has its own rationality."[21] In extreme forms, "nonfoundationalism implies a total relativism of rationalities."[22] Belief systems, like languages, take on the form of a web, in which all beliefs are connected and interconnected without anything anchoring them to reality. Belief systems then, since there are no extra-linguistic parameters by which meta-criticism can occur, are beyond objective critique.[23] Of importance is the coherence connecting and interconnecting all of the beliefs of a belief system. In this sense, nonfoundationalism lends itself to the coherentism discussed above. None of these beliefs, however, are basic or foundational. As will be demonstrated below, nonfoundationalism is equally less favorable than classical foundationalism.

Nonfoundationalism need not be the only alternative to classical foundationalism. While the critiques to this form of foundationalism have been devastating, one need not throw out the epistemological baby with the incorrigible bathwater. Though there may not be basic incorrigible

19. For an example of this claim, see Wittgenstein, *Philosophical Investigations*.

20. Huyssteen, *Essays in Postfoundationalist Theology*, 3.

21. Huyssteen, *Essays in Postfoundationalist Theology*, 3.

22. Huyssteen, *Essays in Postfoundationalist Theology*, 3.

23. See, for example, Kuhn, *The Structure of Scientific Revolutions*. This is not an exact concept drawn from Kuhn. Rather, Kuhn applies this concept to scientific paradigms, claiming that paradigms cannot undergo objective criticism due to the lack of extra-paradigmatic criteria for judgment. All criticisms of paradigms occur from the perspective of another paradigm. The same concept is extrapolated by some and applied to the concepts of language as well as doctrinal systems. See Lindbeck, *Nature of Doctrine*, 59–74.

beliefs on which one founds all of her succeeding beliefs, and though the notion of incorrigibility might be questionable, persons do seem to hold certain beliefs as more foundational, or fundamental, than others. Many will not doubt that they hold certain beliefs with a much higher degree of confidence than others, and these beliefs indeed provide some form of a foundation or core that holds succeeding beliefs together. One can imagine a web of belief that has a number of basic, or core, beliefs at its center, and these beliefs hold this metaphorical web together.[24] Also, these beliefs need not be incorrigible per se, though they might be incorrigible de facto. This concept maintains that there are some forms of foundational, or core, beliefs while highlighting the connectedness and interconnectedness of all other beliefs. This position exemplifies what some refer to as a *postfoundationalist* epistemology.[25]

Van Huyssteen coined the term *postfoundationalism* and appropriated it for theology.[26] More specifically, he appropriates it as his epistemologi-

24. This specific metaphor of *core beliefs* is original to me. Though Grenz provides the metaphor of a "mosaic of belief," in which "some pieces are more central to the 'picture' and others are more peripheral," this is not what I have in mind. Grenz does not clarify the importance of some pieces of the mosaic being more central to the picture than others and implies a weaker appreciation of basic beliefs than do I. Just because some pieces of the mosaic are more central, or important, does not make them more foundational. In my metaphor of the web of belief held together by core beliefs, the concept of core beliefs serves a more foundational role than do the central pieces of Grenz's mosaic. In my metaphor, if one were to remove one of the core beliefs, then the connectors and interconnectors of the web of belief would have to be restructured in order for all beliefs to remain connected and interconnected. The further away from the core beliefs one gets the less restructuring is needed were one of these outer beliefs removed. See Grenz, *Renewing the Center*, 213.

25. Though postfoundationalism is not of the variety of classical foundationalism, I believe that it holds to enough of the theses of general foundationalism to be considered a form of modified, or soft, foundationalism. Like classical foundationalism, soft foundationalism is not a monolithic theory. The reformed epistemology of Alvin Plantinga is one such form of a soft foundationalism. See Plantinga, *Warrant and Proper Function*.

26. Van Huyssteen is not the only theologian to argue for a theological postfoundationalism. Stanley Grenz notes two primary forms that postfoundationlism has taken in theology, one represented by the theology of George Lindbeck and the other represented by the theology of Wolfhart Pannenberg. Lindbeck's form of postfoundationalism takes on a postliberal shape, one that resembles the preferred nonfoundationalist (or antifoundationalist) epistemologies of postmodernism. Panneberg, on the other hand, takes on a form of postfoundationalism that has many resemblances to Peirce's fallibilism. As evidenced by the theological works of Grenz himself, several Evangelical theologians have adopted various postfoundationalist approaches to the task of theology. Examples of these works include Clark, *To Know and Love God*; Grenz, *Renewing the Center*; Grenz,

cal approach to the relationship between theology and the sciences. In *The Shaping of Rationality*, he writes,

> A postfoundationalist model of rationality will take seriously the challenge of much of postmodern thinking, but will carefully distinguish between constructive and deconstructive modes of postmodern thinking. A postfoundationalist model of rationality will therefore especially incorporate into our reasoning strategies the relentless criticism of foundationalist assumptions: we all indeed exercise normative commitments, but the failure to acknowledge those commitments will leave us without any epistemological way of really taking them seriously.[27]

Postfoundationalism takes seriously the criticisms leveled at certain varieties of foundationalism without capitulating into nonfoundationalism. As noted above, nonfoundationalism, or antifoundationalism, often results in radically relativistic views of truth and reality, though these radical views of relativism are de facto and not per se. Technically speaking, one is able to be a nonfoundationalist and a realist simultaneously. Postfoundationalism, unlike radical nonfoundationalism, is able to maintain the criticisms made against varieties of strong foundationalism whilst also maintaining the truth-value of claims to objective truth and objective reality. As stated above, one is able to affirm a postfoundationalist epistemology while being a committed realist. As will be shown below, the philosophy of science known as critical realism naturally lends itself to postfoundationalism. Again, postfoundationalism is *not* antifoundationalism, and it is *not* antirealism.

Peirce is one such philosopher who could be located in the camp of postfoundationalism. As Andrew Robinson points out in *God and the World of Signs*, Peirce, rather than being a foundationalist, was a *fallibilist*.[28] Louis Pojman defines *fallibilism* as "the view, first articulated by C. S. Peirce and later developed by Karl Popper, that any of our beliefs or theories about the world could turn out to be false. Hence, we have no right to be dogmatic about any empirical or metaphysical belief. The theory generally allows that we can be certain about logical truths and beliefs about

Theology for the Community of God; Grenz and Franke, *Beyond Foundationalism*; McGrath, *A Scientific Theology*; Plantinga, *Warranted Christian Belief*; Thiselton, *Hermeneutics of Doctrine*; Thiselton, *Systematic Theology*; Vanhoozer, *Drama of Doctrine*; Wright, *New Testament and the People of God*.

27. Huyssteen, *Shaping of Rationality*, 8.
28. Robinson, *God and the World of Signs*, 51.

immediate experience."[29] Being one of the fathers of modern semiotics, Peirce was well aware that all knowledge, understanding, and experience of the world are mediated through sign systems. This phenomenon does not, however, imply that no external world exists beyond said sign systems, nor does this imply that one is unable to have any knowledge of the external world. Rather, since experience is always mediated via a sign system, one is never able to possess epistemic certainty concerning her experience of the external world. This inability to achieve epistemic certainty emphasizes the finitude of the individual subject's ability to know, implicating that her ability to know things about the external world is *fallible*, hence Peirce's term *fallibilism*.

Peirce provided his clearest explication of this position in his essay "The Fixation of Belief." One of the major topics of this essay is "the end of inquiry."[30] He defined *inquiry* as "the irritation of doubt causes a struggle to attain a state of belief."[31] He claimed that the object of inquiry is "the settlement of opinion."[32] He continued, "We may fancy that this is not enough for us, and that we seek, not merely an opinion, but a true opinion."[33] In summary, the object of inquiry is the settlement of a true opinion. Peirce moved on to discuss different methods for fixing beliefs. These methods included the tenacity method[34], the authority method[35], and the *a priori* method.[36] He concluded that these methods prove unsatisfactory, and he opted for the method of science: "To satisfy our doubts, therefore, it is necessary that a method should be found by which our beliefs may be determined by nothing human, but by some external permanency—by something upon which our thinking has no effect...Such is the method of science."[37] This nonhuman external permanency that should satisfy one's doubts is reality. Peirce wrote,

29. Pojman, *What Can We Know?*, 344.

30. Peirce, "Fixation of Belief," 5.374. All Peirce citations are from the eight-volume *The Collected Papers of Charles Sanders Peirce*. Rather than page numbers, all essays from Peirce, unless otherwise indicated, are referenced by volume number and section number.

31. Peirce, "Fixation of Belief," 5.374.
32. Peirce, "Fixation of Belief," 5.375.
33. Peirce, "Fixation of Belief," 5.375.
34. Peirce, "Fixation of Belief," 5.377–78.
35. Peirce, "Fixation of Belief," 5.379–80.
36. Peirce, "Fixation of Belief," 5.382–83.
37. Peirce, "Fixation of Belief," 5.384.

> There are Real things, whose characters are entirely independent of our opinions about them; those Reals affect our senses according to regular laws, and, though our sensations are as different as are our relations to the objects, yet, by taking advantage of the laws of perception, we can ascertain by reasoning how things really and truly are; and any man, if he have sufficient experience and he reason enough about it, will be led to the one True conclusion.[38]

Reality is the ultimate fixation of belief, according to Peirce. However, as noted previously, one's ability to know reality is mediated through signs, making said knowledge fallible. He wrote elsewhere, "Not only is our knowledge thus limited in scope, but it is even more important that we should thoroughly realize that the very best of what we, humanly speaking, know [we know] only in an uncertain and inexact way."[39] Peirce did not deny the existence of an objective reality, nor did he deny one's ability to know truth concerning objective reality; rather, he denied one's ability to have direct experiences with reality. All experiences of reality are mediated experiences.

On the one hand, one can see that Peirce is a thoroughly committed realist. On the other hand, one can see that Peirce is far from being a foundationalist, especially a classical foundationalist. With the exception of the rules of logic and mathematics, all knowledge of reality is fallible and dubitable. One should not take reality for granted. This state of affairs does not mean, however, that one should withdraw from attempting to know things concerning reality. Peirce did believe that knowledge of the world is possible. As noted above, if one reasons long and well enough, she will arrive at truth eventually. Many *believe*, however, that they have arrived at truth, though, ultimately, they are not able to be *certain* that they have done so. Truth claims are always anticipatory in that they await their final confirmation. One believes, or has *faith*, that she arrived at truth.[40] This belief, however, is fallible.[41]

38. Peirce, "Fixation of Belief," 5.384.

39. Peirce, "Methods for Attaining Truth," 5.587.

40. For more of Peirce on faith, see Peirce, "A Treatise on Metaphysics," 16–20. In this essay, Peirce noted that all knowledge involves inferences and that inferences always involve faith. As such, all knowledge involves faith.

41. As with foundationalism, fallibilism is a family of theories concerning the nature of beliefs rather than one such theory. Karl Popper is another philosopher who espoused a form of fallibilism. His specific version of fallibism is connected with his theory of falsification: "Falsificationists believe . . . that they have discovered logical arguments which show that the programme of the first group [verificationists] cannot be carried out: that we can never give positive reasons which justify the belief that a theory is true.

As will be discussed further below, fallibilism is one of the primary theses of scientific philosophies, namely critical realism. In his ability to affirm an objective reality and question one's ability to know things about reality, Peirce can be viewed as a precursor to postfoundationalism. He is well aware of the interconnectedness of one's beliefs; he is aware that one holds certain beliefs with a larger degree of confidence than others; but he also affirms that, in order to be true, statements and beliefs must correspond with reality.[42] One could understand Peirce to be a postfoundational realist, which is another way of understanding his pragmaticism. He is but one example of how one can be a postfoundationalist, as well as a pragmatist, and still be a realist.

As stated above, Eco's model encyclopedia naturally lends itself to this form of postfoundationalist epistemology. Like his intellectual forefather, Peirce, Eco is a pragmatist, or pragmaticist, as well as a realist. As can be seen in *A Theory of Semiotics* and his *Semiotics and the Philosophy of Language*, he does not deny that an objective reality exists or that signs and sign systems do relate to said reality. The notion of the labyrinth of the encyclopedia, however, does not permit one to be a classical foundationalist. One will notice that Eco's rhizome, when applied to matters of epistemology, does not resemble the metaphor of the edifice on which foundationalism rests. Rather, the model encyclopedia more so resembles Quine's web of interconnected beliefs. Contrary to nonfoundationalists, however, Eco does

---

But . . . we falsificationists believe that we have also discovered a way to realize the old ideal of distinguishing rational science from various forms of superstition, in spite of the breakdown of the original inductivist or justificationist programme. We hold that this ideal can be realized, very simply, by recognizing that the rationality of science lies not in its habit of appealing to empirical evidence in support of its dogmas . . . but solely in the critical *approach*. . . . For us, therefore, science has nothing to do with the quest for certainty or probability or reliability. We are not interested in establishing scientific theories as secure, or certain, or probable. Conscious of our fallibility we are only interested in criticizing them and testing them, hoping to find out where we are mistaken; of learning from our mistakes; and, if we are lucky, of proceeding to better theories." See Popper, *Conjectures and Refutations*, 310.

42. In an unpublished essay, Peirce did discuss his theory of truth. He discussed "truth as correspondence," "truth and satisfaction," and "definitions of truth." Concerning the former, he wrote, "A *state of things* is an abstract constituent part of reality, of such a nature that a proposition is needed to represent it. There is but one *individual*, to completely determinate, state of things, namely the all of reality. A *fact* is so highly a precissively abstract state of things, that it can be wholly represented in a simple proposition, and the term 'simple,' here, has no absolute meaning, but is merely a comparative expression." See Peirce, "Truth," 5.549.

not merely affirm a plurality of labyrinthine encyclopedias of which no external criteria exists by which one can judge them. All local encyclopedias come together in the maximal encyclopedia. In the same way that billions of galaxies are all collected within the universe, local encyclopedias come together in the maximal encyclopedia, which includes everything that has ever been said and everything that has been believed. One should recall also that Eco's notion of the maximal encyclopedia serves as a regulative concept, which hints at the notion of the interconnectedness and coherence of all local encyclopedias.

In *Semiotics and the Philosophy of Language*, Eco applies the model encyclopedia to sememes, or basic units of content. As discussed in chapter two, according to Eco's theory of codes, all signs have an expression plane and a content plane. Within these content planes, the basic unit of content is the sememe. Sememes are not determined based on their so-called *genera* and *species*, as in the model dictionary. As Eco has demonstrated, the model dictionary fails because it is ultimately unable to differentiate between multiple individuals, such as a human and a horse. In order to differentiate between individuals such as these, one must consider other *differentia* and *qualia*, i.e., properties. Eco also rightly points out that there are no extra-categorical or extra-semiotic criteria by which one can judge which properties should be considered and which should not. The closest thing to a standard of criteria for these judgments, as they pertain to words and language, is context. In the encyclopedia, many contents are considered and brought together in the constitution of the verbal sign's content plane. The sememe of a verbal expression is determined by the context in which said expression occurs. This becomes a matter of pragmatics. Sememes, as all content units, are determined based on their connections and interconnections with all other content units.

Items of knowledge, warranted true beliefs, are signs. Again, signs are anything that can stand to someone for something. An item of knowledge stands as a representation to someone for something in reality they have apprehended with the appropriate warrant. As such, knowledge has both an expression plane and a content plane. These content planes are made up of content units, which are grounded in their connections and interconnections with all other content units that exist within an individual's encyclopedia. Since content units, including basic content units, are determined based on their connectedness and interconnectedness with all other content units within the encyclopedia, beliefs, which are signs, are structured in the same way. This rhizomatic labyrinth of the encyclopedia more so resembles the web of belief rather than the edifice of belief. Since the contents of signs are determined by their connectedness and interconnectedness to each other, it makes sense to understand beliefs, since beliefs are signs, as connected and interconnected together.

As noted above, some models of a web of belief lend themselves to relativism. One should be aware, however, that this occurs de facto rather than per se. As stressed above, a rejection of classical foundationalism, or any foundationalism for that matter, does not necessitate a rejection of realism. A web of belief, in which coherence plays an important role in determining whether or not beliefs are warranted properly, need not lend itself to inter–subjective relativism as it does in the works of many postmodern thinkers. One of the benefits of Eco's model encyclopedia for epistemology is that it allows for a broader definition of coherence, the sort for which Plantinga advocates, as noted above. Since Eco primarily adopts Peirce's understanding of semiosis, his semiotic project lends itself to the same realist perspective as does Peirce's. Also, as will be explicated more below, Eco's model encyclopedia lends itself to Peirce's fallibilism. More specifically, the model encyclopedia lends itself to the epistemology known as critical realism.

THE MODEL ENCYCLOPEDIA AND CRITICAL REALISM

As claimed above, Eco's model encyclopedia lends itself to Peirce's fallibilism. Further, the model encyclopedia lends itself to the philosophy of science known as critical realism, a form of epistemic fallibilism. Critical realism is a philosophy of science that Roy Bhaskar proposed in the monograph *A Realist Theory of Science*.[43] In this monograph, Bhaskar proposes a theory of science that affirms the objective nature of reality while simultaneously affirming the fallible nature of the individual's ability to know things.[44]

Generally speaking, much has come from the dialogues between theology and the philosophy of science. Instances of this can be seen in the

---

43. This is not to say that Bhaskar is the founder of critical realism, nor is this to say that he is the one who coined the term. Alister McGrath notes that Roy Wood Sellars coined the term *critical realism* as an alternative to "idealism, pragmatism and realism." See McGrath, *Reality*, 204; Bhaskar, *Realist Theory of Science*.

44. For an introduction to Bhaskar's philosophy of science, see Collier, *Critical Realism*.

works of thinkers such as John C. Polkinghorne,[45] Wolfhart Pannenberg,[46] Thomas F. Torrance,[47] and Alister E. McGrath.[48] The last of these, McGrath, has made, potentially, the most fruitful contribution to the discussion between science and theology amongst contemporary theologians. More specifically, he has sought to develop a theological method that utilizes the methodologies of the natural sciences as the *ancilla theologia* (handmaiden of theology). His primary interlocutor for his three-volume *A Scientific Theology* is Roy Bhaskar, whose version of critical realism McGrath seeks to appropriate as an epistemology for theology.[49]

McGrath discusses the foundations of realism in the natural sciences and critical realism in volume two of *A Scientific Theology*, which he subtitles *Reality*. The goal of the natural sciences, he claims, is to obtain true beliefs about the universe. As such, the universe must be real, and scientists seek to say something concerning this reality. He defines *critical realism* as "reality apprehended by the human mind which attempts to express and accommodate that reality as best it can with the tools at its disposal—such as mathematical formulae or mental models."[50] In other words, critical realism is a version of realism that highlights the role of the knower "in the process of knowing."[51] McGrath notes the varieties of critical realism that have been put forth by different philosophers of science and chooses to utilize the version put forth by Roy Bhaskar due to its prevention of scientific reductionism. He further defines critical realism, stating, "A critical realism recognizes that the observer modulates the process of observation itself; that the quest for truth modifies the truth that is encountered; that the knower affects what can be known."[52] He also notes the contributions of John C. Polkinghorne and Thomas F. Torrance concerning the interaction of theology with critical realism before providing his explication of Bhaskar's specific version.

45. Polkinghorne, *Scientists as Theologians*; Polkinghorne, *One World*.

46. Pannenberg, *Theology and the Philosophy of Science*.

47. Torrance, *Theological Science*; Torrance, *The Ground and Grammar of Theology*; Torrance, *Christian Theology and Scientific Culture*; Torrance, *The Christian Frame of Mind*; Torrance, *Reality and Evangelical Theology*.

48. McGrath, *Nature*.

49. N. T. Wright also appropriates insights from critical realism in his approach to doing history. See Wright, *New Testament and the People of God*, 31–46.

50. McGrath, *Reality*, 195.

51. McGrath, *Reality*, 197.

52. McGrath, *Reality*, 205.

The reason McGrath prefers Bhaskar's version of critical realism is due to the concept of the *stratification of reality*.[53] By *the stratification of reality*, Bhaskar simply means that there are multiple layers to reality. One such stratum is physics, another chemistry, another philosophy, and another theology. Each of these strata is a different layer of reality, and each determines its own method(s) of inquiry. The stratum of physics determines the methods physicists will utilize in physics, and these methods may not work for inquiring into the stratum of chemistry. Even though one can view chemistry as a sub discipline of physics, this does not mean that chemistry can be reduced to physics. This acknowledgment of reality being made up of different strata prevents scientific reductionism, which McGrath claims "states that 'there is an actual identity of subject–matter' between the two disciplines."[54] This claim allows McGrath to maintain that the natural sciences are the *ancilla theologia* without reducing the natural sciences to theology or vice versa. This version of critical realism also prevents theology from being reduced to a branch of philosophy.

What makes critical realism such an appealing dialogue partner for theology is its inherent fallibilism. Critical realists, similar to Peirce, affirm an objective reality while simultaneously affirming the limits of the knowing subject. Also, similar to Peirce, critical realists reject classical foundationalism as an appropriate method for warranting beliefs about the external world. Critical realists also seem to be in agreement that coherentism is not an acceptable alternative to classical foundationalism. They, nonetheless, seek to make statements that correspond to the reality in which they inquire. If strong foundationalism and coherentism do not provide adequate theories of warrant, then how do critical realists seek to warrant their beliefs? They resort to the tools of pragmatism, or pragmaticism. More specifically, they resort to Peirce's notion of *abduction*, or hypothesis.

The theory of abduction concerns how scientists conjecture hypotheses about reality. Whereas Gilbert Harman refers to this as "inference to the best explanation,"[55] Peirce and McGrath refer to this as "abduction to the best explanation."[56] Peirce wrote,

---

53. McGrath, *Reality*, 219. See also Bhaskar, *Realist Theory of Science*, 36; Bhaskar, *The Possibility of Naturalism*, 12.

54. McGrath, *Reality*, 215.

55. Harman, "The Inference to the Best Explanation," 88–95.

56. McGrath, *Reality*, 158. One should note that, for Peirce, an abduced explanation is always a hypothesis. He often uses the terms *hypothesis* and *abduction* interchangeably.

> If you carefully consider the question of pragmatism you will see that it is nothing else than the question of the logic of abduction. That is, pragmatism proposes a certain maxim which, if sound, must render needless any further rule as to the admissibility of hypotheses to rank as hypotheses, that is to say, as explanations of phenomena held as hopeful suggestions.[57]

He understood abduction as "that perceptual judgments contain general elements, so that universal propositions are deducible from them in the manner in which the logic of relations shows that particular propositions usually, not to say invariably, allow universal propositions to be necessarily inferred from them."[58] Whereas deduction begins with premises that necessarily lead to specific consequents, guaranteeing a positive truth-value, assuming a positive truth-value for said premises, and induction begins with a hypothesis and runs a series of tests, or experiments to see whether the hypothesis holds, abduction works differently. Abduction typically begins with a set of data and seeks an explanation for said data. This explanation is what is meant by *abduction to the best explanation*. If a hypothesis is able to explain adequately certain phenomena then one can claim warrant for it; however, should another hypothesis, or abduction, come along that provides more or better explanatory power of the phenomena, then the former is abandoned and one holds to the new hypothesis. Not only is abduction the primary form of reasoning used in the natural sciences, it is also the type of reasoning used when interpreting spoken discourse and texts. Abduction is also the primary form of reasoning utilized in doctrinal development, as doctrines can be viewed as hypotheses concerning the meaning of certain events and/or texts. More will be said on this below in chapter six.

Eco provides his own contributions to the concept of abduction in his essay "Horns, Hooves, Insteps: Some Hypotheses on Three Types of Abduction." He begins by discussing Aristotle's theory on how things are defined. More specifically, he focuses on Aristotle's use of the syllogism for defining things.[59] Eco then shows the similarity between Aristotle's theory of defining and Peirce's theory of abduction:

> There is no difference between what Peirce called Hypothesis or Abduction and the effort by which, according to Aristotle, one figures out a definition, saying *what* a thing is, by explaining

---

57. Peirce, "Pragmatism and Abduction," 5.196.
58. Peirce, "Pragmatism and Abduction," 5.181.
59. Eco, "Horns, Hooves, Insteps," 198–202.

tentatively *why* this is such as it is, so displaying all the elements able to set out a deduction according to which, if the Rule was right, every Result will prove *that* this thing is.[60]

He sets out to reconsider how Peirce defined abduction. For Peirce, one performed induction when she inferred the Rule from the Case and Result. Hypothesis, or abduction, is the inference to the Case from the Result and Rule. Eco also notes Paul Thagard's distinction between "Hypothesis as *inference to a Case*, and Abduction as inference to a Rule."[61] The problem is not whether one first reasons to a Case or to a Rule, but how one simultaneously reasons to both. Eco notes that the middle term of the syllogism, or the argument, is the device that triggers the process of reasoning in this way.[62] He then moves on to discuss four types of abduction: hypothesis, undercoded abduction, creative abduction, and meta-abduction.

Eco defines *Hypothesis*, or *overcoded abduction*, as a form of abduction in which a law is automatically, or semi-automatically, given. He states, "It seems that we usually do this kind of interpretive labor automatically.... To recognize a given phenomenon as the token of a given type presupposes some hypothesis about the context of utterance and the discursive cotext.... This type is close to my notion of *overcoding* as the case-inference to the best explanation."[63] For *undercoded abduction*, Eco states, "The rule must be selected from a series of equiprobable rules put at our disposal by the current world knowledge (or semiotic encyclopedia).... Since the rule is selected as the more plausible among many, but it is not certain whether it is the 'correct' one or not, the explanation is only *entertained*, waiting for further tests."[64] For *creative abduction*, "The law must be *invented ex novo*.... In any case this kind of invention obliges one to make (more than in cases of overcoded or undercoded abductions) a meta-abduction."[65] A *meta-abduction* "consists in deciding as to whether the possible universe outlined by our first-level abductions is the same as the universe of our experience.... We are making a complete 'fair guess' not only about the nature of the result (its cause) but also about the nature of the encyclopedia

---

60. Eco, "Horns, Hooves, Insteps," 202. See also, Aristotle, *Posterior Analytics*, 114–66.

61. Eco, "Horns, Hooves, Insteps," 203. See also Thagard, "Semiosis and Hypothetic Inference in Ch. S. Peirce," 19–20.

62. Eco, "Horns, Hooves, Insteps," 203.

63. Eco, "Horns, Hooves, Insteps," 206.

64. Eco, "Horns, Hooves, Insteps," 206.

65. Eco, "Horns, Hooves, Insteps," 207.

(so that, if the new law results in being verified, our discovery leads to a change of paradigm)."[66] This type of abduction is used by detectives when trying to conjecture explanations of evidence, and it is also the type used in the case of "'revolutionary' scientific discoveries."[67] All four types of abduction that Eco explicates in this essay are utilized by critical realism in the natural sciences. Indeed, all hypotheses are a type of abduction, from those that are small interpretative inferences (overcoded abductions) to those that conjecture entirely new paradigms. All forms of abduction are utilized in navigating the labyrinth of the encyclopedia.

Eco's model encyclopedia organically lends itself to critical realism. Chapter three highlighted that the rhizome was the best labyrinthine model for the encyclopedia in that all of the nodes are either connected or interconnected with each other. One of the main ways the model encyclopedia lends itself to critical realism is through the provisional nature of its connectors and interconnectors. As Eco says, "A rhizome can be broken off at any point and reconnected following one of its own lines."[68] If a connection between two sememes, or content units, is found to be weak or unsatisfactory, one is able to abandon said connection and forge a new one. The model encyclopedia is aware of its own limits. All encyclopedias are fallible, as are those who possess them. Critical realists are aware of their finitude in the process of knowing; they are able to conjecture hypotheses that make sense of phenomena; and should these hypotheses not prove satisfying, or should a better hypothesis come along with more explanatory power, one is able to abandon it and opt for the better one. In this sense, Eco's model encyclopedia also lends itself to abduction.

Eco states, "In a rhizome, blindness is the only way of seeing . . . and thinking means to *grope one's way*."[69] Abduction is how one gets from one node in the labyrinth to the next. Each connector, according to Eco, is a *hypothesis*. He comments on the inability to apprehend the entire labyrinth of the maximal encyclopedia. This fact is because to apprehend the maximal encyclopedia would be to grasp all that has ever been said or thought. One is never outside of the labyrinth, however, not even the labyrinth of a local encyclopedia. One always exists within her encyclopedia. As a result, she is

---

66. Eco, "Horns, Hooves, Insteps," 207.
67. Eco, "Horns, Hooves, Insteps," 207.
68. Eco, *Semiotics and the Philosophy of Language*, 81.
69. Eco, *Semiotics and the Philosophy of Language*, 82.

always navigating from one locale to the next; not even she has a third-person view as one "outside" the labyrinth. As Eco suggests,

> A structure that cannot be described *globally* can only be described as a potential sum of *local* descriptions. In a structure without outside, the describers can look at it only by the inside; as Rosenstiehl ... suggests, a labyrinth of this kind is a *myopic algorithm*; at every node of it no one can have the global vision of all its possibilities but only the local vision of the closest ones: every local description of the net is a *hypothesis*, subject to falsification, about its further course; in a rhizome blindness is the only way of seeing (locally), and thinking means to *grope one's way*.[70]

No one has access to the global encyclopedia; one has access only to a local encyclopedia and she navigates her encyclopedia via abduction.

Not only is every local description of the labyrinth a hypothesis, but all navigation of it is as well. In order to travel from one content unit to another, there must be a connector, or bridge, connecting the two together. This connecting relationship is a hypothesis, or abduction. Whenever one seeks to establish a relationship between two beliefs, she conjectures a hypothesis on how the two are related. If this conjecture fails to connect adequately the two units of content, then the subject abandons it and seeks a new one. This instance is what Eco means when he refers to abduction being one's groping her way through the labyrinth. As one better learns her own encyclopedia, she is able to grope her way through it more efficiently.

This notion of *groping one's way* as a metaphor for abduction can be seen in *The Name of the Rose* as William and Adso better learn their way around the labyrinth of the library. After much *groping* their way around, the characters are finally able to navigate the labyrinth with some ease. Prior, however, they were always *groping* their way around the different corridors and rooms. As William was better able to know which room he was in and what contents the room possessed, he was able to *abduce* his way around the library.[71] This example from *The Name of the Rose* represents how everyone navigates her own encyclopedia; she is always making abductions in order to connect different experiences with different beliefs in her mind. These connections are abductions in that they attempt to connect and explain the relationship between the different contents.

---

70. Eco, *Semiotics and the Philosophy of Language*, 82.
71. Eco, *The Name of the Rose*, 331–47.

As shown in chapter two in the discussion of Eco's *Kant and the Platypus*, individuals tend to organize their cognitive types and contents in a sort of filing system. This cognitive organization is seen also in *The Name of the Rose* concerning the different rooms of the library. Each room preserved certain contents that the others did not. They represent what Eco refers to as a cognitive filing system in *Kant and the Platypus*. As one abduces her way through her encyclopedia, she arrives at different filing systems, each with its own content. All of the contents in each room in the library were connected with each other, and each room was connected with all of the other rooms in the labyrinth. In the same way, in an individual's encyclopedia, all of her cognitive types and their contents, both nuclear and molar, are organized and in some sort of cognitive filing system; and all of these contents within a filing system are connected and interconnected with each other. Also, all of these filing systems are connected and interconnected in one's mind, and she navigates these filing systems and their contents via abduction, just as William and Adso learned to navigate the labyrinth of the library.

Eco's encyclopedia also lends itself to the critical realism of Bhaskar in that it works well with the concept of a stratified reality. What constitutes a stratum of reality for Bhaskar can represent a specialized encyclopedia for Eco. As Eco discusses in *Kant and the Platypus*, encyclopedias contain nuclear contents (NC) and molar contents (MC). MCs represent a specialized form of knowledge, such as the type of knowledge that a zoologist would have about an elephant. Whereas a non-zoologist would have a NC of an elephant by which she understands what it is, she most likely would not possess the type of specialized knowledge of the elephant that a zoologist would have. This specialized knowledge is what Eco refers to as MC, as discussed in chapter two above.

Though this specialized knowledge often can resemble a type of dictionary-like knowledge, this resemblance does not reduce MC to dictionary knowledge. The zoologist has a NC as well as a MC concerning the elephant, and all of these contents are connected with each other within the labyrinth of her encyclopedia. These different types of content represent what Bhaskar would refer to as different strata of reality. The MC of an elephant for a zoologist would represent one type of content, or understanding of the elephant from the standpoint of one stratum of reality; the MC of a geneticist would be a different MC, and the content of the person who cleans out the elephant exhibit at the zoo also would be a different type of content. Though these contents are all different types, they still concern a real elephant. These different types of contents highlight the different strata that make up the reality of the elephant. Eco's distinction of NC and MC within the encyclopedia lends itself to critical realism's notion of a stratified reality. As a matter of fact, both Eco and Bhaskar seem to be saying similar things about the nature of knowledge, each from the local encyclopedia of a different stratum.

CONCLUSION: THE MODEL ENCYCLOPEDIA AND THEOLOGICAL EPISTEMOLOGY

The discussions of postfoundationalism and critical realism have been necessary in that they are contemporary conversation partners of some sort within the discipline of theological prolegomena. As demonstrated above, several theologians have embraced several of postmodernism's critiques of foundationalist theories of epistemic warrant whilst rejecting antifoundationalism. Several theologians, such as Pannenberg and McGrath, have opted for a postfoundationalism, one that affirms a realist understanding of the world. These postfoundationalist theories of epistemic warrant are able to accept some of the contributions of coherentism without rejecting all notions of basic beliefs. As proposed above, one can envision a web of belief that is held together at its center by multiple basic, or core, beliefs. The benefits of this metaphor include its affirmation of realism, the ability of coherence to provide warrant for non–core beliefs, and it stresses the role of coherence sought in most belief–systems.[72]

This discussion of postfoundationalism led to the discussions of pragmaticism and fallibilism. In addition to the role of propositional evidence and coherence serving as epistemic warrant, some note the role of explanatory power of propositions in providing said warrant. Does a statement or belief provide adequate explanatory power over a certain phenomenon? If so, then one can be said to possess the necessary warrant for affirming said belief. This theory affirms the fallible nature of an individual's ability to know. These are the theories of pragmaticism. Pragmaticism does not ignore the role of coherence and propositional evidence in warranting beliefs; rather, it brings the consequences of beliefs to this discussion. The

---

72. This is not to say that coherence is necessary or sufficient for warrant, but that it can function as a form of warrant for further warranting beliefs. Just because some is not necessary or sufficient on its own does not mean that it cannot be helpful. This metaphor simply suggests that coherence can help further warrant beliefs.

pragmaticism of Peirce does not reject the notion of an objective reality, nor does it reject language's ability to relate to reality. Rather, pragmaticism takes into account the possibility that a proposition does not adequately represent reality. Hence it relies on a version of fallibilism.

This realist approach to fallibilism led to the discussion of the philosophy of science known as critical realism. Critical realism, as developed by Bhaskar, is a form of fallibilism that takes into account the role of the knowing subject in the knowing process, and it also helps prevent the fallacy of reductionism. Critical realism, being a form of fallibilism, primarily utilizes the form of reasoning known as abduction. One encounters a certain phenomenon and conjectures a hypothesis to explain said phenomenon. Theologians engage in abduction when they engage God and his revelation. God reveals himself to creation, and persons encounter this revelation. They therefore attempt to make abductions to the best explanation of this phenomenon. This abductive process is especially apparent in how the disciples of Jesus developed their beliefs of his lordship. Faced with the resurrected Jesus, the disciples would have recalled all that he taught and did. Combined with his resurrection, the disciples made the abduction that Jesus was who he claimed to be, and this abduction, being a proposition, provided the best explanation of the data. As such, the disciples possessed both the necessary and sufficient warrant for affirming these beliefs. This form of abductive reasoning is how theologians go about developing doctrine. As will be shown in the following chapters, abduction plays a significant role in hermeneutics and doctrinal development.

As noted above, abduction is the way in which one navigates the labyrinth of the encyclopedia. Not only is this how one navigates the rhizomatic encyclopedia, but it is also how one develops new nodes to appear in the rhizome. As shown above, Eco's model encyclopedia lends itself to these endeavors discussed in this chapter: postfoundationalism and critical realism. These tools have served beneficial purposes in matters pertaining to theological epistemology. Eco's model encyclopedia, however, provides a model that is able to take in these endeavors and serve as a type of meta-theory, or theory that holds all of these together. Eco's encyclopedia is indeed postfoundational, pragmaticist, and fallibilist. Since all of these epistemological matters have proved, thus far, beneficial to theology, and since Eco's encyclopedia is able to bring all these theories together, it can prove useful for theology. Utilizing Eco's model encyclopedia as a model, theology will invoke an epistemology that is postfoundational, pragmaticist, and fallibilist.

The Model Encyclopedia and Theological Epistemology // 109

If a theological abduction does not provide adequate explanatory power, or if another theological abduction surpasses it in explanatory power, then one can abandon it and conjecture a new one or accept the offered replacement. As such, Eco's encyclopedia allows theologians who are critical realists to maintain their critical realism; actually, it encourages them to do so.

This chapter concludes that Eco's model encyclopedia is able to deal adequately with matters of theological epistemology, which is the first test case in determining its adequacy as a model for theology. Attention will turn now to the hermeneutic nature of theology and how Eco's model encyclopedia is able to correlate with it.

5

The Model Encyclopedia and the Hermeneutic Nature of Theology

This chapter will show the relationship between Eco's model encyclopedia and the hermeneutic nature of theology. First, some definitions are in order. *Hermeneutics* does not here refer to the methodic process of interpreting texts (i.e., exegesis), nor does it refer to methods for interpreting the biblical texts (i.e., biblical hermeneutics). *Hermeneutics*, rather, refers to a branch of philosophy that concerns itself with the totality of human understanding (i.e., philosophical hermeneutics or hermeneutic philosophy). This shift in the understanding of the scope of hermeneutics will be discussed more in the first part of this chapter. Major contributors to the field of hermeneutics, as well as important concepts in the field of hermeneutics, will be discussed here. The second part of this chapter will concern itself with showing the relationship of Eco's model encyclopedia to hermeneutic philosophy. Topics of concern here include the semiotics of language, understanding one's horizon of understanding as a local encyclopedia, and understanding what Gadamer calls the *fusion of horizons* as the connections and interconnections between different local encyclopedias. The final part of this chapter will bring Eco's encyclopedia into conversation with the works of significant hermeneutic theologians, namely Wolfhart Pannenberg and Anthony Thiselton. This chapter will conclude with a section evaluating Eco's model encyclopedia as an appropriate 'fit' for the hermeneutic nature of theology.

HERMENEUTICS AS THE PHILOSOPHY OF UNDERSTANDING

The term *hermeneutics* has multiple contemporary uses. Traditionally, *hermeneutics* referred to the study of methods for interpreting written texts.[1] More specifically, *hermeneutics* was used in reference to the *science of interpreting written texts*.[2] More specifically, the term was used as shorthand for the science of interpreting the biblical texts, especially in Christianity. This understanding of hermeneutics, however, encountered its first major shift in the works of Friedrich Schleiermacher, who redefined the term as *the art of understanding*.[3] Thiselton provides the following helpful distinction of terms: "Whereas *exegesis and interpretation* denote the *actual process* of interpreting texts, *hermeneutics* also includes the second-order discipline of asking critically *what exactly we are doing when we read, understand, or apply* texts."[4]

One of Schleiermacher's major contributions to the study of hermeneutics was his notion of the hermeneutic circle, which served a methodological function in his project. The process of understanding, for Schleiermacher, was concerned primarily with the relationship between parts and their wholes. One understands particular statements, or texts, as they relate to the wholes to which they belong. Likewise, one understands a whole as a summation of its particulars.[5] This concept, as will be seen in the work of Pannenberg below, has maintained a strong presence in contemporary hermeneutic philosophy. Schleiermacher's hermeneutic circle had a profound impact on the work of Wilhelm Dilthey, who sought to utilize hermeneutic as a type of scientific method for the human sciences (*Geisteswissenschaften*).[6]

---

1. See Thiselton, *Hermeneutics: An Introduction*, 1.

2. For a diachronic introduction to the topic of hermeneutics, see Grondin, *Introduction to Philosophical Hermeneutics*.

3. Schleiermacher, *Hermeneutics*, 97; and Thiselton, *Hermeneutics: An Introduction*, 2.

4. Thiselton, *Hermeneutics: An Introduction*, 4.

5. Schleiermacher, *Hermeneutics*, 99–100, 110, and 112–27.

6. Dilthey, *Gesammelte Schriften*, 26 vols. (Göttingen: Vandenhoeck & Ruprecht, 1914–2005), especially vol. 5, *Die geistige Welt: Einleitung in das Philosophie des Lebens*, 1924; vol. 7, *Der Aufbau der geschichtlichen Welt in den Geisteswissenschaften*, 1927; vol.

Following Schleiermacher, Dilthey highlighted the historical-conditionedness of both interpreters and the subject matter they seek to interpret. He was the first to extend hermeneutics beyond the scope of language and texts to include "all human institutions beyond language."[7]

Martin Heidegger was one of the major contributors to hermeneutics in the twentieth century. In his early monograph, *Being and Time*, Heidegger went further than Dilthey in defining the scope of hermeneutics. Whereas Dilthey had extended hermeneutics to encompass all human institutions, Heidegger extended hermeneutics to human existence. The concept of *Dasein* was central for this project. *Dasein*, or "being-there," was Heidegger's term for the understanding subject. He wrote, "Everything we talk about, everything we have in view, everything towards which we comport ourselves in any way, is being; what we are is being, and so is how we are. Being lies in the fact that something is, and in its Being as it is; in Reality; in presence-at-hand; in subsistence; in validity; in Dasein; in the 'there is.'"[8] Heidegger defined *Dasein*:

> Thus to work out the question of Being adequately, we must make an entity—the inquirer—transparent in his own Being. The very asking of the question is an entity's mode of *Being*; and as such it gets its essential character from what is inquired about—namely Being. This entity which each of us is himself and which includes inquiring as one of the possibilities of its Being, we shall denote by the term '*Dasein*'.[9]

What is significant here is that *Dasein*'s mode of being, for Heidegger, becomes that of inquiry. He defines *inquiry* as "a cognizant seeking for an entity both with regard to the fact that it is and with regard to its Being as it is. This cognizant seeking can take the form of 'investigating' ['Untersuchen'], in which one lays bare that which the question is about and ascertains its character."[10] The aim of inquiry is understanding, which Heidegger also refers to as a mode of being for *Dasein*: "Understanding always

---

12, *Zur Preussischen Geschichte. Schleiermacher's politische Gesinnung und Wirksamkeit*, 1936; and vols. 13 and 14, *Leben Schleiermachers*, 1966 and 1970. For a brief summary of Dilthey's contributions, see Thiselton, *Hermeneutics: An Introduction*, 161–64; and Grondin, *Introduction*, 84–90.

7. Thiselton, *Hermeneutics: An Introduction*, 163.
8. Heidegger, *Being and Time*, 26.
9. Heidegger, *Being and Time*, 27.
10. Heidegger, *Being and Time*, 24.

has its mood. If we Interpret understanding as a fundamental *existentiale*, this indicates that this phenomenon is conceived as a basic mode of Dasein's *Being*."[11] Each and every person is an instance of *Dasein*, and one of her basic modes of being is understanding. Heidegger thus further extends the scope of hermeneutics to that of existence, specifically "being-there." The final universalization of the scope of hermeneutics would come from Gadamer, a pupil of Heidegger, who was arguably the most significant hermeneutic philosopher of the twentieth century.

As Gadamer defined the scope of philosophical hermeneutics, it

> takes as its task the opening up of the hermeneutical dimension in its full scope, showing its fundamental significance for our entire understanding of the world and thus for all the various forms in which this understanding manifests itself: from interhuman communication to manipulation of society; from personal experience by the individual in society to the way in which he encounters society; and from the tradition as it is built of religion and law, art and philosophy, to the revolutionary consciousness that unhinges the tradition through emancipatory reflection.[12]

Hermeneutics concerns itself with the totality of human understanding. Gadamer's magnum opus, *Truth and Method*, is an exhaustive articulation of just this phenomenon. In this work, Gadamer provided a descriptive theory of human understanding, i.e., hermeneutics. Accepting his mentor's dictum that understanding is one of the basic modes of *Dasein's* being, Gadamer offered a detailed theory of this mode of being, especially in Part II and Part III.[13]

Rhyne Putman provides the following helpful summary of this universal understanding of the scope of hermeneutics:

> While it bears certain similarities to epistemology (i.e., the philosophical study of how we obtain knowledge) and ontology (i.e., the philosophical study of reality), contemporary philosophical hermeneutics probably is best understood as a branch of philosophical anthropology (i.e., the philosophical study of humanity). It is a philosophical exploration of the whole human being, her worldview, and her interpretive experience. Texts may serve as the primary focus of this 'art' of understanding, but hermeneutics also encompasses the *entire communicative*

---

11. Heidegger, *Being and Time*, 182.
12.. Gadamer, "Scope and Function of Hermeneutical Reflection," 18.
13. Gadamer, *Truth and Method*, 268–484.

process, including how texts are read, understood, and applied by their individual and communal interpreters.[14]

Following Heidegger and Gadamer, Putman affirms the universal scope of hermeneutics, noting that it is a sort of philosophical anthropology. This notion of hermeneutics is associated primarily with Gadamer, and Paul Ricoeur. This is the understanding of *hermeneutics* with which this book concerns itself.

Basic Concepts in the Hermeneutic Philosophy of Gadamer and Ricoeur

Before this chapter can bring Eco's model encyclopedia into conversation with the content of philosophical hermeneutics, a basic overview of some hermeneutic concepts is in order. This section will deal primarily with the works of Gadamer and Ricoeur as they were the two most important contributors to contemporary hermeneutic philosophy.[15]

Hans–Georg Gadamer

Gadamer provides his most exhaustive explication of his hermeneutics in *Truth and Method*.[16] He divides this work into three parts: "The Question of Truth as it Emerges in the Experience of Art,"[17] "The Extension of the Question of Truth to Understanding in the Human Sciences,"[18] and "The Ontological Shift of Hermeneutics Guided by Language."[19]

Gadamer begins Part I with a discussion on "transcending the aesthetic dimension."[20] Here, he offers an extended disagreement with Immanuel Kant's reduction of the experience of art to the category of aesthetics. For Kant, the experience of art was concerned primarily with the question of

---

14. Putman, *In Defense of Doctrine*, 46.
15. See Thiselton, *Hermeneutics: An Introduction*, 228.
16. For a brief overview of Gadamer's *Truth and Method*, see Thiselton, *Two Horizons*, 293–326. For a detailed discussion of Gadamer's hermeneutics, one that covers more of his writings than *Truth and Method*, see Grondin, *The Philosophy of Gadamer*.
17. Gadamer, *Truth and Method*, 1.
18. Gadamer, *Truth and Method*, 172.
19. Gadamer, *Truth and Method*, 383.
20. Gadamer, *Truth and Method*, 3.

beauty, and only a subjective judgment can answer this question. As such, aesthetic judgments are fundamentally subjective. Gadamer points out that Kant fails to takes seriously the role of inter-subjectivity in making aesthetic judgments.[21] Previously, he noted the role of the *sensus communis* (sense of the community) as it pertains to one's ability to make judgments and how judgments are connected to the concept of *taste*.[22] These concepts of taste and judgment, Gadamer claims, ought not be reduced merely to subjective aesthetic judgments. Looking back at the concept of the *sensus communis* he discussed previously, he shows the communal nature concerning these concepts. Since there is a communal nature to judgment and taste, there is an objective dimension to them. This notion leads Gadamer to discuss "the ontology of the work of art and its hermeneutic significance."[23]

Gadamer highlights the concept of *play* as it pertains to the experience of art: "When we speak of play in reference to the experience of art, this means neither the orientation nor even the state of mind of the creator or of those enjoying the work of art, nor the freedom of a subjectivity engaged in play, but the mode of being of the work of art itself."[24] One begins to experience art genuinely when she is caught up in the play projected from said work. Consider the game of soccer: the game is governed by a set of rules, and each position has its own guidelines for how that position functions; however, each player brings her own uniqueness to the game. In the act of play, she plays her position in her own way; this is the subjective element. Gadamer asserts, "Play fulfills its purpose only if the player loses himself in play.... The mode of being of play does not allow the player to behave toward play as if toward an object. The player knows very well what play is, and that what he is doing is 'only a game'; but he does not know what exactly he 'knows' in knowing that."[25] Gadamer's notion of play preserves both objective and subjective dynamics in the act of interpretation and the event of understanding. Though a *player* has objective rules and guidelines by which she abides, she also brings her own unique abilities into play.

After discussing a brief history of hermeneutics, Gadamer discusses "the elements of a theory of hermeneutic experience."[26] In this chapter, he

21. Gadamer, *Truth and Method*, 37–87.
22. Gadamer, *Truth and Method*, 17–37.
23. Gadamer, *Truth and Method*, 102.
24. Gadamer, *Truth and Method*, 102.
25. Gadamer, *Truth and Method*, 103.
26. Gadamer, *Truth and Method*, 268.

discusses the concepts of the hermeneutic circle, pre-understanding, authority, the history of effects, the historically effected consciousness, the fusion of horizons, application, and the question–answer dialectic proposed by R. G. Collingwood. Unlike Schleiermacher's hermeneutic circle, which concerned itself primarily with the relationship between parts and wholes, Gadamer's hermeneutic circle, which he gets from Heidegger, concerns the dialogue between the horizons of understanding of the self and the other. Unlike Heidegger, however, Gadamer has a more positive theory of the hermeneutic circle. When one enters the circle, she does so with her own *prejudices*, i. e. pre–understandings, and this is inevitable.[27] As a matter of fact, prejudices are what make understanding possible, as they are what make up the self's horizon of understanding with which she enters into the hermeneutic circle.[28]

This notion of prejudice leads Gadamer to discuss the role of *authority* and *tradition* in understanding. Contra the thinkers of the Enlightenment, he allots a positive function for tradition. Tradition provides one with the prejudices that makeup her horizon of understanding, thus making understanding possible. The Enlightenment's disregard of tradition, as Gadamer points out, was a prejudice against prejudice. As a result, one should restore authority and tradition to their proper place in the hermeneutic process.[29] He concludes, "*Understanding is to be thought of less as a subjective act than as participating in an event of tradition*, a process of transmission in which past and present are constantly mediated. This is what must be validated by hermeneutic theory, which is far too dominated by the idea of a procedure, a method."[30]

Gadamer next discusses the concepts of the history of effects (*Wirkungsgeschichte*) and the historically effected consciousness (*Wirkungsgeschichtliches Bewußtsein*). The history of effects, or effective history, is the concept that one has been conditioned by her place in history, what Heidegger called *thrownness*.[31] Gadamer maintains that

27. Gadamer, *Truth and Method*, 268–73.
28. Gadamer, *Truth and Method*, 274–78.
29. Gadamer, *Truth and Method*, 278–85.
30. Gadamer, *Truth and Method*, 291.
31. Heidegger wrote, "Yet every Dasein always exists factically. It is not a free–floating self-projection; but its character is determined by thrownness as a Fact of the entity which it is; and, as so determined, it has in each case already been delivered over to existence, and it constantly so remains. Dasein's facticity, however, is essentially distinct from the factuality of something present-at-hand. Existent Dasein does not encounter itself as something present-at-hand within-the-world. But neither does thrownness adhere

> historical consciousness must become conscious that in the apparent immediacy with which it approaches a work of art or a traditionary text, there is also another kind of inquiry in play, albeit unrecognized and unregulated. If we are trying to understand a historical phenomenon from the historical distance that is characteristic of our hermeneutical situation, we are always already affected by history. It determines in advance both what seems to us worth inquiring about and what will appear as an object of investigation, and we more or less forget half of what is really there—in fact, we miss the whole truth of the phenomenon—when we take its immediate appearance as the whole truth.[32]

Genuine understanding requires one to be aware of the history of effects; this is what Gadamer refers to as the historically effected consciousness: "Rather, historically effected consciousness ... is an element in the act of understanding itself.... Consciousness of being affected by history ... is primarily consciousness of the hermeneutical situation.... The very idea of a situation means that we are not standing outside it and hence are unable to have any objective knowledge of it."[33] As one seeks genuine understanding, she must be aware of history's effects on her, for the historically effected consciousness is part of her horizon of understanding.

Concerning the concept of *horizon*, Gadamer reminds his reader that one never has complete knowledge of herself, and this finitude is a result from being historically.[34] He states, "The horizon is the range of vision that includes everything that can be seen from a particular vantage point. Applying this to the thinking mind, we speak of narrowness of horizon, of the possible expansion of horizon, of the opening up of new horizons, and so forth."[35] Horizons are not fixed, for as one moves, her respective horizon moves with her. Gadamer also highlights that interpreters are not the only ones to possess a horizon of understanding, but so does the other, even the other of the past.[36] Understanding occurs when a *fusion of the horizons (Horizontverschmelzung)* occurs. Gadamer writes,

---

to Dasein as an inaccessible characteristic which is of no importance for its existence. As something thrown, Dasein has been thrown *into existence*. It exists as an entity which has to be as it is and as it can be." See Heidegger, *Being and Time*, 320–21.

32. Gadamer, *Truth and Method*, 299–300.
33. Gadamer, *Truth and Method*, 301.
34. Gadamer, *Truth and Method*, 301.
35. Gadamer, *Truth and Method*, 301.
36. Gadamer, *Truth and Method*, 302.

> An important part of this testing occurs in encountering the past and in understanding the tradition from which we come. Hence the horizon of the present cannot be formed without the past. There is no more an isolated horizon of the present in itself than there are historical horizons which have to be acquired. *Rather, understanding is always the fusion of these horizons supposedly existing by themselves.* . . . In a tradition this process of fusion is continually going on, for there old and new are always combining into something of living value, without either being explicitly foregrounded form the other.[37]

The fusion of horizons leads to the problem of *application*. Gadamer notes that when a fusion of horizons occurs, there is always application. Contrary to previous theories, namely those of the Enlightenment, the hermeneutic event cannot be dissected into the methodic processes of understanding, interpretation, and application. Gadamer claims, "In the course of our reflections we have come to see that understanding always involves something like applying the text to be understood to the interpreter's present situation. Thus we are forced to go one step beyond romantic hermeneutics, as it were, by regarding not only understanding and interpretation, but also application as comprising one unified process."[38] Where one of these three is present, the other two are as well. Understanding, interpretation, and application are not steps in a method one follows in the hermeneutic process; rather, all three occur simultaneously.

The final major concept in Gadamer's hermeneutics is the notion of "language as the medium of hermeneutic experience."[39] He notes that all understanding occurs through the medium of language: "*Rather, language is the universal medium in which understanding occurs. Understanding occurs in interpreting.*"[40] Actually, language is the primary prejudice that one inherits from her tradition and the primary ingredient that makes up her horizon of understanding, thus enabling a fusion of horizons. Language, according to Gadamer, is not only the means by which all understanding occurs, but it is also one of the primary mediators of effective history. He states, "The linguisticality of understanding is *the concretion of historically effected consciousness*. The essential relation between language and understanding is seen primarily in the fact that the essence of tradition is to exist

---

37. Gadamer, *Truth and Method*, 305.
38. Gadamer, *Truth and Method*, 307.
39. Gadamer, *Truth and Method*, 385.
40. Gadamer, *Truth and Method*, 390.

in the medium of language, so that the preferred *object* of interpretation is a verbal one."[41] As one can see, language, for Gadamer, serves as the sole medium for hermeneutic experience.

Paul Ricoeur

Unlike Gadamer, who waited until late into his career before providing a comprehensive explication of his hermeneutic theory in monograph form, Ricoeur wrote a plethora of monographs throughout his career, none of which provides a comprehensive explication of his own theory. Each work deals with a different aspect of hermeneutic philosophy: the multivalence of meaning, the self, the concept of time as it pertains to historicity, metaphor, and even ethics. Unlike Gadamer, whose concern is primarily phenomenological, Ricoeur is much more interdisciplinary in his approach. He interacts with semiotics (especially structuralism), psychoanalysis, existentialism, literary theory, as well as phenomenology throughout his hermeneutic project. This portion of the chapter will focus on where Ricoeur builds on Gadamer's insights while also providing some important critiques.

Like Gadamer, Ricoeur affirms the concepts of horizon and the historicity of understanding. He does, however, probe deeper into the concept of the interpreting subject. He does this primarily in his monographs *Fallible Man, Freud and Philosophy,* and *Oneself as Another*. In the first of these, Ricoeur highlights the subjective dynamic to individual existence, noting that existence cannot be reduced to scientific objectivity. He highlights the concepts of finitude and the human will, showing that these cannot be explained as some form of objective science. Thiselton notes that, in this work, Ricoeur "betrays the influence not only of [Gabriel] Marcel but also of . . . Martin Buber."[42]

In *Freud and Philosophy*, Ricoeur looks at Freud's psychoanalysis as a conversation partner for hermeneutics. One of the most important developments that he stresses is the importance of both understanding and explanation in interpretation. In *Truth and Method*, Gadamer discusses understanding (*Verstehen*) exclusively concerning interpretation, leaving little to no place for *explanation* (*Erklärung*). Ricoeur seeks to restore the necessary balance:

---

41. Gadamer, *Truth and Method*, 391.
42. Thiselton, *Hermeneutics: An Introduction*, 229.

> According to the one pole, hermeneutics is understood as the manifestation and restoration of a meaning addressed to me in the manner of a message, a proclamation, or as is sometimes said, a kerygma; according to the other pole, it is understood as a demystification, as a reduction of illusion.... From the beginning we must consider this double possibility: this tentions, this extreme polarity, is the truest expression of our 'modernity.'[43]

This tension one holds between understanding and explanation is what aids her in being sensitive to the other. Without a healthy balance between understanding and explanation, one is most likely to see her own reflection at the bottom of the hermeneutical well. This concept is Ricoeur's concept of the *hermeneutics of suspicion*. One should always be aware that she runs the risk of coercing the text to say what she wants it to or thinks it does, hence the need for explanation. At the same time, the text does speak to the interpreting subject, necessitating the need for her to listen. Ricoeur writes,

> The situation in which language today finds itself comprises this double possibility, this double solicitation and urgency: on the one hand, purify discourse of its excrescences, liquidate the idols, go from drunkenness to sobriety, realize our state of poverty once and for all; on the other hand, use the most 'nihilistic,' destructive, iconoclastic movement so as to *let speak* what once, what each time, was *said*, when meaning appeared anew, when meaning was at its fullest. Hermeneutics seems to me to be animated by this double motivation: willingness to suspect, willingness to listen; vow of rigor, vow of obedience. In our time we have not finished doing away with *idols* and we have barely begun to listen to *symbols*.[44]

Understanding and explanation both ought to be involved in interpretation, as it is the only way to respect the text as truly other while also allowing it to speak to the interpreting self. He notes that Freud's psychoanalysis lends itself to stressing explanation at the expense of understanding, which can make hermeneutics reductionistic.

As Ricoeur describes the relationship between explanation and understanding,

> Just as the dialectic of event and meaning remains implicit and difficult to recognize in oral discourse, that of explanation and understanding is quite impossible to identify in the dialogical situation

---

43. Ricoeur, *Freud and Philosophy*, 27.
44. Ricoeur, *Freud and Philosophy*, 27.

> that we call conversation. We explain something to someone else in order that he can understand. And what he has understood, he can in turn explain to a third party. Thus understanding and explanation tend to overlap and to pass over into each other. I will surmise, however, that in explanation we ex-plicate or unfold the range of propositions and meanings, whereas in understanding we comprehend or grasp as a whole chain of partial meanings in one act of synthesis.[45]

As one can see here, explanation is as much part of the hermeneutic enterprise as is understanding. As a matter of fact, explanation is an endeavor in interpretation. As one explains, she brings out what is implicit in the text and makes it explicit, hence it is a form of explication. Ricoeur also informs his reader that explanation finds its best "paradigmatic field of application in the natural sciences."[46] As one encounters phenomenon and conjectures hypotheses to explain nature and then seek verification or falsification of said hypotheses, this is all done with understanding as its aim. Ricoeur rightly argues, contra Gadamer, that both understanding and explanation are necessary in the hermeneutic endeavor. Understanding and explanation both form their own sort of hermeneutic circle: as one understands, she is able to explain; as she explains, she is able to understand better; as she better understands, she is able to explain better, ad infinitum.[47]

In *Time and Narrative*, Ricoeur provides his theory of time, arguing for a narrative view of time, and he shows the implications this has for hermeneutics. He states his thesis as follows: "*Time becomes human to the extent that it is articulated through a narrative mode, and narrative attains its full meaning when it becomes a condition of temporal existence.*"[48] He later states, "My thesis is that history the most removed from the narrative form continues to be bound to our narrative understanding by a line of derivation that we can reconstruct step by step and degree by degree with an appropriate method."[49] For Ricoeur, humans always experience time in the form of narrative. Indeed, every experience of time presupposes the totality of time, and this state of affairs is part of what constitutes the temporal nature of human understanding. Also, for Ricoeur, history is experienced

---

45. Ricoeur, *Interpretation Theory*, 72.
46. Ricoeur, *Interpretation Theory*, 72.
47. See also Ricoeur, "What Is a Text? Explanation and Understanding," 145–64.
48. Ricoeur, *Time and Narrative*, 1.52.
49. Ricoeur, *Time and Narrative*, 1.91.

through the medium of narrative as well. Each person understands herself as a historical being, and thus projects a narrative that she lives out. As several philosophers of worldview have discussed, narratives, or meta-narratives, serve as indispensable elements of worldviews.[50]

Thiselton claims that Ricoeur's *Oneself as Another* is the other of his two "greatest major works."[51] In this work, Ricoeur focuses on the self's identity and the implications this has "for narrative and for ethics."[52] He focuses on Descartes's understanding of the self in the introduction and shows that the problem with this treatment was that it never moved beyond the *what* of the self. Descartes never penetrates to the *who* of the self.[53] After discussing "the shattered cogito,"[54] Ricoeur argues "towards a hermeneutics of the self."[55]

The first two studies of this work focus on the linguistic nature of the self, namely on the self as one who speaks. These provide semantic and pragmatic approaches to the self.[56] Ricoeur goes on to discuss "an agentless semantics of action" in the third study.[57] The thrust of Ricoeur's monograph, however, comes in the fifth and sixth studies, where he discusses "personal identity and narrative identity,"[58] and "the self and narrative identity."[59] Important to understanding the self is understanding the *temporality* of the self. Ricoeur writes, "I propose to reconstruct here a theory of narrative, no longer considered from the perspective of its relation to the constitution of human time, as I did in *Time and Narrative*, but from that of its contributions to the constitution of the self."[60]

Ricoeur discusses the two major notions of identity, those of *sameness* and *selfhood*. He defines *sameness* as "a concept of relation and a relation of relations. First comes *numerical* identity: thus, we say of two occurrences of a thing, designated by an invariable noun in ordinary language, that they

---

50. See Sire, *Universe Next Door*; Sire, *Naming the Elephant*; Wright, *New Testament and the People of God*, 69–80.
51. Thiselton, *Hermeneutics: An Introduction*, 230.
52. Thiselton, *Hermeneutics: An Introduction*, 230.
53. Ricoeur, *Oneself as Another*, 6–7.
54. Ricoeur, *Oneself as Another*, 11.
55. Ricoeur, *Oneself as Another*, 16.
56. Ricoeur, *Oneself as Another*, 27–55.
57. Ricoeur, *Oneself as Another*, 56–87.
58. Ricoeur, *Oneself as Another*, 113.
59. Ricoeur, *Oneself as Another*, 140.
60. Ricoeur, *Oneself as Another*, 114.

do not form two different things but 'one and the same' thing."[61] There is, however, a major weakness in this notion of similitude, and that is "the *uninterrupted continuity* between the first and the last stage in the development of what we consider to be the same individual."[62] Ricoeur then returns his attention to the notion of identity as selfhood, focusing primarily on the concepts of "*character* and *keeping one's word*."[63] By *character*, he means "the set of distinctive marks which permit the reidentification of a human individual as being the same. By the descriptive features that will be given, the individual compounds numerical identity and qualitative identity, *uninterrupted continuity* and *permanence* in time. In this way, the sameness of the person is designated emblematically."[64] The phrase *keeping one's word* is in reference to keeping a promise, which is intimately connected to the notion of *character*. One's decision to keep a promise stems from the character, both of which demonstrate the *uninterrupted continuity* of the self.[65] Thus Ricoeur concludes his study on "personal identity and the self."

Ricoeur then turns his attention to "the self and narrative identity: "The genuine nature of narrative identity discloses itself, in my opinion, only in the dialectic of selfhood and sameness. In this sense, this dialectic represents the major contribution of narrative theory to the constitution of the self."[66] He continues his theory of narrative he developed in *Time and Narrative*, in which the concepts of *the interconnection of events* and *emplotment* importantly figure.[67] This concept of *emplotment* "produces a dialectic of the character which is quite clearly a dialectic of sameness and selfhood."[68] One's *emplotment* in the narrative of history has a determining factor on her existence. This notion of emplotment resembles Heidegger's notion of *thrownness*; however, unlike Heidegger, Ricoeur shows the implications of emplotment for ethics.[69] The rest of *Oneself as Another* develops the implications of these studies on personal identity, selfhood, and narrative for ethics.[70]

61. Ricoeur, *Oneself as Another*, 116.
62. Ricoeur, *Oneself as Another*, 117.
63. Ricoeur, *Oneself as Another*, 118.
64. Ricoeur, *Oneself as Another*, 119.
65. Ricoeur, *Oneself as Another*, 123.
66. Ricoeur, *Oneself as Another*, 140.
67. Ricoeur, *Oneself as Another*, 140.
68. Ricoeur, *Oneself as Another*, 140–41.
69. Ricoeur, *Oneself as Another*, 163–68.
70. In his monograph *Interpreting God and the Postmodern Self*, Anthony Thiselton

Ricoeur's understanding of the relationship between narrative and history, as developed in *Time and Narrative* and *Oneself as Another*, is one of his most significant contributions to the field of hermeneutics. One can see how this concept is an implication of Gadamer's notions of the historicity of understanding as well as his understanding of horizons. History experienced, according to Ricoeur, is history experienced as narrative. Each person lives out this narrative with her own horizon of understanding, and this narrative provides her with her horizon of understanding. This not only has implications for issues concerning personal identity and selfhood, but ethics as well. No one gets to choose where she comes to be in the narrative of history. This is akin to Heidegger's notion of *thrownness* and Gadamer's concept of *givenness*. The individual's horizon of understanding is determined by her placement in this narrative, and it grows as she moves forward in the narrative.

Gadamer and Ricoeur have provided many important insights into the field of hermeneutics, to the point that the term *philosophical hermeneutics* is often limited to the projects of these two.[71] As will now be shown, several theologians have incorporated these insights into their understanding of the nature and task of theology, namely in that they have chosen to see the nature of theology as hermeneutical. These theologians include Wolfhart Pannenberg and Anthony Thiselton.[72]

THE HERMENEUTIC NATURE OF THEOLOGY

Now that sufficient attention has been given to hermeneutics as the philosophy of understanding, with special attention given to Gadamer and Ricoeur, I now want to turn attention to the hermeneutic nature of theology. Numerous theologians have given careful attention to this, such as Karl Barth, Rudolf Bultmann, Gerhard Ebeling, Jürgen Moltmann, Kevin Vanhoozer, and several others. However, space only allows for discussion of two significant contributions on this topic, namely those of Wolfhart

---

utilizes Ricoeur's *Oneself as Another* extensively in refuting many postmodern perspectives of God and the self, namely those that relate to the hermeneutics of suspicion practiced by socio–critical and socio–pragmatic hermeneutics.

71. Grondin, *Introduction to Philosophical Hermeneutics*, 2.

72. The majority of material in this section will focus on the contributions of Pannenberg, as his are the most foundational for the others. The majority of Thiselton's project presupposes Pannenberg's accomplishments in *Theology and the Philosophy of Science*. As a result, the treatment of his work will be substantially shorter.

Pannenberg and Anthony Thiselton. These two have provided what is perhaps the most significant work on the topic in recent years, with Pannenberg's coming much earlier than Thiselton's. This is not to say that the contributions of other important theologians, such as those mentioned above, do not merit discussion, only that the space allowed for this discussion in this chapter does not permit it. What makes the contributions of Pannenberg and Thiselton so noteworthy is multifaced. Pannenberg demonstrates how all scientific inquiry is hermeneutic at its very foundation. For him, hermeneutic provides a sort of foundational method that can bring together both the natural and human sciences, which has important implications for theology, which he defines as the science of God. Thiselton's work, which is a sort of continuation of Pannenberg's program, demonstrates not only the positive implications hermeneutics has for theology as a science, but the benefits it has for spirituality in general. He demonstrates this by paying careful attention to the role of formation in doing theology and doctrine. As such, his treatment in *The Hermeneutics of Doctrine* merits discussion here.

Wolfhart Pannenberg

One of the clearest expressions of the hermeneutic nature of theology is that of Wolfhart Pannenberg. In his monograph *Theology and the Philosophy of Science*, he attempts to discuss the scientific nature and task of theology. He begins by discussing some basic issues concerning the development of the philosophy of science, especially noting the logical positivism of the Vienna Circle and the critical rationalism of Karl Popper. He discusses the strengths that both of these philosophies of science put forth while also being critical of the weaknesses they entail. Logical positivism, the position that a statement only has literal meaning if one can verify it,[73] is unable to account for the many statements that few would doubt have literal meaning but are unable to be verified. The problem here is that this view limits language to a descriptive function. One can say the same of Karl Popper's critical rationalism.[74] Though this latter position is more satisfactory than verificationism, it still proves unsatisfactory.

73. See Ayer, *Language, Truth, and Logic*, 5.
74. Popper questioned the logic verificationism of logical positivism. Namely, when one conjectures a hypothesis she does so in the form of a material conditional: if *A* then *B*. She would then perform an experiment of some form to test this hypothesis, which

Pannenberg then turns his attention to the divide between the natural and human sciences. He affirms that both branches of science utilize different methodologies for carrying out their inquiries, and he is not opposed to these decisions. He does, however, oppose the chasm that appears between the two divisions of science. He affirms that both are indeed sciences and that some foundational methodology must link the two together. This foundational methodology will also serve as an appropriate mode of inquiry for theology. He claims that this foundational method is none other than hermeneutic.[75]

According to Pannenberg, "the aim of hermeneutic is the understanding of meaning, and meaning is to be understood in this context as the relation of parts to a whole within a structure of life or experience."[76] Hermeneutic is the most basic form of inquiry of any science, whether it be physics, theology, or sociology. Whenever a scientist inquires of a certain phenomenon, what she gleans from this inquiry has implications for her understanding of everything else. As discussed at length in chapter four above, all truth is connected and interconnected. Pannenberg holds that every system, whether it is individual and temporal or universal and timeless, always includes a relationship of particulars to wholes, which results in every system being meaningful.[77] Here, his view of history (*Geschichte*) provides a unifying theme for his project. History, according to Pannenberg, "is the most comprehensive horizon of Christian theology. All theological questions and answers are meaningful only within the framework of the history which God has with humanity and through humanity with his whole creation—the history moving toward a future still hidden from the

---

would result in *B*. The problem here, as Popper points out, is that this "verification" seems to commit the formal fallacy of affirming the consequent. As a result, Popper put forth his theory of falsification, which claims that, provisionally, one can hold a conjectured hypothesis is true if she was not able to falsify via her experiment. This is not a case of verificationism, but a lack of falsification. See Popper, *Conjectures and Refutations*, 43–86.

75. Pannenberg uses the term *hermeneutic* to refer to the type of method that the sciences presuppose in their inquiry, and he uses the term *hermeneutics* to refer to the philosophical discipline.

76. Panneberg, *Theology and the Philosophy of Science*, 156.

77. Pannenberg, *Theology and the Philosophy of Science*, 156. Pannenberg makes this explicitly clear in his discussions concerning history in hermeneutics. In his essay "Hermeneutic and Universal History," he states, "Of course, every event has its peculiar character and meaning only within the nexus of events to which it belongs from the very beginning" (98). See also, Pannenberg, *Anthropology in Theological Perspective*, 486, 511–12.

world but already revealed in Jesus Christ."[78] History is the sphere in which all human experience occurs, and it is also the realm in which all truth occurs. As such the unity of history is fundamental. Pannenberg summarizes elsewhere, "Human life, whether it is the life span of the individual or the larger story of peoples and states, takes concrete form in history."[79] Since all human experience and existence take place in history, one must grapple not only with historiography and the philosophy of history but also with "the whole of human reality."[80]

Since truth exists in unity with all other truth, then there must be some form of unity in the history in which said truth occurs. Hence, Pannenberg claims, "Of course, every event has its peculiar character and meaning only within the nexus of events to which it belongs from the very beginning."[81] One can see a form of narrative understanding to history in Pannenberg's thought here.[82] In the same way that a particular event in a narrative derives its meaning from its relationship to the totality of the narrative, so do particular events in history. Each individual event in history presupposes the totality of history for the determination of its meaning. This presupposition is the case with all instances of meaning, not just historical meaning. Every instance of meaning presupposes the totality of meaning. Pannenberg writes,

> In so far as there exists, for any semantic whole, a context which transcends it, the whole itself possesses its meaning only in relation to that context, as its 'reference' within it. It follows from this that no unity of meaning and no perception of meaning is autonomous in itself. Every specialised meaning depends on a final, all-embracing totality of meaning in which all individual meanings are linked to form a semantic whole. Because every individual meaning depends

---

78. Pannenberg, "Redemptive Event and History," 15.

79. Pannenberg, *Anthropology in Theological Perspective*, 485. Pannenberg is also clear that *history* is not something projected by the individual as a means of processing experience, but is something experienced by all persons. He states, "The universality of history marks human life itself and is inseparable from the coming into existence and passing away of this life. As a result, history belongs to the shared world of human beings, despite the fact that historical processes repeatedly dissolve, transform, and destroy the order of the shared human world." See Pannenberg, *Anthropology in Theological Perspective*, 486.

80. Pannenberg, *Anthropology in Theological Perspective*, 486.

81. Pannenberg, "Hermeneutic and Universal History," 98.

82. A lot of similarity exists between Pannenberg's narrative view of history and that espoused by Ricoeur above, though the latter's magnum opus had not be written at the time of the former's major developments in his philosophy of history.

o this whole, the latter is implicitly invoked in every experience of particular meaning. This is not to say that this semantic whole is somehow present in fully defined form in every perception of particular meaning. The proposition, in particular the affirmative proposition, possesses a relative autonomy of definition, as does a complete section of discourse, but they too are admitted into their 'unexpressed semantic horizon'. Within this they are surrounded by a greater or lesser area of definition, but beyond this the boundaries of meaning shade off into indefiniteness. This combination of definition and indefiniteness also exists in language; indeed it is only because the words of a language are incompletely defined that propositions can be formulated with precise definition. The proposition's comparative autonomy of meaning exists as the semantic anticipation of an indefinite semantic whole which transcends it and which is revealed in the proposition and acquires explicit, though only partial, definition in it.[83]

The meaning of each individual statement is determined by the totality of statements in which it occurs. All propositions, assuming they are intended as truth claims, presuppose the totality of true propositions in their own assertion. Here, the question of meaning relates to science. As one can see, Pannenberg opts for a contextual understanding of meaning rather than a referential or intentional understanding.[84] As will be discussed below, this contextual understanding of meaning has a lot in common with Eco's semiotics.

83. Pannenberg, *Theology and the Philosophy of Science*, 216–17.

84. Pannenberg, *Theology and the Philosophy of Science*, 211. Pannenberg disregards the referential view in that it was the view of logical positivism, which he has already shown to be a failed epistemology. He also disregards the "intentional" view of meaning in that though it provides the human sciences their own playing field, it does not make a connection between it and that of the natural sciences. He opts for a contextual understanding of meaning asking, "Is the meaning of an expression that to which the speaker is *in fact* referring, or that to which he *thinks* his utterance refers, or that to which the *interpreter* thinks the speaker is referring, or that to which his utterance would naturally refer in normal usage? That such questions can be asked shows that the relation of a linguistic utterance to its object cannot be determined without a consideration of its social and historical context." He notes that this understanding of meaning arose in linguistic analysis in the works of the later Wittgenstein, namely in his concept of the "language–game [*Sprachspiele*]." Particular words find their meanings in their relationship to the other particulars, and ultimately the whole, of the sentence; and the sentence finds its meaning in the wider context in which it is found. Instead of asking what the meaning of a word is, one should inquire instead into the context in which it is *used*. Pannenberg praises Wittgenstein for his notion of the language–game in that it depends on what he, Wittgenstein, referred to as "life–forms [*Lebensform*]" of a society. See also Wittgenstein, *Philosophical Investigations*, 8, 11.

Pannenberg discusses the question of truth as it pertains to meaning. He notes that though a consensus theory of truth is as incomplete as the classical correspondence theory of truth, "the correspondence of a statement with the facts cannot be determined without reference to the judgment of others."[85] These "others" must be experts or intelligent judges. Pannenberg states, "Since it is possible only for *subjects* to learn about facts, interpersonal agreement retains a predominance in decisions about the truth of statements."[86] Since this is the case, truth and meaning coincide in the totality of meaning. To this extent, part of the hermeneutical process is to make judgments concerning the truth–value of statements. Pannenberg here notes the anticipatory element of truth by making reference to the concept of the assertion. He claims that every assertion anticipates truth in that though the proposition it contains puts itself forward as true, it also puts itself forward to be refuted. All assertions, or truth claims, anticipate their future verification.[87]

Pannenberg then discusses what he calls "comprehensive networks of meaning."[88] He claims that networks of meaning appeared in the forms of myth in the ancient times. He then notes that philosophy and science seek to produce these networks in the modern day, though they do so differently. He states, "Philosophy and science differ from myth in producing systematic interpretations in the form of models of meaning which are intended to be free from internal contradiction and contain no more than what can be shown to be logically necessary for the explanation of networks of phenomena."[89] The sciences differ from philosophy in that the sciences restrict statements to a formal language and/or to statements that the scientific community can empirically verify or falisify. Philosophical statements cannot be subjected to the criterion used by the sciences because if they are, then they lose the feature of what Pannenberg calls their "unrestricted reflection."[90] Unrestricted reflection, he notes, cannot cease until it reveals

---

85. Pannenberg, *Theology and the Philosophy of Science*, 219.

86. Pannenberg, *Theology and the Philosophy of Science*, 220.

87. Pannenberg, *Theology and the Philosophy of Science*, 220. This notion of "anticipation" permeates through much of Pannenberg's other works as well. See also Pannenberg, "On Historical and Theological Hermeneutic," 137–81; Pannenberg, "What is Truth?," 1–27; Pannenberg, "Eschatology and the Experience of Meaning," 192–210.

88. Pannenberg, *Theology and the Philosophy of Science*, 220.

89. Pannenberg, *Theology and the Philosophy of Science*, 221.

90. Pannenberg, *Theology and the Philosophy of Science*, 221.

"the totality of meaning which encompasses all experience."[91] After discussing how the empirical sciences produce their networks of meaning, he then discusses the networks of meaning that belong to history [*Geschichte*]:

> The networks of meaning which the historian describes in past phenomena depend on a present understanding of reality (which the historian shares with his contemporaries) and on a future which is still open. At this point, consideration of the semantic networks constructed by the historian leads into philosophical consideration of the totality of meaning.[92]

Unlike the natural sciences, history is not able to devote itself entirely to its material and verification/falsification of its theories and hypotheses. Instead, it functions in the same manner as philosophy, in that it is always anticipating the totality of the meaning of experience.[93] Pannenberg shows that philosophical analyses of meaning operate by describing the totality of meaning in a systematic manner.[94] This system, however, is only "an anticipation of the implicit and only partly defined totality of meaning of all experience, to which it is related and in which it possesses its truth."[95] This system can demonstrate truth only by integrating and illuminating experiences of meaning. Pannenberg closes this chapter of *Philosophy and the Theology of Science* by asserting that theology, like philosophy and history, concerns itself with the totality of meaning of experience and "must be aware of this if it is to know what it is saying" concerning its talk of God.[96]

In summary, hermeneutic plays an inseparable role in theology in that it is the methodology that theology utilizes according to Pannenberg. Theology is a hermeneutical task because it is hermeneutic in nature. Hermeneutic concerns itself with meaning and meaning is concerned with the relationship of particulars to their wholes. Pannenberg approves Gadamer's hermeneutic project in that it explicitly makes one aware of the finitude of her experience and reminds her of the alien nature of the other that she seeks to understand.[97] One can see that, for Pannenberg, there is not a dichotomy separating epistemology and hermeneutics as they both come

---

91. Pannenberg, *Theology and the Philosophy of Science*, 222.
92. Pannenberg, *Theology and the Philosophy of Science*, 223.
93. See also Pannenberg, "Redemptive Event and History," 15–80.
94. Pannenberg, *Theology and the Philosophy of Science*, 224.
95. Pannenberg, *Theology and the Philosophy of Science*, 224.
96. Pannenberg, *Theology and the Philosophy of Science*, 224.
97. Pannenberg, *Theology and the Philosophy of Science*, 164–69.

together in scientific inquiry. Theology is thus a science that is grounded on the methodology of hermeneutic, for it is hermeneutic at its very nature.

Anthony Thiselton

Though Pannenberg provides what is, perhaps, the most detailed explication of the hermeneutic nature of theology, he is by no means the only one to do so. In contemporary theology, Anthony Thiselton explicitly discusses the hermeneutic nature of theology. More specifically, he discusses the hermeneutic nature of the development of Christian doctrine. He begins by making reference to Gadamer's distinction between historically conditioned *questions that arise* and *free-floating problems*.[98] Drawing from the work of R. G. Collingwood, Gadamer stated, "We can understand a text only when we have understood the question to which it is an answer.... This is the nerve of all historical knowledge."[99] In this sense, the problems of philosophy are tied to the questions of history. Philosophical problems are not simply abstract problems floating around "out there." Rather, they arise within the realm of history as a result of a lack of understanding concerning something else. Gadamer states, "Critiquing the concept of the problem by appealing to a logic of question and answer must destroy the illusion that problems exist like stars in the sky. Reflection on the hermeneutical experience transforms *problems* back to *questions that arise* and that derive their sense from their motivation."[100] This transformation is how all understanding occurs, including theological understanding. As one encounters the phenomenon of God's revelation in history, certain questions arise concerning said phenomenon.

Thiselton draws heavily from the project of Pannenberg set forth in *Theology and the Philosophy of Science*, namely on emphasizing how theology can be both hermeneutical and scientific.[101] He points out, however, that despite Pannenberg's extensive interaction with Gadamer, he does not dialogue with Gadamer's hermeneutic concept of *Bildung*, or formation. Important to Gadamer's hermeneutic philosophy is the formative role of understanding on the individual.[102] Put another way, the hermeneutic

---

98. Thiselton, *Hermeneutics of Doctrine*, 3. See also Gadamer, *Truth and Method*, 363–71.
99. Gadamer, *Truth and Method*, 363–64. See also Collingwood, *An Autobiography*.
100. Gadamer, *Truth and Method*, 369–70. Italics mine.
101. Thiselton, *Hermeneutics of Doctrine*, 156–62.
102. I have discussed this at length in my M. A. thesis in which I utilized Gadamer's

circle, the never-ending dialogue that occurs between the self and the other, always has a formative effect on the self. Not only is this effect formative, but it is transformative as well.[103] Jens Zimmerman deploys a slightly modified version of Gadamer's hermeneutic circle in which the other is replaced with God, the one who is truly other.[104] He adopts this revised circle from John Calvin, who opened his *Institutes of the Christian Religion* with the following statement: "Our wisdom, insofar as it ought to be deemed true and solid wisdom, consists almost entirely of two parts: the knowledge of God and of ourselves."[105] If one desires to possess true understanding of herself then she must have a true understanding of who God is; and she can only understand who God, the truly other, is by understanding who she is before him. As the hermeneutic circle furthers the understanding of the self and the Truly Other, the self is formed and transformed further.

According to Thiselton, this *formation* is one of the primary roles of doctrine. He discusses the relationship between beliefs and patterns of behavior, making special reference to H. H. Price's monograph *Belief*.[106] In this work, Price developed a *dispositional* account of belief. One's disposition, or patterns of behavior, displays what she truly believes. Price referred to cases in which one professes a belief and her disposition affirms these claims only when it is beneficial to her as *half-belief*. According to Thiselton, doctrines, at the fundamental level, are beliefs and as such, following Price, ought to result in certain dispositions, or patterns of behavior, rather than others. He shows this dispositional account of belief to be the case in the early Christian confessions of faith and creeds. He writes, "Christian doctrine is the communal endorsement and transmission of such belief, as expressed in life, worship, and action."[107] Thiselton spends the last two-thirds of this monograph approaching specific Christian doctrines, such as the Work of Christ, as problems that arose in the church's experience of God's revelation and history, and how these doctrines have continued to develop throughout history as more questions have arisen. He also highlights the formative

---

concept of *Bildung* as a conversation partner for *Christian discipleship*. See Hollingsworth, "Hans-Georg Gadamer and a Hermeneutics of Discipleship."

103. Thiselton refers to this notion as "the transformative power of texts." See Thiselton, *New Horizons in Hermeneutics*, 31–35.

104. Zimmerman, *Recovering Theological Hermeneutics*, 86.

105. Calvin, *Institutes of the Christian Religion*, 4.

106. Price, *Belief*.

107. Thiselton, *Hermeneutics of Doctrine*, 34, 36–42.

effects these beliefs have had on the church throughout history and how they can continue to have these effects today.

ECO'S MODEL ENCYCLOPEDIA AND HERMENEUTIC THEOLOGY

Eco's model encyclopedia naturally lends itself to the hermeneutic nature and task of theology. As discussed above, hermeneutics is the philosophy of human understanding. All understanding takes place from the standpoint of a particular horizon. In Eco's terms, all understanding occurs from the standpoint of a particular encyclopedia. As discussed in chapter three above, no individual, or culture for that matter, has access to the maximal encyclopedia. Individuals and cultures have access only to local encyclopedias. A local encyclopedia is made up of cultural knowledge, and individuals operate out of these encyclopedias. Encyclopedias include language, the medium that makes knowledge and understanding possible. As noted by Gadamer above, all cognition occurs through the medium of language, and language is the primary ingredient in one's horizon of understanding. As such, the fusion of horizons, or the event of understanding, is a type of agreement between two users of language. What Gadamer does not discuss, however, is the phenomenon of language being a sign system. This is where Eco's encyclopedia is able not only to strengthen this position but take it further.

One of the things that make language unique is that it is a shared phenomenon. No individual speaks her own language; rather, she participates in a shared language. As discussed above, all thinking occurs through the medium of language. Eco and Gadamer agree on this point. Communication is made possible in that languages are shared sign systems. As Eco discusses at length in *A Theory of Semiotics*, all sign systems, especially conventional sign systems such as language, presuppose a theory of codes that dictate how one produces signs and interprets them. In this sense, codes are a type of grammar that tell signs how to behave. What makes communication and interpretation possible is the shared nature of these signs with their codes. A given local encyclopedia contains not only the signs that individuals and cultures use to communicate, but it also contains the codes that tell them how to use these signs.

One of the first parallels one might see in Eco's encyclopedia and the hermeneutic nature of theology is found in Pannenberg's discussion above, namely how every instance of meaning presupposes the totality of meaning.

This concept has implications concerning the question of truth: every true statement presupposes the totality of true statements. In this sense, the question of meaning and truth coincide, according to Pannenberg's hermeneutic. All inquiry is concerned with how parts relate to wholes. This notion also parallels the following that was said in chapter four above: what is true of one discipline, such as physics, must also be true of another, such as theology. Concerning meaning, this is connected, for Pannenberg, in the meaning of history. The totality of history determines the meaning, or significance, of any and all historical events. At the same time, the totality of history is an amalgamation of all historical events. So in this sense, the parts determine the whole and the whole determines the parts.

In Eco's model encyclopedia, all sememes, or basic content units, presuppose the totality of sememes. This totality of sememes is how particular sememes are determined. The content, or meaning, of a sign is determined by its relationship to all of the other signs in its respective sign system. Not only this, but every sign system is connected and interconnected in the maximal encyclopedia, i.e., the totality of meaning. Drawing from Peirce's theory of interpretants, Eco claims that all interpretants become their own sign in that they also require interpretation, ad infinitum. This phenomenon is what Peirce and Eco refer to as *unlimited semiosis*. Contrary to many postmodern thinkers, such as deconstructionists, however, this unlimited semiosis, the process by which signs are understood by more and more signs, does not lead to a hermetic drift in which one never arrives at the meaning of a sign. Whereas, according to the theory of the hermetic drift, one always *drifts away* from the meaning of a sign through this semisosic process of deferment, for Peirce and Eco, the contrary is the case. Unlimited semiosis does not remove one further from the meaning of a sign; rather, it reveals to the interpreter how much meaning, i.e., connectedness and interconnectedness, the expressed sign has. Again, sememes are determined by their connectedness and interconnectedness to all other sememes in the encyclopedia. Every sememe presupposes the totality of sememes, not only in the local encyclopedia in which it appears but in the maximal encyclopedia as well. This is what Eco means when he claims that the maximal encyclopedia serves as a regulative idea.

One can apply this concept in turn to the concept of doctrine, namely in that doctrines can be viewed as signs, possessing both an expression and a content plane. Consider, for example, the doctrine of the Work of Christ. *The Work of Christ* serves as the expression plane to which is attached a content plane. The content of *The Work of Christ* is not determined based off of some *genera* or *species* that is innate in the expression, as in the model dictionary. Rather, the content, or sememe, of *The Work of Christ* is determined by its connections and interconnections with other doctrines such as *Creation, the Incarnation, Eschatology*, and even *The Lord's Supper*. Each instance of doctrine presupposes the entire system, or encyclopedia, of doctrine in which it occurs. One might refer to this local, or specialized, encyclopedia as Christian Theology, which in turn appears in the maximal encyclopedia, connected and interconnected to all other localized and specialized encyclopedias, such as psychology, Hinduism, and economics. In this way, the localized encyclopedia presupposes the maximal encyclopedia and is determined by its place in the maximal encyclopedia. The meaning of a doctrine is determined by its place in its local encyclopedia and also by its place in the maximal encyclopedia. Again, as a regulative rule, all meaning, or sememes, presuppose the maximal encyclopedia as a regulative idea. As discussed in Pannenberg's project above, the question of meaning and truth coincide with doctrine as well. The truth–value of a doctrine also presupposes the totality of true statements. One might say that every truth claim presupposes the maximal encyclopedia of true statements since coherence is a necessary condition for a statement to be true.

Eco's encyclopedia also lends itself to the formative concerns of Thiselton's project. As Thiselton himself agrees with Gadamer, all understanding occurs from within a particular horizon. Horizons are not static, for as the self moves about in the narrative of history, her horizon broadens. Eco's labyrinthine library in *The Name of the Rose* can provide a helpful analogy here. As one is willing to leave her own room in the library, symbolic of her own local encyclopedia, she can cross through the connecting hallways and corridors into the next room. As she encounters the new contents of this next room, her own encyclopedia broadens, as it never truly leaves her. Not only does she broaden her own horizon in this way, she better learns how to navigate the labyrinth of the maximal encyclopedia, or the library of libraries. This learning to navigate is a formative effect on the self. The more one explores the labyrinth of the encyclopedia, the more she is formed and transformed into one who better knows her way around the labyrinth, and this formation cannot be undone. As with William and Adso in the library, once they had groped their way around the labyrinth to the point of familiarity, they no longer had the problem of getting lost. They had broadened their horizons, so to say.

Not only does the navigation of the encyclopedia have the ability to form one into someone who knows how better to navigate the encyclopedia, it also forms her through the accrual of new knowledge. As discussed above, as one comes to learn more she is able to sympathize with positions and horizons of understanding other than her own. This learning to sympathize is also a formative effect. One can consider the example of doctrine again. When someone encounters new horizons of understanding concerning a familiar doctrine, and if this someone truly listens, she is able to broaden her own horizon by taking in this new information. The more one broadens her horizons, i.e., ventures into new encyclopedias, she is able to make more apt judgments concerning the meaning and truth-value of doctrines. One only need think of the current debates over the doctrine of justification to see this point. Throughout her existence, a self might have encountered only one horizon of understanding concerning the doctrine of justification. In this example, this horizon of understanding represents the traditional Lutheran view of justification. As the self encounters a new understanding of justification, say that espoused by N. T. Wright's version of the New Perspective on Paul position, she has the ability to explore new potential content for her own understanding of justification, namely the traditional Lutheran view. The more she knows concerning these different perspectives, she is equipped more to make better judgments concerning which position is more true than the other.[108] This equipping has a formative effect on her.

Thiselton refers to Hans Robert Jauss's notion of the *interruption of one's horizon of expectation* in regards to the above discussion.[109] When one encounters something other, such as a text, she typically possesses a horizon of expectation concerning it. Horizons of expectation, however, can be interrupted when encountering the other. This happened when Luther encountered the writings of Paul concerning justification and the righteousness of God.[110] Prior to encountering Paul's letters and allowing them

---

108. I say "more true" because since no individual is privileged with access to the maximal encyclopedia in an objective sense, she is constantly testing propositional contents, such as the contents of doctrines, for their potential truth-value. When she is unable to determine the truth-value of a doctrine based on its correspondence with reality, she will resort to testing its explanatory power over the concerned phenomenon, as well will she test it for coherence with other doctrinal positions she has judged as being truth-value positive.

109. Thiselton, *Hermeneutics of Doctrine*, 98–104. See also Jauss, *Toward an Aesthetic of Reception*, 22–32.

110. Thiselton, *Hermeneutics of Doctrine*, 96.

to speak for themselves, from their own horizon, Luther had a particular horizon of expectation concerning the righteousness of God. Upon encountering Paul's letters, his horizon of expectation was interrupted by the otherness of the text. This interruption of the horizon of expectation had a tremendous formative effect on Luther. One can see also Gadamer's claim that *application* is something that coincides with interpretation and understanding. Simply by gaining this new understanding, said understanding is *applied* to the self's own encyclopedia. New connections and interconnections with other contents occur without the self even consciously doing so. When a fusion of horizons occurs, application always occurs, consciously or subconsciously.

Ricoeur's notion of the need for both explanation and understanding in interpretation finds a home in Eco's model encyclopedia as well. *Understanding* is one's navigating her way through the labyrinth of the encyclopedia; it is a form of abduction. As one gropes her way through the encyclopedia, she gains a better understanding of the layout of the labyrinth and is able to navigate it more efficiently. An implication of this better understanding is that she is in turn able to *explain* it. Whereas *understanding* is a form of abduction, *explanation* serves as a form of map that tells one how to better go about *understanding*. One explains in order to better understand, but one must understand first in order to explain. *Explanation* aids one in navigating the theological encyclopedia and is able to make theological *understanding* easier. Though *explanation* serves as a guide to *understanding*, one should note that *explanation* itself occurs through the medium of signs, which presupposes an *understanding* of the signs that are used to explain. In the same sense that explanation and understanding undergo a dialectic between themselves in interpretation, so do they as concerns the semiotic encyclopedia. This dialectic is at work in abduction, which, as mentioned multiple times above, is the type of reasoning used in making interpretative judgments. Interpretation, being a form of abduction, is a way in which one gropes her way through the encyclopedia.

CONCLUSION

As one can see, Eco's model encyclopedia naturally lends itself to the hermeneutic nature of theology. Drawing from the insights of Gadamer and Ricoeur, Pannenberg and Thiselton show that theology itself is hermeneutic in both its nature and task. Understanding always takes place from a particular horizon, a concept that parallels Eco's concept of a local encyclopedia. Pannenberg highlights that every instance of meaning presupposes the totality of meaning, and in this sense the questions of meaning and truth coincide. This concept also parallels Eco's discussion of how signs relate to one another in the model encyclopedia. The content of a sign, or the sememe of a sign, is determined by a sign's relationship to all other signs in the encyclopedia. Every sememe presupposes the totality of sememes in the maximal encyclopedia. In this sense, every utterance presupposes the totality of language in its being uttered. In the model encyclopedia, doctrines are signs possessing expression planes and content planes. These contents that fill these planes are determined by their connections and interconnections with all other contents. The contents, or sememes, of doctrines are determined by their connectedness and interconnectedness to all other doctrines. Eco's model encyclopedia lends itself to this aspect of the hermeneutic nature of theology.

As one further navigates the maximal encyclopedia, she broadens her horizons, which has a formative effect on her. As she encounters new contents in different localized encyclopedias, she is able to make more apt judgments concerning the truth–value of these contents. These better judgments are a formative effect of the broadening of horizons, or exploring new encyclopedias. Not only this, but one is able to have her horizon of expectation interrupted when navigating other encyclopedias. Upon having her horizon of expectation interrupted, a self is able to see the other in a new light, which is a formative effect of the hermeneutic circle. As one explores new local encyclopedias, she stands in a position to have her previous horizon of expectation concerning the contents of said encyclopedias interrupted. As a result, new connections and interconnections are made between one's own encyclopedia and the other encyclopedia.

As has been shown above, Eco's model encyclopedia lends itself to the hermeneutic nature and task of theology, thus successfully dialoging with the second question that I have posed as a test case to determine the adequacy of Eco's encyclopedia as a model for theology. One can see this especially in how each doctrine presupposes the totality of doctrines within the theological encyclopedia and how this encyclopedia presupposes all other localized and specialized encyclopedias within the maximal encyclopedia. Questions concerning doctrinal development, however, have not been discussed in this chapter. These questions deserve a chapter of their own, and attention will turn now to deal with them in chapter six.

6

The Model Encyclopedia and the Development of Doctrine

This chapter will explore how Eco's model encyclopedia lends itself to doctrinal development. This discussion serves as the third and final test case for appropriating the model encyclopedia as a model for theology. After providing a brief discussion on the nature of doctrine and the phenomenon of doctrinal development, I will bring Eco's model encyclopedia into dialogue with three different approaches to doctrine and doctrinal development: the hermeneutic approach of Anthony Thiselton, the theodramatic approach of Kevin Vanhoozer, and the scientific approach of Alister McGrath. I will show then how Eco's model encyclopedia lends itself to all three of these approaches, and I will provide a conclusion as to whether or not it passes this third test case.

THE NATURE OF DOCTRINE AND THE PHENOMENON OF DOCTRINAL DEVELOPMENT

In *An Essay on the Development of Christian Doctrine*, John Henry Newman stated, "It is the characteristic of our minds to be ever engaged in passing judgment on the things which come before us. No sooner do we apprehend that we judge: we allow nothing to stand by itself: we compare, contrast, abstract, generalize, connect, adjust, classify: and we view all our knowledge in the associations with which these processes have invested it."[1] Throughout the history of ideas and learning, new knowledge consistently has come to light. When a new idea is put forth, it is synthesized with already existing knowledge and even newer ideas are produced as a result. All knowledge is constantly developing. The same is the case with Christian doctrine.

Broadly defined, the term *Christian doctrine* denotes *Christian teaching*. In this sense, *doctrine* has a strong connection to theology. Alister McGrath writes,

> The use of the word 'doctrine' implies reference to a tradition and a community, where 'theology' more properly designates the views of individuals, not necessarily within this community or tradition, who seek to explore ideas without any necessary commitment to them. Doctrine defines communities of discourse, possessing a representative character, attempting to describe or prescribe the beliefs of a community.[2]

Whereas individuals have a theology, or theologies, communities, especially religious ones, have doctrines. As McGrath defines it, *Christian doctrine* denotes the communally binding teaching possessed by the Christian religion. In this sense, doctrine serves as a form of boundary marker. When beliefs, or teachings, fall outside the parameters of Christian doctrine, they cease to be Christian. McGrath further comments,

> Doctrine entails a sense of commitment to a community, and a sense of obligation to speak on its behalf, where the corporate mind of the community exercises a restraint over the individual's perception of truth. Doctrine is an *activity*, a process of transmission of the collective wisdom of a community, rather than a passive set of deliverance.[3]

Christian doctrine is an activity performed by the Christian community for the Christian community. As Karl Barth stated,

> Dogmatics is a theological discipline. But theology is a function of the Church. The Church confesses God as it talks about God. . . . Fortunately the reality of the Church does not coincide

---

1. Newman, *Essay on the Development of Christian Doctrine*, 33.
2. McGrath, *Genesis of Doctrine*, 10–11.
3. McGrath, *Genesis of Doctrine*, 11.

with its action. But its action coincides with the fact that alike in its existence in believers and its communal existence as such it speaks about God. Its action is 'theology' in both the broader and the narrower sense.[4]

In other words, theology and doctrine, according to Barth, is done by the Church, in the Church, for the Church.

George Lindbeck's Postliberal Approach

Perhaps the most popular twentieth-century monograph on the nature of doctrine is George Lindbeck's *The Nature of Doctrine*. In this seminal work, Lindbeck provides three understandings of the nature of doctrine: the cognitive-propositional, the experiential-expressive, and the cultural-linguistic, the latter being the theory he develops and proposes. The first of these approaches, the cognitive-propositional approach, "emphasizes the cognitive aspects of religion and stresses the ways in which church doctrines function as informative propositions or truth claims about objective realities. Religions are thus thought of as similar to philosophy or science as these were classically conceived."[5] Charles Hodge's three-volume *Systematic Theology* serves as an example of this approach.[6] The second of these, the experiential-expressive approach, "focuses on . . . the 'experiential-expressive' dimension of religion, and it interprets doctrines as noninformative and nondiscursive symbols of inner feelings, attitudes, or existential orientations."[7] One can find a prime example of this approach in Friedrich Schleiermacher's *The Christian Faith*.[8] Lindbeck notes that several thinkers have attempted to reconcile these two approaches to doctrine, the most notable being Karl Rahner and Bernard Lonergan; however, these have been unsuccessful.[9] He then begins to develop his cultural-linguistic approach to doctrine.

According to Lindbeck, doctrine functions in religious communities in the same way that grammar functions in a linguistic community:

---

4. Barth, *Church Dogmatics I*, 3.
5. Lindbeck, *The Nature of Doctrine*, 2.
6. See Hodge, *Systematic Theology*.
7. Lindbeck, *Nature of Doctrine*, 2.
8. Schleiermacher, *The Christian Faith*.
9. Lindbeck, *Nature of Doctrine*, 2. See also Rahner, *Foundations of Christian Faith*; and Lonergan, *Method in Theology*.

> The function of church doctrines that becomes most prominent in this perspective is their use, not as expressive symbols or as truth claims, but as communally authoritative rules of discourse, attitude, and action. This general way of conceptualizing religion will be called in what follows a 'cultural–linguistic' approach, and the implied view of church doctrine will be referred to as a 'regulative' or 'rule' theory.[10]

Doctrine does not provide the content of what is said; instead, it provides the grammar that structures what is said. In other words, rather than being the content of faith, doctrine serves as the structuring mechanism of faith. He continues, "Doctrines regulate truth claims by excluding some and permitting others, but the logic of their communally authoritative use hinders or prevents them from specifying positively what is to be affirmed."[11] Doctrine provides faith with its shape rather than its content. Lindbeck also notes that grammar does not have a truth–value and that grammars vary amongst linguistic communities or cultures. As such, each culture determines its own grammar, and one culture's grammar is not more or less true than that of another. Hence Lindbeck refers to his approach as *cultural–linguistic*.

Lindbeck rightly points out the regulative role of doctrine. Approaches that emphasize the propositional nature of doctrine while neglecting its regulative nature are unsatisfactory. Likewise, the experiential–expressive approach is dissatisfactory due to its neglect of communal authority in favor of emphasizing the role of the individual undergoing the experience. At the same time, however, Lindbeck's approach seems to create more problems than it solves. First, if doctrine does not provide faith with its content, then what is the content of faith? Lindbeck is unclear on this point. Second, if doctrine serves only to structure faith, then what can be said concerning the truth–value of faith or its doctrine? If doctrine is merely the grammar of faith, then it ultimately fails to say anything.[12]

Lindbeck is a figure in theological prolegomena who contemporary theologians cannot ignore. Though there are problems with his cultural–linguistic theory of doctrine, he has been monumental in contemporary understandings of doctrine. However, several critics have engaged

---

10. Lindbeck, *Nature of Doctrine*, 4.
11. Lindbeck, *Nature of Doctrine*, 5.
12. For more critiques on Lindbeck's project, see McGrath, *Science of God*, 101–5.

Lindbeck's work, especially from the Evangelical community.[13] Not all of these critics are completely negative concerning his work; there are some who sympathize with certain elements of his project.

Kevin Vanhoozer's Theodramatic Approach

Kevin Vanhoozer is one who, while having qualms with the majority of the cultural-linguistic approach, is able to sympathize with several of Lindbeck's concerns.[14] While concerned with the diminished role of Scripture in Lindbeck's project, Vanhoozer affirms that doctrine is something that should have behavioral implications in the life of the believer.[15] Doctrine is something that is performed as well as believed. As a result, Vanhoozer argues for a *canonical-linguistic* approach to doctrine as opposed to Lindbeck's *cultural-linguistic* approach. He offers the model of *drama* as a model for doing doctrine.

Vanhoozer divides the drama of redemption, which he calls the theodrama, into five acts:

> Doctrine helps the church understand where it has been 'thrown' and what role it is to play there. The church now lives between the times (of Jesus' first and second comings), between the acts of a divine drama of redemption. Each act of the play is set in motion by an act of God. The first act is creation (Genesis 1–3), the setting for everything else that follows. Act 2 (beginning from Genesis 12 and running through the rest of the Old Testament) concerns God's election, rejection, and restoration of Israel. The third pivotal and climactic act is Jesus: God's definitive Word/Act. Act 4 begins with the risen Christ sending his Spirit to create the church. The fifth and final act is the eschaton, the consummation of all things, and the consummation of God's relationship with Israel and the church. The church lives at present between the definitive event of Jesus and the concluding event of the eschaton, poised between memory and hope.[16]

---

13. Not all evangelicals are critics of Lindbeck's cultural-linguistic approach to doctrine. Though he has some reserves, Stanley Grenz is one who has been an advocate for Lindbeck's approach within Evangelicalism. See Grenz, *Theology for the Community of God*, 1–25; and Grenz, *Renewing the Center*.
14. Vanhoozer, *Drama of Doctrine*.
15. Vanhoozer, *Drama of Doctrine*, 10–12.
16. Vanhoozer, *Drama of Doctrine*, 2–3.

Doctrine informs the church on how to be the church as it waits for Act 5. Vanhoozer defines doctrine as "the reward that faith finds at the end of its search for the meaning of the apostolic testimony to what God was doing in the event of Jesus Christ."[17] As such, doctrine does have a cognitive-propositional dimension to its nature, and one derives these propositions from the Bible. Whereas Lindbeck grounded doctrine in linguistic communities, or cultures, Vanhoozer grounds doctrine in the biblical canon itself, hence the name *canonical-linguistic*. He states, "The *canonical*-linguistic approach to be put forward in the present book has much in common with its cultural-linguistic cousin. Both agree that meaning and truth are related closely to language use; however, the canonical-linguistic approach maintains that the normative use is ultimately not that of ecclesial *culture* but of the biblical *canon*."[18] In this sense, Vanhoozer's proposal is *postconservative* whereas Lindbeck's is *postliberal*.[19]

After giving many pages to the discussion of the nature of doctrine, Vanhoozer turns his attention to doctrinal development. He states, "It is one thing to define the *nature* of doctrine, quite another to formulate actual doctrines. It is often neither simple nor straightforward to decide just what constitutes a 'fitting' participation in the drama of redemption. . . . Moreover, the drama of redemption is, in some sense, ongoing."[20] He further states, "Present-day Christians find themselves stretched between two poles: we are audience to the historical drama and participants in its ongoing development."[21] Since the theo-drama continues, doctrine must also continue. Doctrine must develop. Vanhoozer writes, "To participate in the drama rightly, it is necessary that our speech and action fit with Scripture *and* with our concrete situation. Doctrine's direction must therefore be susceptible of fresh appropriations in new cultural-historical settings."[22] How does one know whether the church is developing doctrine properly? This question is where Scripture, the "script" of the theo-drama, comes into play. Since Scripture serves as the script for the theo-drama then it serves as the norm by which the church checks its performance as it awaits Act 5, i.e., the eschaton. As one better knows the Script(ure), she is better

---

17. Vanhoozer, *Drama of Doctrine*, 4.
18. Vanhoozer, *Drama of Doctrine*, 16.
19. Vanhoozer, *Drama of Doctrine*, 278–91.
20. Vanhoozer, *Drama of Doctrine*, 110–11.
21. Vanhoozer, *Drama of Doctrine*, 111.
22. Vanhoozer, *Drama of Doctrine*, 111.

equipped to perform her role in the drama of redemption, which includes the development of doctrine.

Anthony Thiselton's Hermeneutical Approach

Throughout the course of its history, the Christian religion has prioritized its doctrine. Hence the early Christians formulated confessions of faith and creeds. In *The Hermeneutics of Doctrine*, Anthony Thiselton notes the role these confessions of faith and creeds play in historic Christianity.[23] Confessions of faith and creeds are formalized statements of belief. Thiselton, here, adopts for a *dispositional* account of belief, namely that proposed by H. H. Price:

> When we say of someone, 'he believes the proposition', it is held that we are making a dispositional statement about him, and that is equivalent to a series of conditional statements describing what he *would* be likely to say or do or feel if such and such circumstances were to arise. For example, he would assert the proposition (aloud or privately to himself) if he heard someone else denying it or expressing doubt of it. . . . If circumstances were to arise in which it made a practical difference whether *p* was true or false, he would act as if it were true. If *p* were falsified he would be surprised, and he would feel no surprise if it were verified.[24]

One demonstrates what she believes by her actions. When one's actions do not correspond to her alleged beliefs, then she can be accused of non-belief or half-belief.[25] These behaviors are not merely private behaviors; rather, they are corporate, or public, behaviors. Thiselton writes, "Christian doctrine is the communal endorsement and transmission of such belief, as expressed in life, worship, and action."[26] When Christians make a confession of faith, they are making what J. L. Austin refers to as a *performative utterance*.[27] Through their confession, Christians commit themselves to

23. Thiselton, *Hermeneutics of Doctrine*, 19–42.
24. Price, *Belief*, 20.
25. According to Price, *half-belief* is when an individual's actions correspond to her alleged beliefs only when she deems it beneficial for herself. See Price, *Belief*, 302–14.
26. Thiselton, *Hermeneutics of Doctrine*, 34.
27. According to Austin's Speech Act Theory, utterances fall into two primary categories: constative utterances and performative utterances. Constative utterances function primarily as *descriptive* utterances in that they primarily aim at description. The aim in making a descriptive utterance is to get one's words to match the world, and the aim in

certain patterns of behavior and not others. Being formalized confessions of faith, creeds have the same performative character. The doctrines contained in these confessions of faith, therefore, possess a performative nature as well, namely that of self-involvement. Since doctrine is a community activity, the formation of doctrine can be seen as a communal performative of self-involvement. When the church develops her teaching and beliefs concerning God, she commits herself to the patterns of behavior implicated by these beliefs. As this commitment is the case, doctrine and ethics are closely connected. Beliefs and behaviors that fall outside those put forth by the Christian community are not therefore described as *Christian*. One can see here the boundary-making role of doctrine, especially those doctrines espoused in confessions of faith and creeds.

Christian doctrine, however, is not static; rather, it develops throughout the course of history. As Thiselton notes, doctrine develops in order to address what Hans-Georg Gadamer refers to as *questions that arise*.[28] Following R. G. Collingwood, Gadamer held that one understands a text only when she understands the questions that it answers, for all texts serve as an answer to a question, though this need not necessarily be a single question.[29] Thiselton writes, "The process of understanding concerns not one question or even one set of questions, but those from an earlier context in which the statement or subject matter arose *as well as* questions that emerge from within *present* horizons of understanding."[30] These questions arise from historical situations; they are not abstract problems. For example, the early Christians worshipped Jesus as God, though they knew that there was only one true God worthy of worship, namely YHWH. Jesus, therefore, must be God; but how can he and YHWH both be God if he, God, is one? They are clearly distinct persons, as Jesus himself prayed to YHWH; however, it is possible that they share the same being, i.e., *homoousios*. As a result of these questions that arose, Christologies such as that presented in the Nicene Creed were developed. This instance is a clear case of the hermeneutic nature of doctrinal development.

---

making a performative utterance is in getting the world to match one's words. A promise is an example of a performative. When one makes a promise, she commits herself to certain patterns of behavior and not others. She aims to make her world match her words. See Austin, *How to Do Things with Word*.

28. Thiselton, *Hermeneutics of Doctrine*, 3. See also Gadamer, *Truth and Method*, 363.
29. Gadamer, *Truth and Method*, 363–64. See also Collingwood, *An Autobiography*.
30. Thiselton, *Hermeneutics of Doctrine*, 4.

Doctrines develop as Christians further understand the meaning of God's self-revelation in the person of Jesus of Nazareth as well as Holy Scripture. Jesus and Scripture shed light on the questions of meaning as they pertain to individuals, communities, and the totality of creation. Doctrines develop because of new and further understanding. In Gadamerian terminology, doctrines develop as there are new fusions of horizons. As the horizon of the present continues to engage the horizon of the past, there will continue to be new fusions of these horizons. As these horizons continue to fuse, understanding grows and develops. As such, doctrinal development is clearly a hermeneutic phenomenon.[31]

Alister McGrath's Scientific Approach

McGrath discusses theory and theory formation in volume three of *A Scientific Theology*. In this three-volume work, he has sought to bring insights from the methods of the natural sciences to bear on the methods for theology, claiming that the natural sciences are the prime choice to be the handmaiden of theology. In volume one, he demonstrates that the scientific concept of *nature* is best understood as *creation* for the scientific theologian, and in volume two he argues for the epistemological approach known as *critical realism* for theology. He turns his attention to theory in volume three. McGrath defines *theory* as "an attempt to render in words the great wonders and mysteries of faith."[32] He begins by giving attention to the debate amongst scientists as to whether or not the scientific community should seek to develop theories at all.[33] There are those, such as the romanticists, who argue that theory is overly reductionist in nature and diminishes one's understanding of particulars as a result. Reductionism, however, need not be the case. As McGrath shows, scientists must offer theories as a means of explaining the phenomena of reality. Developing theories is inevitable. The problem of theory, however, is not in its nature but in its use.[34] McGrath agrees that theory is reductionist by nature, but this need not make theorizing illegitimate:

---

31. See also Putman, "Postcanonical Doctrinal Development as Hermeneutical Phenomenon;" Putman, *In Defense of Doctrine*.
32. McGrath, *Theory*, 3.
33. McGrath, *Theory*, 29–42.
34. McGrath, *Theory*, 34.

> Granted that there is at least some substance to the Romantic agenda, it is entirely proper to make two points in refutation of their concerns. First, the scientific quest for theories is not undertaken by discarding the phenomena once a theoretical explanation has been derived. . . . Second, the Romantic refusal to reflect *theoretically* on what they observed in nature must ultimately be regarded as intellectually indefensible.[35]

Again, the primary concern is that one will prioritize theories over particulars. McGrath shows, however, that reductionism is not a necessary implication of theory development.

McGrath goes on to discuss "theory and the redemption of particulars."[36] The temptation for one to allow particulars to be determined a priori by theories always exists. A scientific theology, however, seeks to avoid this, and instead allows particulars to determine theories; it is an a posteriori approach to theory development.[37] He states, "Theory exists in a highly ambivalent relation to particulars. On the one hand, it owes its existence to them; on the other, they perpetually threaten to undermine or over throw it. . . . The same facts that seem to disconfirm a theory one day may confirm it the next."[38]

According to McGrath, *doctrines* function as theological theories.[39] As the church continues to engage the particulars of God's revelation in Jesus and Scripture, she forms theories, or doctrines, as a means of understanding and explaining these particulars. In this sense, the development of theories is both scientific and hermeneutic.[40] These doctrines, being theories, are not static or infallible; rather, they are always subject to correction. This understanding of theory development, being grounded in critical realism, presupposes fallibilism, as discussed above in chapter four. The particulars that theories seek to make sense of must be the guiding factor in theory development. Translated to doctrinal development, doctrines must allow the particulars of revelation be the guiding factor in developing doctrine.

Since a scientific theology makes the particulars of revelation the guiding factor in doctrinal development, the type of reasoning in use here

---

35. McGrath, *Theory*, 35.
36. McGrath, *Theory*, 38.
37. McGrath, *Theory*, 39.
38. McGrath, *Theory*, 39.
39. McGrath, *Theory*, 24.
40. See Thiselton, *Hermeneutics of Doctrine*, 145–73.

is that of abduction.[41] As one encounters the particulars of God's revelation, she conjectures hypotheses as a means of explaining them. Doctrines are instances of conjectured hypotheses and theories that seek to make sense of the particulars of revelation. As such, they are fallible and subject to potential correction. In the same way that theories are proposed and accepted by the scientific community, doctrines are proposed and accepted by the theological community, i.e., the church.[42]

The community of faith, the church, plays an important role in doctrinal development in the same way the scientific community plays an important role in the development of scientific theories. As scientists examine particular phenomena and propose theories as a means of explanation, these theories are subject to criticism by the wider scientific community. One scientist might conjecture a theory concerning a certain phenomenon, and another might conduct an experiment to test the theory. This experiment has the potential either to verify or falsify the theory or hypothesis proposed. Not only this, but others in the wider scientific community are able to provide criticism of the proposed theory as well. They might know something from their own scientific field with a higher degree of certainty that has the potential to overturn the proposed theory. The point here is that subjects do not practice science in individual autonomy but within the boundaries of a community. In the same way, subjects do not develop doctrine in individual autonomy but within the boundaries of the theological community. A systematic theologian might propose a new understanding of a doctrine, say the doctrine of the work of Christ, and this doctrine is subject to the criticism of the wider theological community. A biblical theologian, for example might have insights that overthrow or correct the proposed doctrine of the systematic theologian. Since all doctrines are instances of abduction, they are fallible and subject to criticism by the theological community.

As one can see, the approaches to the nature and development of doctrine put forth by Thiselton, Vanhoozer, and McGrath work well together. Each highlights a unique dimension of the problem of doctrinal development: Thiselton highlights the hermeneutic dimension, Vanhoozer the dramatic dimension, and McGrath the scientific dimension. None of these precludes the others, and each, in some sense, seems to presuppose the others. Each of these understandings of doctrine and development works

41. McGrath, *Theory*, 154.
42. McGrath, *Theory*, 3.

well with Umberto Eco's model encyclopedia. Eco's encyclopedia naturally lends itself to the problem of doctrinal development and allows for the approaches proposed by Thiselton, Vanhoozer, and McGrath.

THE MODEL ENCYCLOPEDIA AND DOCTRINAL DEVELOPMENT

How might Eco's model encyclopedia lend itself to doctrinal development? One will notice here that there are multiple similarities as to how the encyclopedia lends itself to doctrinal development as it lends itself to the hermeneutic nature of theology. As demonstrated in chapter three and repeated in following chapters, the model encyclopedia functions as a network of signs. All signs have expression and content planes. According to Eco, the meaning of a sign is a cultural unit. The most basic unit of content, or meaning, is a sememe. Sememes, as well as all contents, are determined by their connections and interconnections with all other sememes and contents. Encyclopedias are not purely subjective; rather, they are a communal phenomenon. One's encyclopedia is made up of all the contents she possesses. A local encyclopedia contains all of the knowledge possessed by any given culture. When someone speaks, she presupposes the totality of her local encyclopedia as well as the maximal encyclopedia. One should remember also that no individual or culture has access to the maximal encyclopedia, and the maximal encyclopedia serves a regulative role. The model encyclopedia is represented best by the rhizomatic labyrinth, in which all nodes are connected and interconnected.

Of special significance here is Eco's discussion concerning the boundaries of the model encyclopedia. According to him, the model encyclopedia has no set boundaries. As a result, it is ever growing and developing. New expressions and contents are developing constantly within languages. New connections and interconnections, as a result, are constantly being formed. The way one sign relates to the rest might change, as these connections can shift to different nodes. The encyclopedia, in other words, undergoes a form of restructuring. Not only this, but as new expressions are developed and as contents are assigned to them, the labyrinth of the encyclopedia continues to grow. This boundaryless nature of the model encyclopedia allows for and encourages doctrinal development.

Doctrines function as signs, possessing content planes. The contents of doctrines are determined by their connections and interconnections with all other doctrines. Since the model encyclopedia, which is being appropriated as a model for theology, is without boundaries, doctrine is able to develop. One is able to add new doctrinal expressions and contents to her local encyclopedia as she better understands the particulars of God's revelation. As new doctrinal expressions are added to the doctrinal encyclopedia, new connections and interconnections are introduced. As a result, the contents of all other doctrines change as well, since the contents are determined by their connections and interconnections with all other doctrinal expressions. Since all expressions and their contents, including those of doctrine, presuppose the totality of expressions and contents within the encyclopedia, then those of new additions are presupposed as well. In other words, suppose a new doctrinal expression is formulated and a content unit is assigned to it. Whenever one makes the doctrinal expression, all of the others within the encyclopedia are presupposed in the utterance. Likewise, if one were to make a doctrinal expression that exists already in the encyclopedia, then even this new doctrinal expression is presupposed in the utterance. As such, the content of all the doctrines within the encyclopedia alter because the new addition contributes to the contents of all the others.

Eco's model encyclopedia also lends itself to Vanhoozer's dramatic approach to doctrinal development.[43] According to Vanhoozer, doctrine develops as the church learns how to improvise her role in the drama of redemption as it moves from Act Four to Act Five. In the *Drama of Doctrine*, he notes how many postmodern thinkers have rejected foundationalism in favor of a form of coherentism; they have exchanged the edifice of belief for a web of belief. I have discussed already this above in chapter four, as well as the weaknesses that come with models of the web of belief, such as the one proposed by Willard V. O. Quine. In exchange, I have proposed a modified web of belief, one that has central, or core, beliefs that hold the rest of the web together. Vanhoozer offers a similar model, namely that of a map.[44] Beliefs and propositions function as locations on a map where Scripture functions as the compass that tells one how to navigate the map. Vanhoozer

---

43. Since Lindbeck's postliberal approach was found wanting, I have not set out to demonstrate how it might work with the model encyclopedia. Instead, I have opted only to show how Vanhoozer's dramatic approach appears as a better alternative to Lindbeck's approach.

44. Vanhoozer, *Drama of Doctrine*, 295–301. Vanhoozer provides the following clarifying statement: "A map is an interpretative framework, not a foundation of basic facts. The proof: there is no such thing as a universal, all-purpose map" (296).

states, "A map is a text, a combination of words and images governed by a set of conventions that aim to communicate a certain sense of place. Fully to understand a map requires one to be able to use it in the way it was intended, and this means in turn being conversant with its conventions."[45] As one better understands Scripture, she better knows how to navigate this map. As she is able to navigate this map better, she is able to navigate better her place in reality.

Vanhoozer's metaphor of the map and Eco's model encyclopedia fit well together. According to Vanhoozer, as one better understands the "script" of the drama of redemption provided by Scripture, she is able to perform better her role in this theo–drama. This concept translates well into Eco's model encyclopedia. As one better understands the encyclopedia of Scripture, she is able to navigate her own encyclopedia better, as well is she able to develop new connections and interconnections between the two. The key here is one's ability to know the encyclopedia of Scripture. In a drama, the script tells the actors how to perform, as well does it provide one with the inference clues needed to improvise. As the church awaits Act Five of the theo–drama, she must learn to improvise her way in the drama of redemption. Doctrinal development is an instance of this improvisation. If one is going to develop new doctrinal expressions and contents adequately, she must know adequately the encyclopedia of Scripture, i.e., she must adequately know the script of the theo–drama. If one is going to make useful abductions in order to navigate better the model encyclopedia, she must adequately know the local encyclopedias necessary, namely those of Scripture and its contexts.

Eco's model encyclopedia lends itself to Thiselton's hermeneutic approach to doctrinal development. As discussed above, according to Thiselton, doctrine develops as a result of new questions that arise and demand answers. These questions arise within a given local encyclopedia, which, as discussed in chapter five above, forms one's horizon of understanding. One should recall that, according to Gadamer, one's horizon is not fixed or static; rather, it continues to move as the one who bears it moves. As the interpreter's present horizon of understanding continues to grow, new fusions of the horizons of the past and the present come about. This phenomenon translates into Eco's semiotic encyclopedia in the following way: as one's local encyclopedia continues to grow and develop, new connections and interconnections develop as she engages with

---

45. Vanhoozer, *Drama of Doctrine*, 296.

the encyclopedia of Scripture. As a result, new abductions must occur in order for one to navigate the reconfigured and enlarged encyclopedia. One should recall that, according to Eco, abduction is the way in which one gropes her way through the labyrinth of the encyclopedia. As new doctrinal expressions and their contents are added to the encyclopedia, new connections and interconnections come about as well. As a result, one must learn to navigate these new corridors of content, which occurs via abduction.

Finally, Eco's model encyclopedia lends itself to McGrath's scientific approach to doctrinal development as well. According to McGrath, doctrines function for Christian theology as theories function for the natural sciences. As one encounters the particulars of reality, namely specific patterns, she proposes theories as a way of making sense of them. Theories are much like hypotheses but with experiments and observations strengthening them. In the natural sciences, theories are developed a posteriori rather than a priori. Scientific theology, likewise, attempts to develop doctrine a posteriori.

Eco's semiotics can shed some light on the nature of theory as well. Theories function as signs, containing expression planes and content planes. As such, the content of a theory is determined by its connections and interconnections with all other scientific knowledge and theories. As such, each theory presupposes the totality of theories contained by the scientific encyclopedia. These new theory expressions and their contents, being additions to the scientific encyclopedia, require one to make new abductions as a means of navigating the labyrinth.

As shown above, theories are instances of abduction. In other words, new theories develop via abductive reasoning. As one encounters the particulars of reality, she conjectures hypotheses and theories that make these particulars understandable and explainable. As one encounters new phenomena in reality, she formulates new expressions to identify them, and she assigns contents to these expressions. This assigning of expressions and contents itself is an exercise in abduction. As these new doctrinal theories are added to the encyclopedia, new connection and interconnections are made within the encyclopedia, resulting in the need for new ways of navigating the encyclopedia.

Another important correlation between McGrath's scientific theology and Eco's encyclopedia is the role of the community. McGrath notes that scientists do not work in individual autonomy; rather, they work in community with each other. The wealth of knowledge that makes up the scientific encyclopedia is a shared encyclopedia. The terminology, the knowledge, the theories, indeed, all scientific contents are encompassed within this encyclopedia, and this encyclopedia is shared with the totality of the scientific community. The same is the case with theology and doctrine. One does not develop doctrine in autonomy, and her doctrinal encyclopedia is a shared encyclopedia. This doctrinal encyclopedia and all of its contents are shared with the rest of the theological community, i.e., the church. As a result, each attempt at doctrinal development is subject to criticism. As Eco notes about the model encyclopedia, if a connector or interconnector is deemed unfit, then the community can choose to do away with it. As such, doctrinal development presupposes a form of fallibism. New doctrines are always subjected to Scripture and the church for acceptance or rejection in the same way that new expressions and their contents are subjected to linguistic communities, either for acceptance or rejection.

CONCLUSION

This chapter has demonstrated that Umberto Eco's model encyclopedia naturally lends itself to doctrinal development. The model encyclopedia is an important notion for doctrinal development in three ways. First, it understands doctrine to function semiotically, i.e., it sees doctrines as signs composed of expressions and contents. Second, it allows for doctrine to develop due to its lack of boundaries. Third, it allows specific traditions to develop doctrine from within their own local encyclopedias. A brief discussion on the nature of doctrine and the problem of development was provided before engaging different understandings of the nature of doctrine and approaches to doctrinal development. These different understandings and approaches come from the works of Anthony Thiselton, George Lindbeck, Kevin Vanhoozer, and Alister McGrath. Lindbeck was discussed primarily as the catalyst for a new understanding of the nature of doctrine; however, his cultural–linguistic approach ultimately was found wanting. After providing brief discussions on the approaches to doctrinal development by Thiselton, Vanhoozer, and McGrath, I demonstrated that Eco's model encyclopedia lends itself to all three of these approaches: the hermeneutic, the dramatic, and the scientific. How Eco's model encyclopedia lends itself to doctrinal development was the third and final test case for appropriating it as a model for theology to follow. Eco's encyclopedia has been demonstrated to allow not only for the continuance of doctrinal development, but its boundaryless nature encourages this development. The model encyclopedia, therefore, passes this final test case.

Conclusion

This monograph has been an interdisciplinary endeavor in constructive theology seeking to bring semiotics and systematic theology into dialogue with one another. Theologians have dialogued with multiple branches of philosophy throughout history in order to discover languages and thought categories that can help them clearly articulate Christian doctrine. In doing so, however, the majority of theologians have overlooked the discipline of semiotics, the science and study of signs and signification. This oversight is not altogether surprising, seeing that semiotics is a relatively new discipline. Though philosophers since Plato and Aristotle have discussed language and signification, semiotics did not come into its own until the late nineteenth century.

The research problem this book addressed was the lack of dialogue between theology and semiotics. Since all thinking and inquiry, including that of theology, takes place through language, a conventional sign system, semiotics has much to offer theology concerning its nature and task. I sought to contribute to the solution of this problem by showing the usefulness of a concept from the work of a major semiotician for theology, namely the model encyclopedia of Umberto Eco. How might Umberto Eco's semiotic project aid systematic theologians in matters pertaining to theological prolegomena? The research thesis was that Eco's model encyclopedia could provide a model for systematic theology, one that would be especially useful concerning matters of theological prolegomena. I then argued that Eco's model encyclopedia could provide an adequate model for theology due to its ability to facilitate contemporary endeavors in theological epistemology, the hermeneutic nature of theology, and doctrinal development. The methodology was simple: after providing an overview of the history of semiotics and an overview of Eco's semiotic project, I would provide a detailed explication of the model encyclopedia, and then I would show its usefulness for matters pertaining to epistemology, hermeneutics, and doctrinal development in the chapters that followed, thus demonstrating the encyclopedia's adequacy as a model for theology.

Chapter one gave a brief history of semiotics in order to provide the appropriate context for understanding Eco's semiotics. While noting the discussions on signs and signification in ancient and medieval thinkers, this chapter focused on modern semitoticians from Ferdinand de Saussure to Charles Sanders Peirce. Saussure, on the one hand, argued that signs were dyads comprised of a signifier and a signified. Peirce, on the other hand, claimed that signs were triads comprised of a representamen (signifier), an interpretant (signified), and the object. The former focused primarily on conventional signs, while the latter focused on both natural and conventional signs. Structuralism, poststructuralism, and deconstruction arose from thinkers adopting Saussure's approach to semiology, while pansemiotics and zoosemiotics arose from thinkers following Peirce's project. Eco, while primarily Peircean in his understanding of semiosis, adopts a structrualist methodology for his own semiotics.

Chapter two provided an overview of Eco's semiotic project. He developed the foundation of his semiotics in *A Theory of Semiotics* and showed the implications of *Theory* in the works that followed. In *The Role of the Reader*, he applied insights from *Theory* to textual interpretation and textual semiotics. He likewise applies semiotics to the philosophy of language in *Semiotics and the Philosophy of Language*. In *The Limits of Interpretation*, Eco revisits textual interpretation and the role of semiotics in reading in order to respond against deconstructionists. Though he argues for the multivalence of meaning in texts, he does not affirm that texts have an unlimited number of potential meanings. Eco turns his attention to cognition and language in *Kant and the Platypus*. These works are not the only works in which Eco makes recourse to semiotics, but they are his most important works on the subject. This chapter was necessary to provide the appropriate context for discussing the model encyclopedia, which finds a place in all five of Eco's aforementioned works.

I provided a detailed explication of Eco's model encyclopedia in chapter three. Rather than constructing a systematic treatment of this topic, I approached it in a chronological manner. Eco's most thorough treatments of the model encyclopedia appear in *Semiotics and the Philosophy of Language* and his essay "From the Tree to the Labyrinth." I summarized this concept by making recourse to Eco's novel *The Name of the Rose*, in which the labyrinthine library represents the model encyclopedia. Whereas the Porphyrian Tree best represents the model dictionary, the labyrinth, namely the rhizome, best represents the model encyclopedia. This labyrinth is without boundaries and is ever growing. The contents for expressions are grounded in their connections and interconnections with all other expressions and contents. Eco refers to these basic content units as sememes, and one navigates the encyclopedia via abduction.

In chapter four, I showed the usefulness of Eco's model encyclopedia for theological epistemology. The model encyclopedia resembles the web of belief of coherentism more so than the edifice, or chain, of belief of classical foundationalism. However, it does not necessitate one over the other. I provided my own understanding of the structures of belief in this chapter, namely as a web of belief that has more foundational beliefs at its core. I refer to these as core beliefs. This model, which works well with Eco's model encyclopedia, represents a postfoundationalist understanding of epistemology. Being postfoundational, the model encyclopedia presupposes fallibilism and lends itself to the philosophy of science known as critical realism, which theologians such as Alister McGrath have shown to be useful for theology.

I brought Eco's model encyclopedia into dialogue with the hermeneutic nature of theology in chapter five. After showing that hermeneutics has become the philosophy of human understanding rather than simply the science of interpreting written texts, I show how theologians such as Wolfhart Pannenberg and Anthony Thiselton have demonstrated the hermeneutic nature of theology. Eco's model encyclopedia lends itself to the hermeneutic nature of theology in the following ways. First, the notion of *horizons of understanding*, made popular by Gadamer, finds a parallel in Eco's *local encyclopedia*. A local encyclopedia makes up one's horizon. I then showed that all hermeneutical endeavors, namely interpretation, understanding, and explanation, all rely on abductive reasoning. All hermeneutic endeavors, including theological endeavors, presuppose and rely on the model encyclopedia.

Chapter six showed the usefulness of the model encyclopedia for doctrinal development. More specifically, I showed how the model encyclopedia explains doctrinal development and how it allows for doctrine to continue to be developed. As discussed in chapter six, doctrines are types of signs, having expressions and contents. These contents, in the model encyclopedia, are determined by their connections and interconnections with all other expressions and contents. I noted the contributions of Thiselton, Vanhoozer, and McGrath in this chapter concerning the hermeneutic, theo-dramatic, and scientific natures of development. Doctrinal development, in semiotic terms, can be seen as the exploration from one local encyclopedia into a new local encyclopedia, resulting in new connections and interconnections between them. The model encyclopedia allows not only for doctrinal development but also encourages it via its boundaryless nature. Since doctrines develop in the same way that theories develop in science, they engage in the process of abduction. Doctrinal development, presupposing the model encyclopedia, is an abductive process.

Chapters four, five, and six served as test cases for my thesis. Chapter four demonstrated the model encyclopedia's ability to facilitate matters of epistemology; chapter five demonstrated the encyclopedia's ability to facilitate the hermeneutic nature of theology; and chapter six demonstrated its ability to facilitate and advance doctrinal development. As a result, I affirm that Eco's model encyclopedia can serve as an adequate model for theology to follow. Not only does it provide helpful descriptions of the nature and task of theology, but it also provides normative insights for the future of theology, specifically as it pertains to doctrinal development. As such, I have contributed to the solution of the aforementioned research problem: the lack of dialogue between theology and semiotics.

In summary, all experience of reality, especially thinking, is mediated to the thinking subject via sign systems. As such, semiotics can provide useful categories for understanding human experience and cognition. Since all thinking takes place via sign systems, all thinking presupposes the model encyclopedia. Not only thinking, but all speaking makes this presupposition as well. Theology, being a cognitive endeavor, does not avoid this phenomenon. All understanding, including the understanding of God and Scripture, presupposes the model encyclopedia. Not only does one think and understand from the locale of her own local encyclopedia, but she presupposes the maximal encyclopedia when making theological truth claims. Since no theologian has access to the maximal encyclopedia, which contains everything that has ever been thought or spoken, all of her truth claims are provisional, with the exception of things necessarily known, i.e., a triangle has three sides, the law of noncontradiction, etc.

160 \\ Conclusion

Not only this, but since all thinking occurs via signs, doctrines function as signs as well. Doctrines, being signs, are made up of expressions and contents, and these contents are determined by their relationships to all of the other signs in the sign system, or local encyclopedia. The content of a doctrine, therefore, is determined by its relationships to all of the other doctrines within its theological system, a type of local encyclopedia. As doctrines develop, new contents are added to the encyclopedia, and new connections and interconnections are added between its preexisting contents. The model encyclopedia, in summary, functions as both a descriptive and normative model for theology.

Bibliography

Aichele, George. *Sign, Text, Scripture: Semiotics and the Bible*. Sheffield: Sheffield, 1997.
Alkier, Stefan. "Intertextuality and the Semiotics of Biblical Texts." In *Reading the Bible Intertextually*, edited by Richard B. Hays, Stefan Alkier, and Leroy A. Huizenga, 3–21. Waco, TX: Baylor University Press, 2008.
———. "New Testament Studies on the Basis of Categorical Semiotics." In *Reading the Bible Intertextually*, edited by Richard B. Hays, Stefan Alkier, and Leroy A. Huizenga, 223–48. Waco, TX: Baylor University Press, 2008.
———. *The Reality of the Resurrection: The New Testament Witness*. Translated by Leroy A. Huizenga. Waco, TX: Baylor University Press, 2013.
———. *Wunder und Wirklichkeit in den Briefen des Apostels Paulus*. Tübingen: Mohr Siebeck, 2001.
Almeder, Robert. *The Philosophy of Charles S. Peirce: A Critical Introduction*. Totowa: Rowman and Littlefield, 1980.
Apel, Karl-Otto. *Charles S. Peirce: From Pragmatism to Pragmaticism*. Translated by John Michael Krois. Amherst: University of Massachusetts Press, 1981.
Aristotle, *De Interpretatione*. In *The Complete Works of Aristotle*, vol.1, edited by Jonathan Barnes, 25–38. Princeton: Princeton University Press, 1984.
———. *Posterior Analytics*. In *The Complete Works of Aristotle*, vol.1, edited by Jonathan Barnes, 114–66. Princeton: Princeton University Press, 1984.
Augustine, St. *On Christian Teaching*. Translated by R. P. H. Green. Oxford: Oxford University Press, 1997.
Austin, J. L. *How to Do Things with Words* 2nd ed. Cambridge: Harvard University Press, 1975.
Ayer, Alfred Jules. *Language, Truth, and Logic* 2nd ed. New York: Dover, 1952.
Ayim, Maryann. "Abduction." In *Encyclopedic Dictionary of Semiotics: A-M*, edited by Thomas A. Sebeok and Marcel Danesi, 1–2. 3rd ed. Berlin: De Gruyter Mouton, 2010.
Bains, Paul. *The Primacy of Semiosis: An Ontology of Relations*. Toronto: University of Toronto Press, 2006.
Bakhtin, Mikhail Mikhailovich. *The Dialogic Imagination*. Edited by Michael Holquist. Translated by Caryl Emerson and Michael Holquist. Austin: University of Texas Press, 1981.

———. *Speech Genres and Other Late Essays*. Edited by Caryl Emerson and Michael Holquist. Translated by Vern McGee. Austin: University of Texas Press, 1986.

Balthasar, Hans Urs von. *Theo-Drama: Theological Dramatic Theory*. 5 Vol. San Francisco: Ignatius, 1988.

Barth, Karl. *Church Dogmatics I.1: The Doctrine of the Word of God*. 2nd ed. Translated by G. W. Bromiley. Edited by G. W. Bromiley and T. F. Torrance. Peabody, MA: Hendrickson, 2010.

Barthes, Roland. *A Barthes Reader*. Edited by Susan Sontag. New York: Barnes and Noble, 2009.

———. *Elements of Semiology*. Translated by Annette Lavers and Colin Smith. New York: Hill and Wang, 1967.

———. *Fashion System*. New York: Hill & Wang, 1983.

———. *S/Z: An Essay*. Translated by Richard Miller. New York: Hill and Wang, 1974.

Bartholomew, Craig G. *Introducing Biblical Hermeneutics: A Comprehensive Framework for Hearing God in Scripture*. Grand Rapids: Baker, 2015.

Bernstein, Richard J. *Perspectives on Peirce: Critical Essays on Charles Sanders Peirce*. New Haven, CT: Yale University Press, 1965.

Bhaskar, Roy. *The Possibility of Naturalism: A Philosophical Critique of the Contemporary Human Sciences*. 3rd ed. London: Routledge, 1998.

———. *A Realist Theory of Science*. London: Verso, 2008.

Billings, J. Todd. *The Word of God for the People of God: An Entryway to the Theological Interpretation of Scripture*. Grand Rapids: Eerdmans, 2010.

Briggs, Richard S. *Words in Action: Speech Act Theory and Biblical Interpretation—Toward a Hermeneutic of Self-Involvement*. New York: T&T Clark, 2001.

Buber, Martin. *I and Thou*. Translated by Ronald Gregor Smith. New York: Scribner Classics, 1986.

Buczynska-Garewicz, Hanna. "Semiotics and Deconstruction." In *Reading Eco: An Anthology*, edited by Rocco Capozzi, 163–72. Bloomington: Indiana University Press, 1997.

Bultmann, Rudolf K. *Existence and Faith: Shorter Writings of Rudolf Bultmann*. Meridian: Meridian, 1960.

———. *Jesus Christ and Mythology*. Upper Saddle River: Prentice Hall, 1958.

———. *New Testament and Mythology and Other Basic Writings*. Edited and translated by Schubert M. Ogden. Philadelphia: Fortress, 1984.

———. *Theology of the New Testament*. Translated by Kendrick Grobel. 2 vols. Waco: Baylor University Press, 2007.

Caesar, Michael. *Umberto Eco: Philosophy, Semiotics, and the Work of Fiction*. Cambridge: Polity, 1999.

Calvin, John. *Institutes of the Christian Religion*. Translated by Henry Beveridge. Peabody: Hendrickson, 2008.

Capozzi, Rocco. "Interpretation and Overinterpretation. The Rights of Texts, Readers and Implied Authors." In *Reading Eco: An Anthology*, edited by Rocco Capozzi, 217–34. Bloomington: Indiana University Press, 1997.

———ed. *Reading Eco: An Anthology*. Bloomington: Indiana University Press, 1997.

Chandler, Daniel. *Semiotics: The Basics*. 2nd ed. London: Routledge, 2007.

Clark, David K. *To Know and Love God: Method for Theology*. Wheaton, IL: Crossway, 2003.

Clarke, D. S. *Principles of Semiotic*. London: Routledge and Kegan Paul, 1987.

Cobley, Paul, and Litza Jansz. *Introducing Semiotics: A Graphic Guide*. London: Icon, 2010.
Collier, Andrew. *Critical Realism: An Introduction to Roy Bhaskar's Philosophy*. London: Verso, 1994.
Congdon, David W. *The God Who Saves: A Dogmatic Sketch*. Eugene, OR: Cascade, 2016.
Corrington, Robert S. *A Semiotic Theory of Theology and Philosophy*. Cambridge: Cambridge University Press, 2000.
Culler, Jonathan. *The Pursuit of Signs: Semiotics, Literature, Deconstruction*. Ithaca, NY: Cornell University Press, 1981.
Danesi, Marcel. *Encyclopedic Dictionary of Semiotics, Media, and Communications*. Toronto: University of Toronto Press, 2000.
———. *Messages and Meanings: An Introduction to Semiotics*. Toronto: Canadian, 1994.
———. *The Quest for Meaning: A Guide to Semiotic Theory and Practice*. Toronto: University of Toronto Press, 2007.
Deely, John. *Basics of Semiotics*. Bloomington: Indiana University Press, 1990.
———. *Four Ages of Understanding: The First Postmodern Survey of Philosophy from Ancient Times to the Turn of the Twentieth Century*. Toronto: University of Toronto Press, 2001.
———. "Looking back on *A Theory of Semiotics*." In *Reading Eco: An Anthology*, edited by Rocco Capozzi, 82–110. Bloomington: Indiana University Press, 1997.
Deledalle, Gerard. *Charles S. Peirce's Philosophy of Signs: Essays in Comparative Semiotics*. Bloomington: Indiana University Press, 2000.
Derrida, Jacques. *Of Grammatology*. Translated by Gayatri Chakravorty Spivak. Baltimore, MD: Johns Hopkins University Press, 2016.
———. *Writing and Difference*. Translated by Alan Bass. Chicago: University of Chicago Press, 1978.
Descartes, René. *A Discourse on the Method*. Translated by Ian Maclean. Oxford: Oxford University Press, 2006.
———. *Meditations on First Philosophy*. Translated by Desmond M. Clarke. New York: Penguin, 2003.
Desogus, Paolo. "The Encyclopedia in Umberto Eco's Semiotics." *Semiotica* 192 (2012) 501–21.
Diller, Kevin. *Theology's Epistemological Dilemma: How Karl Barth and Alvin Plantinga Provide a Unified Response*. Downers Grove: IVP, 2014.
Dilthey, Wilhelm. *Gesammelte Schriften*. 26 vols. Göttingen: Vandenhoeck & Ruprecht, 1914–2005.
Doležel, Lubomir. "The Themata of Eco's Semiotics of Literature." In *Reading Eco: An Anthology*, edited by Rocco Capozzi, 111–20. Bloomington: Indiana University Press, 1997.
Downing, Crystal L. *Changing Signs of Truth: A Christian Introduction to the Semiotics of Communication*. Downers Grove, IL: IVP, 2012.
Dulles, Avery. *The Craft of Theology: From Symbol to System*. New York: Crossroad: 1992.
Eco, Umberto. *The Aesthetics of Chaosmos: The Middle Ages of James Joyce*. Translated by Ellen Esrock. Boston: Harvard University Press, 1989.
———. *The Aesthetics of Thomas Aquinas*. Translated by Hugh Bredin. Cambridge: Harvard University Press, 1988.
———. "An Author and His Interpreters." In *Reading Eco: An Anthology*, edited by Rocco Capozzi, 59–70. Bloomington: Indiana University Press, 1997.

———. *Art and Beauty in the Middle Ages*. Translated by Hugh Bredin. New Haven, CT: Yale University Press, 1986.
———. *Baudolino: A Novel*. Translated by William Weaver. New York: Harcourt, 2000.
———. *The Book of Legendary Lands*. New York: Rizzoli, 2013.
———. *Chronicles of a Liquid Society*. Translated by Richard Dixon. Boston: Harcourt, 2017.
———. *Confessions of a Young Novelist*. Cambridge: Harvard University Press, 2011.
———. *Experiences in Translation*. Translated by Alastair McEwen. Toronto: University of Toronto Press, 2000.
———. *Faith in Fakes: Travels in Hyperreality*. Translated by William Weaver. London: Vintage, 1998.
———. *Five Moral Pieces*. Translated by Alastair McEwen. San Diego, CA: Harcourt, 2001.
———. *Foucault's Pendulum*. Translated by William Weaver. Orlando, FL: Harvest, 2007.
———. *From the Tree to the Labyrinth: Historical Studies on the Sign and Interpretation*. Translated by Anthony Oldcorn. Cambridge: Harvard University Press, 2014.
———. *Kant and the Platypus: Essays on Language and Cognition*. Translated by Alastair McEwen. San Diego, CA: Harcourt, 1999.
———. *The Limits of Interpretation*. Bloomington: Indiana University Press, 1990.
———. *The Role of the Reader: Explorations in the Semiotics of Texts*. Bloomington: Indiana University Press, 1979.
———. *Semiotics and the Philosophy of Language*. Bloomington: Indiana University Press, 1984.
———. *A Theory of Semiotics*. Bloomington: Indiana University Press, 1976.
———. *History of Beauty*. New York: Rizzoli, 2010.
———. "Horns, Hooves, Insteps: Some Hypotheses on Three Types of Abduction." In *The Sign of Three: Dupin, Holmes, Peirce*, edited by Umberto Eco and Thomas A. Sebeok, 198–200. Bloomington: Indiana University Press, 1984.
———. *How to Travel with a Salmon and Other Essays*. Translated by William Weaver. San Diego, CA: Harcourt, 1995.
———. *How to Write a Thesis*. Translated by Caterina Mongiat Farina and Geoff Farina. Cambridge: MIT Press, 2015.
———. *The Infinity of Lists: An Illustrated Essay*. Translated by Alistair McEwen. New York: Rizzoli, 2009.
———. "Innovation and Repetition: Between Modern and Post-Modern Aesthetics." In *Reading Eco: An Anthology*, edited by Rocco Capozzi, 14–33. Bloomington: Indiana University Press, 1997.
———. *Inventing the Enemy and Other Occasional Writings*. Translated by Richard Dixon. Boston: Houghton Mifflin Harcourt, 2012.
———. *The Island of the Day Before*. Translated by William Weaver. New York: Penguin, 1995.
———. *Misreadings*. Translated by William Weaver. San Diego, CA: Harcourt, 1993.
———. *Mouse or Rat?: Translation as Negotiation*. London: Phoenix, 2004.
———. *The Name of the Rose*. Translated by William Weaver. Boston: Mariner, 2014.
———. *Numero Zero*. Translated by Richard Dixon. Boston: Mariner, 2016.
———. *On Literature*. Translated by Martin McLaughlin. San Diego, CA: Harcourt, 2004.
———. *On Ugliness*. New York: Rizzoli, 2011.
———. *The Open Work*. Translated by Ana Cancogni. Cambridge: Harvard University Press, 1989.

———. *The Prague Cemetery*. Translated by Richard Dixon. Boston: Mariner, 2011.
———. *The Search for the Perfect Language*. Translated by James Fentress. Malden: Blackwell, 1994.
———. *Semiotics and the Philosophy of Language*. Bloomington: Indiana University Press, 1984.
———. "Semiotics and the Philosophy of Language." In *Reading Eco: An Anthology*, edited by Rocco Capozzi, 1–13. Bloomington: Indiana University Press, 1997.
———. *Serendipities: Language and Lunacy*. Translated by William Weaver. San Diego, CA: Harcourt, 1999.
———. "Sign." In *Encyclopedic Dictionary of Semiotics: N-Z*, edited by Thomas A. Sebeok and Marcel Danesi, 959–64. 3rd ed. Berlin: De Gruyter Mouton, 2010.
———. *Six Walks in the Fictional Woods*. Cambridge: Harvard University Press, 1994.
———. "Social Life as a Sign System." In *Structuralism: An Introduction*, edited by David Robey, 57–72. Oxford: Clarendon, 1973.
———. *Turning Back the Clock: Hot Wars and Media Populism*. Translated by Alistair McEwen. San Diego: Harcourt, 2007.
———. "Two Problems in Textual Interpretation." In *Reading Eco: An Anthology*, edited by Rocco Capozzi, 34–52. Bloomington: Indiana University Press, 1997.
———. "Universe of the Mind. A Semiotic Theory of Culture." In *Reading Eco: An Anthology*, edited by Rocco Capozzi, 53–58. Bloomington: Indiana University Press, 1997.
Eco, Umberto, and Constantino Marmo, eds. *On the Medieval Theory of Signs*. Amsterdam: John Benjamins, 1989.
Eco, Umberto, and Cardinal Martini. *Belief or Nonbelief?: A Confrontation*. Translated by Minna Proctor. New York: Helios, 2012.
Eco, Umberto, Richard Rorty, Jonathan Culler, and Christine Brooke-Rose. *Interpretation and Overinterpretation*. Edited by Stefan Collini. Cambridge: Cambridge University Press, 1992.
Eco, Umberto, Marco Santambrogio, and Patrizia Violi, eds. *Meaning and Mental Representations*. Bloomington: Indiana University Press, 1988.
Eco, Umberto, and Thomas A. Sebeok, ed. *The Sign of Three: Dupin, Holmes, Peirce*. Bloomington: Indiana University Press, 1984.
Erickson, Millard. *Christian Theology*. 3rd ed. Grand Rapids: Baker, 2013.
Evans, Robert. *Reception History, Tradition and Biblical Interpretation: Gadamer and Jauss in Current Practice*. London: Bloomsbury, 2014.
Fee, Gordon D., and Douglas Stuart. *How to Read the Bible for All Its Worth*. Grand Rapids: Zondervan, 2003.
Fish, Stanley. *Is There a Text in This Class?: The Authority of Interpretive Communities*. Cambridge: Harvard University Press, 1980.
Fitzgerald, John J. *Peirce's Theory of Signs as Foundation for Pragmatism*. Studies in Philosophy 11. The Hague: Mouton & Co., 1966.
Foucault, Michel. *The Archaeology of Knowledge*. London: Tavistock, 1974.
———. *The Order of Things*. London: Tavistock, 1970.
———. *This Is Not a Pipe*. Berkeley: University of California Press, 1983.
Fowl, Stephen E. *Engaging Scripture: A Model for Theological Interpretation*. Eugene, OR: Wipf and Stock, 1998.
Gadamer, Hans-Georg. *Hermeneutics, Religion, and Ethics*. Translated by Joel Weinsheimer. New Haven: Yale University Press, 1999.

———. *Philosophical Hermeneutics*. trans. David Linge. Berkeley: University of California Press, 1976.

———. *Truth and Method*. 2nd ed. Translated by Joel Weinsheimer and Donald G. Marshall. New York: Continuum, 1975.

Garrett, James Leo., Jr. *Systematic Theology: Biblical, Historical, and Evangelical*. 2 vols. Grand Rapids: Eerdmans, 1990.

Green, Joel B., and Max Turner ed. *Between Two Horizons: Spanning New Testament Studies and Systematic Theology*. Grand Rapids: Eerdmans, 2000.

Gregersen, Niels Henrik, and J. Wentzel van Huyssteen, eds. *Rethinking Theology and Science: Six Models for the Current Dialogue*. Grand Rapids: Eerdmans, 1998.

Greimas, Algirdas J. *On Meaning: Selected Writings in Semiotic Theory*. Translated by Paul J. Perron and Frank H. Collins. London: Frances Pinter, 1987.

———. *Structural Semantics*. Lincoln: University of Nebraska Press, 1983.

Greimas, Algirdas J., and Joseph Courtés. *Semiotics and Language: An Analytical Dictionary*. Translated by L. Crist, D. Patte et al. Bloomington: Indiana University Press, 1982.

Grenz, Stanley J. *Renewing the Center: Evangelical Theology in a Post-Theological Era*. Grand Rapids: Baker, 2006.

———. *Theology for the Community of God*. Grand Rapids: Eerdmans, 2000.

Grenz, Stanley J., and John R. Franke. *Beyond Foundationalism: Shaping Theology in a Postmodern Context*. Louisville, KY: Westminster John Knox, 2001.

Grenz, Stanley J., and Roger E. Olson. *20th Century Theology: God and the World in a Transitional Age*. Downers Grove, IL: IVP, 1992.

Grondin, Jean. *Introduction to Philosophical Hermeneutics*. New Haven, CT: Yale University Press, 1994.

———. *The Philosophy of Gadamer*. Translated by Kathryn Plant. Montreal: McGill-Queen's University Press, 2003.

Gundry, Stanley N., and Gary T. Meadors, ed. *Moving beyond the Bible to Theology: Four Views*. Grand Rapids: Zondervan, 2009.

Haiman, John. "Dictionaries and Encyclopedias." *Lingua* 50 (1980) 329–57.

———. "Dictionaries and Encyclopedias Again." *Lingua* 56 (1982) 353–55.

Hall, Sean. *This Means This, This Means That: A User's Guide to Semiotics*. London: Laurence King, 2007.

Harman, Gilbert. "The Inference to the Best Explanation." *Philosophical Review* 74 (1965) 88–95.

Hawkes, Terence. *Structuralism and Semiotics*. 2nd ed. London: Routledge, 2003.

Hays, Richard B., Stefan Alkier, and Leroy A. Huizenga, eds. *Reading the Bible Intertextually*. Waco, TX: Baylor University Press, 2008.

Heidegger, Martin. *Being and Time*. New York: Harper and Row, 1962.

Hirsch, E. D., Jr. *Validity in Interpretation*. New Haven: Yale University Press, 1967.

Hjelmslev, Louis. *Prolegomena to a Theory of Language*. Translated by Francis J. Whitfield. Madison: University of Wisconsin Press, 1961.

Hoffmeyer, Jesper. "A Biosemiotic Approach to the Question of Meaning." *Zygon* 45 (June 2010) 367–90.

Hollingsworth, Andrew. "'Ecos' in the Labyrinth: Systematic Theology as Semiotic Phenomenon." PhD diss., New Orleans Baptist Theological Seminary, 2018.

———. "Hans-Georg Gadamer and a Hermeneutics of Discipleship." MA thesis. New Orleans Baptist Theological Seminary, 2014.

Humboldt, Wilhelm von. *On Language: On the Diversity of Human Language Construction and its Influence on the Mental Development of the Human Species*. Edited by Michael Losonsky. Translated by Peter Heath. Cambridge: Cambridge University Press, 1999.

Hume, David. *An Enquiry Concerning Human Understanding*. Edited by Peter Millican. Oxford: Oxford University Press, 2007.

Huyssteen, J. Wentzel van. *Duet or Duel?: Theology and Science in a Postmodern World*. Harrisburg: Trinity International, 1998.

———. *Essays in Postfoundationalist Theology*. Grand Rapids: Eerdmans, 1997.

———. *The Shaping of Rationality: Toward Interdisciplinarity in Theology and Science*. Grand Rapids: Eerdmans, 1999.

———. *Theology and the Justification of Faith: Constructing Theories in Systematic Theology*. Grand Rapids: Eerdmans, 1989.

Innis, Robert E., ed. *Semiotics: An Introductory Anthology*. Bloomington: Indiana University Press, 1985.

Jakobson, Roman. *Main Trends in the Science of Language*. London: Allen & Unwin, 1973.

Jauss, Hans Robert. *Aesthetic Experience and Literary Hermeneutics*. Translated by Michael Shaw. Minneapolis: University of Minnesota Press, 1982.

———. *Toward an Aesthetic of Reception*. Translated by T. Bahti. Minneapolis: University of Minnesota Press, 1982.

Johnson, Alfred M., Jr. "A Bibliography of Semiological and Structural Studies of Religion." In *Bibliographia Tripotamopolitana: A Series of Bibliographies Published Occasionally by the Barbour Library Pittsburgh Theological Seminary*. Pittsburgh: Pittsburgh Theological Seminary, 1979.

Kant, Immanuel. *Critique of Judgment*. Translated by J. H. Bernard. New York: Dover, 2005.

———. *Critique of Practical Reason*. Translated by Thomas Kingsmill Abbott. New York: Dover, 2004.

———. *Critique of Pure Reason*. Translated by Norman Kemp Smith. New York: Palgrave Macmillan, 2007.

Katz, J. J., and J. A. Fodor. "The Structure of a Semantic Theory." *Language* 39 (1963) 170210.

Kevelson, Roberta. "Eco and Dramatology." In *Reading Eco: An Anthology*, edited by Rocco Capozzi, 196–209. Bloomington: Indiana University Press, 1997.

Klink, Edward W., III, and Darian R. Lockett. *Understanding Biblical Theology: A Comparison of Theory and Practice*. Grand Rapids: Zondervan, 2012.

Kristeva, Julia. *Desire in Language: A Semiotic Approach to Literature and Art*. Edited by Leon S. Roudiez. Translated by Thomas Gora, Alice Jardine, and Leon S. Roudiez. New York: Columbia University Press, 1980.

———. *The Kristeva Reader*, ed. Moi, Toril, ed. New York: Columbia University Press, 1986.

———. *Revolution in Poetic Language*. Translated by Margaret Waller. New York: Columbia University Press, 1984.

Kuhn, Thomas S. *The Structure of Scientific Revolutions* 4th ed. Chicago: University of Chicago Press, 2012.

Lacan, Jacques. *Écrits*. Translated by Alan Sheridan. London: Tavistock, 1980.

———. *The Language of the Self*. Translated by Anthony Wilden. Baltimore, MD: Johns Hopkins Press, 1968.

Langford, Justin M. *Defending Hope: Semiotics and Intertextuality in 1 Peter*. Eugene, OR: Wipf and Stock, 2013.

———. "'Signs' of Hope in the Midst of Suffering: A Semiotic Investigation of the Use of Isaiah in 1 Peter." PhD diss., New Orleans Baptist Theological Seminary, 2012.

Lévi-Strauss, Claude. *Structural Anthropology*. Translated by Claire Jacobson and Brooke Grundfest Schoepf. Harmondsworth: Penguin, 1972.

Lindbeck, George A. *The Nature of Doctrine: Religion and Theology in a Postliberal Age*. Louisville: Westminster John Knox, 2009.

Liszka, James Jakób. *A General Introduction to the Semiotic of Charles Sanders Peirce*. Bloomington: Indiana University Press, 1996.

Lonergan, Bernard J. F. *Method in Theology*. Toronto: University of Toronto Press, 1990.

Longoni, Anna. "Esoteric Conspiracies and the Interpretative Strategy." In *Reading Eco: An Anthology*, edited by Rocco Capozzi, 210–16. Bloomington: Indiana University Press, 1997.

Lotman, Yuri. *Universe of the Mind: A Semiotic Theory of Culture*. Translated by Ann Shukman. Bloomington: Indiana University Press, 1990.

Lowe, Walter. *Theology and Difference: The Wound of Reason*. Bloomington: Indiana University Press, 1993.

Magli, Patrizia. "Cultural Unit." *Encyclopedic Dictionary of Semiotics: A-M*, edited by Thomas A. Sebeok and Marcel Danesi, 170. 3rd ed. Berlin: De Gruyter Mouton, 2010.

Martin, R. M. *Semiotics and Linguistic Structure*. Albany: State University of New York Press, 1978.

McCall, Thomas H. *An Invitation to Analytic Christian Theology*. Downers Grove, IL: IVP, 2015.

McGrath, Alister E. *The Genesis of Doctrine: A Study in the Foundation of Doctrinal Criticism*. Grand Rapids: Eerdmans, 1997.

———. *The Science of God*. New York: T&T Clark International, 2004.

———. *A Scientific Theology*. 3 vols. Grand Rapids: Eerdmans, 2001.

McGrew, Timothy. *The Foundations of Knowledge*. Lanham: Littlefield Adams Books, 1995.

Meland, Bernard E. *Fallible Forms and Symbols: Discourses of Method in a Theology of Culture*. Philadelphia: Fortress, 1976.

Merrell, Floyd. *Peirce, Signs, and Meaning*. Toronto: University of Toronto Press, 1997.

Misak, Cheryl, ed. *The Cambridge Companion to Peirce*. Cambridge: Cambridge University Press, 2004.

Morris, Charles. *Foundations of the Theory of Signs*. International Encyclopedia of Unified Science, vol. 1. Chicago: University of Chicago Press, 1938.

———. *Signification and Significance: A Study of the Relations of Signs and Values*. Cambridge: MIT Press, 1964.

———. *Signs, Language and Behavior*. New York: Prentice-Hall, 1946.

———. *Writings on the General Theory of Signs*. Approaches to Semiotics 16. Edited by Thomas A. Sebeok. The Hague: Mouton, 1971.

Mueller-Vollmer, Kurt, ed. *The Hermeneutics Reader*. New York: Continuum, 1985.

Newman, John Henry Cardinal. *An Essay on the Development of Christian Doctrine*. Notre Dame, ID: University of Notre Dame Press, 1989.

Nida, Eugene A. *Componential Analysis of Meaning: An Introduction to Semantic Structures*. Paris: Mouton, 1975.

Nöth, Winfried. *Handbook of Semiotics*. Bloomington: Indiana University Press, 1990.
Olson, Roger E. *The Journey of Modern Theology: From Reconstruction to Deconstruction*. Downers Grove, IL: IVP, 2013.
Ormerod, Neil, and Christiaan Jacobs-Vandegeer. *Foundational Theology: A New Approach to Catholic Fundamental Theology*. Minneapolis: Fortress, 2015.
Pannenberg, Wolfhart. *Anthropology in Theological Perspective*. Translated by Matthew J. O'Connell. Philadelphia: Westminster, 1985.
———. *Basic Questions in Theology: Collected Essays*. 2 vols. Translated by George H. Kelm. Fortress, 1970–1971.
———. *The Idea of God and Human Freedom*. Philadelphia: Westminster, 1973.
———. *Systematic Theology*. 3 vols. Translated by Geoffrey W. Bromiley. Grand Rapids: Eerdmans, 1991–1998.
———. *Theology and the Philosophy of Science*. Translated by Francis McDonagh. Philadelphia: Westminster, 1976.
Parris, David Paul. *Reception Theory and Biblical Hermeneutics*. Eugene, OR: Pickwick, 2009.
Peckham, John C. *Canoncial Theology: The Biblical Canon, Sola Scriptura, and Theological Method*. Grand Rapids: Eerdmans, 2016.
Peirce, Charles S. *Charles S. Peirce: Selected Writings*. Edited by Philip P. Wiener. New York: Dover, 1958.
———. *The Collected Papers of Charles Sanders Peirce*. Edited by Charles Hartshorne and Paul Weiss. Cambridge: Belknap, 1960.
———. *Peirce on Signs: Writings on Semiotic by Charles Sanders Peirce*. Edited by James Hoopes. Chapel Hill: University of North Carolina Press, 1991.
Perron, Paul, and Patrick Debbèche. "On Truth and Lying: U. Eco and A. J. Greimas." In *Reading Eco: An Anthology*, edited by Rocco Capozzi, 185–95. Bloomington: Indiana University Press, 1997.
Peters, Ted. *God—The World's Future: Systematic Theology for a New Era* 3rd ed. Minneapolis: Fortress, 2015.
Petrilli, Susan. "Towards Interpretation Semiotics." In *Reading Eco: An Anthology*, edited by Rocco Capozzi, 121–36. Bloomington: Indiana University Press, 1997.
Plantinga, Alvin. *Warrant and Proper Function*. Oxford: Oxford University Press, 1993.
———. *Warranted Christian Belief*. Oxford: Oxford University Press, 1999.
Plato. *Phaedrus and Letters VII and VIII*. Translated by Walter Hamilton. Harmondsworth: Penguin, 1973.
———. *Cratylus*. Translated by C. D. C. Reeve. Indianapolis: Hackett, 1998.
Pojman, Louis P. *What Can We Know?: An Introduction to the Theory of Knowledge* 2nd ed. Belmont: Wadsworth, 2001.
Polkinghorne, John C. *One World: The Interaction of Science and Theology*. Princeton: Princeton University Press, 1986.
———. *Scientists as Theologians: A Comparison of the Writings of Ian Barbour, Arthur Peacocke and John Polkinghorne*. London: SPCK, 1996.
Popper, Karl. *Conjectures and Refutations: The Growth of Scientific Knowledge*. New York: Routledge, 2006.
Poythress, Vern S. *In the Beginning Was the Word: Language—A God Centered Approach*. Wheaton, IL: Crossway, 2009.
———. *Philosophy, Science, and the Sovereignty of God*. Phillipsburg: P & R, 2004.

———. *Redeeming Philosophy: A God-Centered Approach to the Big Questions*. Wheaton: Crossway, 2014.
———. *Redeeming Science: A God-Centered Approach*. Wheaton: Crossway, 2006.
———. *Science and Hermeneutics: Implications of the Scientific Method for Biblical Interpretation*. Grand Rapids: Zondervan, 1988.
———. *Symphonic Theology: The Validity of Multiple Perspectives in Theology*. Grand Rapids: Zondervan, 1987.
Price, H. H. *Belief*. London: Allen & Unwin, 1969.
Putman, Rhyne R. *In Defense of Doctrine: Evangelicalism, Theology, and Scripture*. Minneapolis, MN: Fortress, 2015.
———. "Postcanonical Doctrinal Development as Hermeneutical Phenomenon." PhD diss., New Orleans Baptist Theological Seminary, 2012.
Putnam, Hilary. *The Many Faces of Realism*. Chicago: Open Court Publishing, 1988.
———. *Mathematics, Matter and Method: Philosophical Papers—Volume 1*. Cambridge: Cambridge University Press, 1979.
———. *Mind, Language and Reality: Philosophical Papers—Volume 2*. Cambridge: Cambridge University Press, 1979.
———. *Realism and Reason: Philosophical Papers—Volume 3*. Cambridge: Cambridge University Press, 1985.
———. *Representation and Reality*. Denver: Bradford, 1991.
Putti, Joseph. *Theology as Hermeneutics: Paul Ricoeur's Theory of Text Interpretation and Method in Theology*. Bethesda: International, 1994.
Quillian, Ross. "Semantic Memory." *Semantic Information Processing*, edited by Marvin Minksy, 227–70. Cambridge: MIT Press, 1968.
Quine, W. V. *Quintessence: Basic Readings from the Philosophy of W. V. Quine*. Edited by Roger F. Gibson Jr. Cambridge: Belknap, 2004.
———. *Word and Object*. New York: MIT Press, 2013.
Quine, W. V., and J. S. Ullian. *The Web of Belief*. 2nd ed. New York: Random House, 1978.
Rahner, Karl. *Foundations of Christian Faith: An Introduction to the Idea of Christianity*. Translated by William V. Dych. New York: Crossroad, 1982.
Rauch, Irmengard. "Openness, Eco, and the End of Another Millennium." In *Reading Eco: An Anthology*, edited by Rocco Capozzi, 137–46. Bloomington: Indiana University Press, 1997.
Ricoeur, Paul. *The Conflict of Interpretations: Essays in Hermeneutics*. Edited by Don Ihde. Evanston: Northwestern University Press, 1974.
———. *Fallible Man*. Revised and Translated by Charles A. Kelbley. New York: Fordham University Press, 1985.
———. *Freud and Philosophy: An Essay on Interpretation*. trans. D. Savage. New Haven, CT: Yale University Press, 1970.
———. *Hermeneutics and the Human Sciences*. Cambridge: Cambridge University Press, 1981.
———. *Interpretation Theory: Discourse and the Surplus of Meaning*. Fort Worth, TX: TCU Press, 1976.
———. *Oneself as Another*. Translated by Kathleen Blamey. Chicago: University of Chicago Press, 1992.
———. *The Rule of Metaphor: The Creation of Meaning in Language*. Translated by Robert Czerny with Kathleen McLaughlin and John Costello, SJ. New York: Routledge, 2003.
———. *The Symbolism of Evil*. Translated by Emerson Buchanan. Boston: Beacon, 1967.

———. *Time and Narrative*. 3 vols. Translated by Kathleen McLaughlin and David Pellauer. Chicago: University of Chicago Press, 1984.

Riffaterre, Michael. "The Interpretant in Literary Semiotics." In *Reading Eco: An Anthology*, edited by Rocco Capozzi, 173–84. Bloomington: Indiana University Press, 1997.

Robey, David, ed. *Structuralism: An Introduction*. Oxford: Clarendon, 1973.

Robinson, Andrew. *God and the World of Signs: Trinity, Evolution, and the Metaphysical Semiotics of C. S. Peirce*. Boston: Brill, 2010.

Robinson, Andrew, and Christopher Southgate. "Semiotics as a Metaphysical Framework for Christian Theology." *Zygon* 45 (September 2010) 689–712.

Rorty, Richard. *Consequences of Pragmatism: Essays: 1972–1980*. Minneapolis, MN: University of Minnesota Press, 1982.

———. *Philosophy and the Mirror of Nature*. Princeton: Princeton University Press, 2017.

Rossi, Ino, ed. *The Unconscious in Culture: The Structuralism of Claude Lévi-Strauss in Perspective*. New York: Dutton, 1974.

Rush, Rajka. "Religion and Semiosphere: From the Religious to the Secular and Beyond." PhD diss., Western Michigan University, 2006.

Saussure, Ferdinand de. *Course in General Linguistics*. Translated by Roy Harris. London: Duckworth, 1983.

Schleiermacher, Friedrich. *Brief Outline of Theology as a Field of Study* 3rd ed. Translated by Terrance N. Tice. Louisville: Westminster John Knox, 2011.

———. *The Christian Faith*. 2nd ed. Translated by H. R. Mackintosh and J. S. Stewart. Edinburgh: T&T Clark, 1928.

———. *Hermeneutics and Criticism and Other Writings*. Translated and Edited by Andrew Bowie. Cambridge: Cambridge University Press, 1998.

———. *Hermeneutics: The Handwritten Manuscripts*. Edited by Heinz Kimmerle. Translated by James Duke and J. Forstman. Missoula: Scholars, 1977.

Scholes, Robert. *Semiotics and Interpretation*. New Haven, CT: Yale University Press, 1982.

Searle, John R. *Expression and Meaning: Studies in the Theory of Speech Acts*. Cambridge: Cambridge University Press, 1985.

———. *Mind, Language, and Society: Philosophy in the Real World*. New York: Basic, 1998.

———. *Speech Acts: An Essay in the Philosophy of Language*. Cambridge: Cambridge University Press, 1969.

Sebeok, Thomas A. *Global Semiotics*. Bloomington: Indiana University Press, 2001.

———. *A Perfusion of Signs*. Bloomington: Indiana University Press, 1977.

———. *A Sign is Just a Sign*. Bloomington: Indiana University Press, 1991.

———. *Signs: An Introduction to Semiotics*. Toronto: University of Toronto Press, 1994.

Sebeok, Thomas A., and Marcel Danesi, eds. *Encyclopedic Dictionary of Semiotics*. 3 vols. Berlin: DeGruyter Mouton, 2010.

Seed, David. "The *Open Work* in Theory and Practice." In *Reading Eco: An Anthology*, edited by Rocco Capozzi, 73–81. Bloomington: Indiana University Press, 1997.

Short, T. L. *Peirce's Theory of Signs*. Cambridge: Cambridge University Press, 2007.

Sire, James. *Naming the Elephant: Worldview as a Concept*. Downers Grove, IL: IVP, 2004.

———. *The Universe Next Door: A Basic Worldview Catalog*. 5th ed. Downers Grove, IL: IVP, 2009.

Stewart, Robert B. *The Quest for the Hermeneutical Jesus: The Impact of Hermeneutics on the Jesus Research of John Dominic Crossan and N. T. Wright*. Lanham: University Press of America, 2008.

Taylor, Charles. *The Language Animal: The Full Shape of the Human Linguistic Capacity.* Cambridge: Belknap, 2016.
Taylor, Mark C. *Erring: A Postmodern A/theology.* Chicago: University of Chicago Press, 1984.
Tejera, Victorino. "Eco, Peirce and the Necessity of Interpretation." In *Reading Eco: An Anthology,* edited by Rocco Capozzi, 147–62. Bloomington: Indiana University Press, 1997.
Thagard, Paul R. "Semiosis and Hypothetic Inference in Ch. S. Peirce." *Versus* (1978) 19–20.
Thiselton, Anthony C. *Doubt, Faith, and Certainty.* Grand Rapids: Eerdmans, 2017.
———. *Hermeneutics: An Introduction.* Grand Rapids: Eerdmans, 2009.
———. *The Hermeneutics of Doctrine.* Grand Rapids: Eerdmans, 2007.
———. *Interpreting God and the Postmodern Self: On Meaning, Manipulation, and Promise.* Grand Rapids: Eerdmans, 1995.
———. "Knowledge, Myth, and Corporate Memory." In *Thiselton on Hermeneutics: Collected Works with New Essays,* 701–25. Grand Rapids: Eerdmans, 2006.
———. *New Horizons in Hermeneutics: The Theory and Practice of Transforming Biblical Reading.* Grand Rapids: Zondervan, 1992.
———. *Systematic Theology.* Grand Rapids: Eerdmans, 2015.
———. *Thiselton on Hermeneutics: Collected Works with New Essays.* Grand Rapids: Eerdmans, 2006.
———. *The Two Horizons: New Testament Hermeneutics and Philosophical Description.* Grand Rapids: Eerdmans, 1980.
Thomas, Heath A. *Poetry and Theology in the Book of Lamentations: The Aesthetics of the Open Text.* Sheffield: Sheffield Phoenix, 2013.
Tillich, Paul. *Systematic Theology.* 3 vols. Chicago: University of Chicago Press, 1951.
Tilling, Chris. *Paul's Divine Christology.* Grand Rapids: Eerdmans, 2012.
Torrance, Thomas F. *The Christian Frame of Mind: Reason, Order, and Openness in Theology and Natural Science.* Colorado Springs: Helmers & Howard, 1989.
———. *Christian Theology and Scientific Culture.* Oxford: Oxford University Press, 1981.
———. *The Ground and Grammar of Theology.* Charlottesville: University of Virginia Press, 1980.
———. *Reality and Evangelical Theology: The Realism of Christian Revelation.* Downers Grove, IL: InterVarsity, 1999.
———. *Theological Science.* Oxford: Oxford University Press, 1969.
Tracy, David. *The Analogical Imagination: Christian Theology and the Culture of Pluralism.* New York: Crossroads, 1981.
Vanhoozer, Kevin J. *Biblical Authority after Babel: Retrieving the Solas in the Spirit of Mere Protestant Christianity.* Grand Rapids: Brazos, 2016.
———. *Biblical Narrative in the Philosophy of Paul Ricoeur: A Study in Hermeneutics and Theology.* Cambridge: Cambridge University Press, 1990.
———. *The Drama of Doctrine: A Canonical Linguistic Approach to Christian Theology.* Louisville, KY: Westminster John Knox, 2005.
———. *Faith Speaking Understanding: Performing the Drama of Doctrine.* Louisville, KY: Westminster John Knox, 2014.
———. *First Theology: God, Scripture, and Hermeneutics.* Downers Grove, IL: International Varsity, 2002.

———. *Is There a Meaning in This Text?: The Bible, the Reader, and the Morality of Literary Knowledge*. Grand Rapids: Zondervan, 1998.
Veeneman, Mary M. *Introducing Theological Method: A Survey of Contemporary Theologians and Approaches*. Grand Rapids: Baker, 2017.
Warburton, Nigel. *A Little History of Philosophy*. New Haven, CT: Yale University Press, 2011.
Wells, Samuel. *Improvisation: The Drama of Christian Ethics*. London: SPCK, 2004.
Wildman, Wesley J. "A Semiotic Theory of Theology and Philosophy." *The Journal of Religion* 82 (October 2002) 657–58.
Wittgenstein, Ludwig. *Philosophical Investigations* 4th ed. Translated by G. E. M. Anscombe, P. M. S. Hacker, and Joachim Schulte. Malden: Wiley-Blackwell, 2009.
Wolterstorff, Nicholas. *Divine Discourse: Philosophical Reflections on the Claim That God Speaks*. Cambridge: Cambridge University Press, 1995.
Wright, N.T. *Jesus and the Victory of God*: Minneapolis, MN: Fortress, 1997.
———. *The Last Word: Beyond the Bible Wars to a New Understanding of the Authority of Scripture*. San Francisco: Harper, 2005.
———. *The New Testament and the People of God*. Minneapolis, MN: Fortress Press, 1992.
———. *The Resurrection of the Son of God*. Minneapolis, MN: Fortress Press, 2003.
———. *Paul and the Faithfulness of God*. 2 vols. Minneapolis, MN: Fortress Press, 2013.
———. *Scripture and the Authority of God: How to Read the Bible Today*. New York: HarperOne, 2011.
Yaghjian, Lucretia B. *Writing Theology Well: A Rhetoric for Theological and Biblical Writers*. 2nd ed. London: Bloomsbury, 2015.
Yong, Amos. "God and the World of Signs: Trinity, Evolution, and the Metaphysical Semiotics of C. S. Peirce." *Perspectives on Science and Christian Faith* 65 (December 2013) 269–70.
Zimmerman, Jens. *Recovering Theological Hermeneutics: An Incarnational-Trinitarian Theory of Interpretation*. Grand Rapids: Baker, 2004.

Index

abduction, 3, 11, 12, 49, 54, 61, 71, 85, 86, 101, 102, 103, 104, 105, 106, 107, 108, 109, 137, 149, 152, 153
abduction, creative, 103
abduction, meta, 103, 104
abduction, overcoded, 103
abduction, undercoded, 103
Alkier, Stefan, 7, 8, 11
antifoundationalism, 88, 92, 107
anti-realism, 88, 94
application, 116, 117, 137
Aquinas, Thomas, 16
Aristotle, 15, 16, 48, 50, 59, 61, 72, 102
Augustine, 16
Austin, J. L., 145, 146
author, 44, 55
authority, 116
Ayer, A. J., 125

Bacon, Francis, 17
Barth, Karl, 124, 140, 141
Barthes, Roland, 26, 27
being, 57, 58, 112
belief, 132, 145–147, 151
belief, half, 132, 145
belief, web of, 91, 92, 93, 99
beliefs, basic, 89, 90, 91, 92, 93, 107
Berkeley, George, 17
Bhaktin, Mikhail, 6, 27
Bhaskar, Roy, 99, 100, 101, 106, 108
biosemiotics, 6, 27
Buber, Martin, 119

Bultmann, Rudolf, 124

Caesar, Michael, 29, 30, 37, 48, 57
Calvin, John, 132
categories, Peircean, 5, 6
certainty, epistemic, 95
Chandler, David, 22
Cobley, Paul, 23, 27
code, 32, 33, 37, 49, 51, 69, 133
codes, theory of, 31, 36, 42, 67, 68, 82, 98, 133
cognition, 56, 59, 82, 85
coherentism, 90, 91, 101, 107, 151
Collingwood, R. G., 116, 131, 146
communication, 1, 3, 6, 23, 31, 32, 51, 57
connotation, 21, 22, 26, 35, 67
content, 10, 19, 22, 34, 35, 36, 41, 50, 62, 63, 67, 69, 71, 98, 105, 106, 134, 135, 150–155
content, molar, 62, 63, 65, 83, 84, 85, 106
content, nuclear, 60, 62, 63, 65, 83, 84, 85, 106
contracting, 65, 85
Corrington, Robert, 4, 5
critical realism, 11, 88, 94, 99–107, 108, 109, 147–150
cultural unit, 3, 37, 47, 71, 150

Danesi, Marcel, 15, 16, 21
Dasein, 112
deconstruction, 25, 51, 52, 54

deduction, 3, 102
denotation, 22, 35, 62, 67
Derrida, Jacques, 10, 25, 54
Descartes, René, 89, 90, 92, 122
designatum, 23, 24
dictionary, model, 10, 37, 49, 58, 63, 64, 66–87, 98, 106
différance, 26
différence, 26
differentiae, 49, 58, 73, 98
Dilthey, Wilhelm, 111, 112
directories, 64, 65, 84, 106
discourse, universe of, 8
doctrinal development, 11, 13, 139–155
doctrine, 131, 132, 134, 135, 136, 138, 139–155
doctrine, canonical-linguistic theory of, 143–145
doctrine, cultural-linguistic theory of, 141–143
dogmatics, 3, 9, 140
Downing, Crystal, 6, 7
dyad, 18, 24, 32

Ebeling, Gerhard, 124
encyclopedia, local, 50, 81, 98, 104, 133, 135, 138, 150, 152
encyclopedia, maximal, 50, 80, 81, 82, 98, 104, 133, 134, 135, 138, 150
encyclopedia, median, 80, 81, 82
encyclopedia, model, 2, 7, 10, 29, 37, 44, 46, 49, 50, 54, 58, 63, 64, 65, 66–87, 88, 89, 97, 98, 103, 104, 105, 105, 107, 108, 109, 110, 114, 133–138, 139, 150–155
encyclopedia, special, 80, 81, 106, 135
Epicureans, 15, 16
epistemology, 88–109, 113, 130
ethics, 123, 146
explanation, 119, 120, 121
expression, 10, 22, 34, 35, 41, 43, 50, 67, 69, 98, 134, 135, 150–155

fabula, 45
fallacy, referential, 35
fallibilism, 94, 95, 96, 97, 99, 101, 104, 107, 108, 147, 149
files, 64, 65, 84, 106

firstness, 5, 6, 20, 21
Fodor, Jerry A., 37, 72
formation, 125, 131, 132, 135, 136
forms, 16
Foucault, Michel, 25
foundationalism, 88, 89, 90, 92, 96, 99, 107, 151
foundationalism, classic, 88, 89, 90, 92, 96, 97, 99, 101
Freud, Sigmund, 24, 119, 120

Gadamer, Hans‚Georg, 2, 13, 61, 91, 110, 113, 114–119, 121, 124, 130, 131, 132, 133, 135, 137, 146, 147
genera/genus, 10, 49, 58, 72, 73, 82, 98, 135
glossematics, 21, 27
Greimas, Algirdas Julien, 26, 27
Grenz, Stanley, 90, 93, 94, 143

Habermas, Jürgen, 7
Harman, Gilbert, 101
Heidegger, Martin, 57, 112, 114, 116
hermeneutic circle, 111, 116, 131, 132
hermeneutics, 1, 13, 110,138, 145–147, 148
hermeneutics of suspicion, 120
hermetic drift, 53, 54, 134
historically effected consciousness, 116, 117, 118
history, 121, 122, 123, 124, 126, 127, 130, 131, 132, 134
history of effects, 116, 117, 118
Hjelmslev, Louis, 21, 26, 27, 28, 32, 72
Hodge, Charles, 141
Hoffmeyer, Jasper, 7
horizon/horizon of understanding, 116, 117, 118, 119, 124, 133, 135, 136, 137, 138, 146, 152
horizon of expectation, 136, 137
horizons, fusion of, 116, 117, 118, 133, 135, 137, 147, 152
Huizenga, Leroy, 8, 11
Huyssteen, J. Wentzel van, 92, 93, 94
hypoconism, 65

icon, 39, 40
iconism, 40, 65

idealism, 17, 18
ideas, 16, 17, 18
incorrigible, 89, 92, 93
index, 39
indubitable, 89
induction, 3, 102
interpretant, 20, 23, 24, 37, 46, 49, 62, 74, 79, 134
interpretation, 51, 52, 53, 54, 69, 102, 110–138
intertextuality, 7, 8, 9, 26, 28
invention, 41
isotopy, 27, 44, 51, 70

Jakobson, Roman, 22, 23, 24, 28
Jauss, Hans-Robert, 136
judgments, perceptual, 60, 61

Kant, Immanuel, 20, 59, 60, 114
Katz, Jerrold J., 37, 72
KF Model, 37, 67, 68
knowledge, 88–109
Kristeva, Julia, 6, 26, 27

labyrinth, 10, 11, 50, 52, 54, 66–87, 97, 98, 99, 104, 105, 106, 135, 137, 150, 153
Lacan, Jacques, 24
Langford, Justin, 9, 11, 14
language, 2, 18, 21, 22, 24, 25, 27, 47, 56, 58, 64, 66–87, 91, 118, 119, 120, 133
language, philosophy of, 47, 50, 57, 66–87
langue, 19, 24
Lévi-Strauss, Claude, 24, 26
lexeme, 70
Lindbeck, George, 13, 141–143, 154
linguistics, 18, 21, 23
Locke, John, 17
Lonergan, Bernard, 141
Lotman, Yuri, 7
Luther, Martin, 136, 137

McGrath, Alister, 2, 13, 100, 101, 107, 139, 140, 147–150, 153, 154
McGrew, Timothy, 89

meaning, 3, 13, 19, 37, 46, 50, 52, 54, 62, 65, 71, 110–138
mentioning, 39
metaphysics, 4, 5, 16, 58
Model Q, 37, 68, 69, 74, 78
Moltmann, Jürgen, 124
morpheme, 10
Morris, Charles, 23, 27

nature, 4, 5, 147
negotiation, 65, 85, 86
Newman, John Henry, 139
nominalism, 16, 17
nonfoundationalism, 92, 94, 97
Nöth, Martin, 16, 21, 22, 24, 25, 27

object, 19, 20, 25, 39, 46, 57
object, dynamical, 57
object, immediate, 57
Ockham, William of, 16
ontology, 113, 115
ostension, 41
overcoding, 38, 44, 68, 70

Pannenberg, Wolfhart, 2, 11, 13, 100, 107, 110, 111, 124, 125–131, 133, 134, 135, 137, 138
parole, 19, 24
Peirce, Charles Sanders, 3, 5, 6, 7, 11, 13, 18, 19, 20, 21, 23, 24, 27, 32, 37, 39, 48, 57, 59, 65, 71, 85, 86, 94, 95, 96, 99, 101, 102, 103, 108, 134
Plantinga, Alvin, 90, 91, 99
Plato, 14, 15
play, 115, 116
Poinsot, John, 17
Pojman, Louis, 94
Polkinghorne, John, 100
Popper, Karl, 94, 125
Porphyry, 73
positivism, logical, 125
postfoundationalism, 88–99, 107, 108
poststructuralism, 25, 26, 28
pragmatics, 23, 24
pragmaticism, 19, 54, 97, 101, 107, 108
pragmatism, 19, 97, 101, 102
pragmatism, neo, 54
pre-judgment, see "pre-understanding"

prejudice, see "pre-understanding"
pre-understanding, 116
Price, H. H., 132, 145
primitives, 73
psychoanalysis, 5, 24, 28, 119, 120
psychosemiotics, 5
Putman, Rhyne, 13, 113, 114

Quillian, Ross, 37, 80
Quine, Willard V. O., 13, 75, 97, 151

Rahner, Karl, 6, 141
rationalism, critical, 125
reader, 44, 55
reader, empirical, 43
reader, model, 8, 43, 55
realism, 88, 94, 96, 99, 107
reality, stratification of, 101, 106
recognition, 64, 82
referent, 35, 36
referring, 39
relativism, 99
representamen, 19, 20, 46
rhizome, 11, 50, 77, 80, 97, 99, 104, 150
Ricoeur, Paul, 13, 114, 119-124, 137
Robinson, Andrew, 5, 6, 7, 10, 94
Rorty, Richard, 54
Rush, Rajka, 7

s-codes, 33, 51, 68
Saussure, Ferdinand de, 5, 6, 18, 19, 22, 24, 26, 27, 32
schema/schemata, 59, 60, 61, 64
Schleiermacher, Friedrich, 111, 112, 116, 141
science, human, 125, 126
science, natural, 100, 101, 102, 125, 126, 130, 147
science, philosophy of, 99, 125-131, 147-150
Sebeok, Thomas, 27
secondness, 5, 6, 20, 21
semantics, 23, 24
semantics, extensional, 36
semantics, intensional, 36
sememe, 3, 10, 45, 46, 49, 50, 66-87, 98, 104, 134, 138, 150-155
semiology, 3, 18

semiosis, 19, 20, 27, 38, 47, 58, 60, 72, 79, 82, 84, 99
semiosis, unlimited, 26, 37, 46, 54, 74, 134
semiotics, 1, 2, 5, 6, 7, 8, 10, 14,28, 20, 31, 47, 48, 57, 119
semiotics, categorical, 8
semiotics, connotative, 21
semiotics, text, 42
sensus communis, 115
Shults, F. Leron, 7
sign, 1, 3, 8, 10, 14,28, 35, 36, 48, 54, 57, 72
sign, conventional, 14, 15, 16, 19, 23
sign, natural, 14, 15, 16, 23
sign function, 34, 35, 45
sign production, theory of, 31, 36, 37, 40, 42
signal, 34
signification, 25, 27, 31, 32, 36, 38, 47, 48
signified, 18, 19, 24, 25, 37
signifier, 18, 19, 24, 25, 37
Southgate, Christopher, 7
species, 10, 49, 58, 72, 73, 82, 98, 135
Stoics, 15, 16
structuralism, 18, 19, 21, 22, 24, 25, 26, 27, 28
subcode, 35
symbol, 6, 7, 39, 49, 50, 120
syntactics, 23, 24

Taylor, Mark C., 10
text, 35, 41, 43, 46, 50, 52, 68, 74, 110-138
text, aesthetic, 42, 50
text, open, 9, 43, 45, 46
Thagard, Paul, 103
theodrama, 143-145
theology, 1, 5, 6, 7, 10, 125, 140, 141
theology, hermeneutic, 124-133, 150
theology, systematic, 1, 3, 9, 11
theory, 147-150, 153
theory, speech act, 69, 145, 146
thirdness, 5, 6, 20, 21
Thiselton, Anthony, 2, 11, 13, 110, 111, 119, 124, 125, 131-133, 135, 136, 137, 139, 145-147, 149, 150, 152, 154

Thomas, Heath, 9, 11, 68, 81
thrownness, 116, 124, 143
time, 121, 122, 123, 124, 127, 137
token, 40, 61, 80
Torrance, Thomas F., 100
trace, 26
tradition, 91, 92, 116, 117, 118, 140
Tree, Porphyrian, 10, 37, 72
triad, 19, 20, 32
truth, 95, 96, 127, 129, 134, 135, 136
type, 40, 61, 80
type, cognitive, 60, 61, 62, 63, 65, 83, 84, 85, 100

undercoding, 38
understanding, 2, 110–138

Vanhoozer, Kevin, 13, 124, 139, 143–145, 149, 150, 151, 152, 154

warrant, epistemic, 90, 91, 101, 107
Weber, Bruce, 7
Wildman, Wesley, 5
Wilkins, John, 52
Wright, N. T., 136

Yong, Amos, 6

Zimmerman, Jens, 132
zoosemiotics, 24, 27

www.ingramcontent.com/pod-product-compliance
Lightning Source LLC
Chambersburg PA
CBHW071231170426
43191CB00032B/1318